ETHICS, EQUITY AND COMMUNITY DEVELOPMENT

RETHINKING COMMUNITY DEVELOPMENT SERIES

P

Series editors: Mae Shaw, University of Edinburgh, **Rosie R. Meade,** University College Cork and **Sarah Banks**, University of Durham

The *Rethinking Community Development Series* is an international book series that offers the opportunity for a critical re-evaluation of community development. Rethinking what community development means in theory as well as in practice, it aims to draw together a broad range of international, cross-disciplinary and cross-generational perspectives.

Each book in the series:

- provides an international perspective on community development;
- theorises issues and practices in a way that encourages diverse audiences to consider the potentiality and future directions of community development;
- encourages practitioners to engage more critically with their work.

Also available:

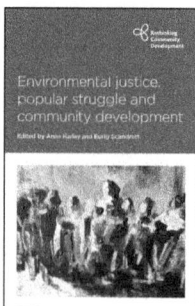

Information on all titles is available on our website:

https://policy.bristoluniversitypress.co.uk/rethinking-community-development

Rethinking Community Development

ETHICS, EQUITY AND COMMUNITY DEVELOPMENT

Edited by
Sarah Banks and Peter Westoby

P

Rethinking
Community
Development

First published in Great Britain in 2019 by

Policy Press
University of Bristol
1-9 Old Park Hill
Bristol
BS2 8BB
UK
t: +44 (0)117 954 5940
pp-info@bristol.ac.uk
www.policypress.co.uk

North America office:
Policy Press
c/o The University of Chicago Press
1427 East 60th Street
Chicago, IL 60637, USA
t: +1 773 702 7700
f: +1 773-702-9756
sales@press.uchicago.edu
www.press.uchicago.edu

British Library Cataloguing in Publication Data
A catalogue record for this book is available from the British Library

Library of Congress Cataloging-in-Publication Data
A catalog record for this book has been requested

978-1-4473-4510-7 hardback
978-1-4473-4512-1 paperback
978-1-4473-4511-4 ePdf
978-1-4473-4513-8 ePub
978-1-4473-4514-5 Mobi

Cover design by Liam Roberts
Front cover image: Ian Martin

Contents

List of figures and tables

Figures

Tables

Rethinking Community Development

Communities are a continuing focus of public policy and citizen action worldwide. The purposes and functions of work with communities of place, interest and identity vary between and within contexts and change over time. Nevertheless, community development – as both an occupation and as a democratic practice concerned with the demands and aspirations of people in communities – has been extraordinarily enduring.

This book series aims to provide a critical re-evaluation of community development in theory and practice, in the light of new challenges posed by the complex interplay of emancipatory, democratic, self-help and managerial imperatives in different parts of the world. Through a series of edited and authored volumes, *Rethinking Community Development* will draw together international, cross-generational and cross-disciplinary perspectives, using contextual specificity as a lens through which to explore the localised consequences of global processes. Each text in the series will:

- *promote critical thinking*, through examining the contradictory position of community development, including the tensions between policy imperatives and the interests and demands of communities.
- *include a range of international examples*, in order to explore the localised consequences of global processes.
- *include contributions from established and up-and-coming new voices*, from a range of geographical contexts.
- *offer topical and timely perspectives*, drawing on historical and theoretical resources in a generative and enlivening way.
- *inform and engage a new generation of practitioners*, bringing new and established voices together to stimulate diverse and innovative perspectives on community development.

If you have a broad or particular interest in community development that could be expanded into an authored or edited collection for this book series, contact:

Mae Shaw
mae.shaw@ed.ac.uk

Rosie R. Meade
r.meade@ucc.ie

Sarah Banks
s.j.banks@durham.ac.uk

Acknowledgements

This book developed from our initial ideas at Peter's dining table in Brisbane in July 2014 to our discussions of the first and last chapters in Dublin in July 2018. The journey has seemed quite long and sometimes tortuous, but very worthwhile, as we have learnt much from the process and the people accompanying us along the way.

We offer profound thanks to all the contributors to the book, for hanging in there with our demands and deadlines, navigating the editorial pen, and stretching themselves into new spaces. We are also very grateful to Ian Martin, who has generously given one of his original paintings for the front cover. Finally, we would like to thank our editors at Policy Press, Isobel Bainton, Emily Watt and Sarah Bird, and the anonymous referees for their helpful advice and encouragement.

We each have particular acknowledgements to those who have helped us over the years:

Sarah: I would like to thank the many people, locally and internationally, who have contributed to the development of my practice and thinking about community development over several decades. I am particularly grateful to community members and workers in North-East England and colleagues and students at Durham University, including many cohorts of students on community and youth work programmes and members of the Centre for Social Justice and Community Action. These have provided fertile grounds for collaborating in growing ideas about ethics and communities.

Peter: Deep thanks to community members in numerous places over the past 30 years that have challenged me in everyday ethics work. Not always easy, but nevertheless, leading to growth. Many thanks too for colleagues and comrades in the Queensland and global community development 'community of practice' that keep modelling ethical community development practice ('walking the talk') and deliberating ethical dilemmas.

Sarah Banks, Durham, UK and
Peter Westoby, Brisbane, Australia

Notes on contributors

Sarah Banks is Professor of Applied Social Sciences, Department of Sociology, and Co-director, Centre for Social Justice and Community Action, Durham University, UK. She teaches and researches on professional ethics, community development and participatory action research. Books include: *Critical community practice* (Policy Press, 2007, with Butcher, Henderson and Robertson); *Managing community practice* (Policy Press, 2013, 2nd edn, edited with Butcher, Orton and Robertson); *Ethical issues in youth work* (Routledge, 2010, editor); *Ethics and values in social work* (4th edn, Palgrave Macmillan, 2012) and *Practising social work ethics around the world: Cases and commentaries* (Routledge, 2012, edited with Kirsten Nøhr).

Neil Barringham is a community worker who has worked with others in his home and neighbourhood to facilitate inclusion and community supports. Neil is part of Praxis Community Co-operative, a worker's cooperative in Brisbane through which he enjoys interacting with passionate people in the mental health and disability fields about ways to build community-based supports and opportunities for participation. Neil has postgraduate qualifications in social work.

Sowmyaa Bharadwaj works with Praxis Institute for Participatory Practices, New Delhi, India. She has been involved with several participatory research studies, monitoring designs, assessments and evaluations across a range of thematic areas of development. An experienced facilitator and a practitioner of participatory approaches, she has been involved in various trainings and capacity building initiatives with a range of organisations and community groups across India.

Jennie Buchanan grew up in the South West of Western Australia. She is a research associate in the School of Indigenous Studies at the University of Western Australia. She trained and practised as a youth and community worker and has since worked for many Aboriginal community-controlled organisations, a range of universities and has taught community development at Murdoch University.

Len Collard is a *Wadjuk Balladong Noongar* from the South West of Western Australia. He is a professor of Indigenous Studies at the

University of Western Australia. He first trained in youth work and has been working on many Aboriginal community-controlled projects since the 1980s, incorporating *Noongar* language, culture and knowledge systems into his practice and the work of others.

Mike de Kreek has been a lecturer and researcher at the Amsterdam University of Applied Sciences since 1999. Since his master's studies in computational linguistics, he has been interested in learning as a social process. At the Amsterdam Research Institute for Societal Innovation, he has been coordinating and teaching the research courses in the Masters in Social Work programme since 2008. In his PhD dissertation called 'Collective empowerment through local memory websites', Mike analysed how participants learn to balance between group interest and the common good.

Gradon Diprose is a researcher at Manaaki Whenua Landcare Research, Wellington, New Zealand. He conducts research in community economies and community development and planning across Australasia.

Jeroen Gradener is Associate Professor, Amsterdam University of Applied Sciences, the Netherlands. He lectures in Community Development Practice and Theory, Human Rights Advocacy and Cultural Psychology. He has 15 years of experience in professional higher education. Since 2011, he combined his lectureship with a PhD project on professional legitimation in community development practices, 'Keys to the community', a multiple and comparative case study on professional legitimation in community development, conducted in South Africa, the US and the Netherlands.

Ann Hill is Assistant Professor in Education, University of Canberra, Australia. She teaches and conducts research in Australia and Asia in the areas of community development and community education for sustainable worlds. She is a human geographer and diverse economies scholar by training, with specific interests in collective ethics and methods for living in a climate and resource-changing world. She is a member of the Community Economies Collective and the Community Economies Research Network, international cross-disciplinary networks of academic and lay researchers committed to opening the economy to ethical debate and exploring different community development practices and pathways.

Bipin Jojo is Professor, School of Social Work (Mumbai Campus), and Centre for Social Justice and Governance, Tata Institute of Social Sciences, India. He is engaged with teaching, research and outreach work with communities and organisations. His area of work has been on social work with a tribal/indigenous perspective, tribal education, working with groups, development-induced displacement and resettlement and rehabilitation, mining and participatory development.

Pradeep Narayanan is associated with Praxis Institute for Participatory Practices, New Delhi, India. He has been implementing participatory action research programmes with communities facing marginalisation. Lately he has been working on issues related to human rights and business and mainstream voices of bonded labour and communities affected by businesses.

Dave Palmer was raised in Adelaide, but has lived in Western Australia for the last 30 years or so. His family comes from Great Britain and he is a senior lecturer in Sociology and Community Development at Murdoch University. In a 'previous life' he was a community worker and now spends lots of time travelling along with projects that have been designed by and with Indigenous community groups.

Keith Popple is Emeritus Professor and previously Head of Social Work at London South Bank University, UK. Formerly Editor of the *Community Development Journal* and presently a member of the editorial board, he has written and lectured widely in the area of community, community development and social policy and is author of *Analysing community work: Theory and practice* (2nd edn, 2015, Open University Press). He is a Visiting Professor at Bournemouth University, Newman University and Honorary Fellow in the School of Applied Social Science at the University of Brighton. He is Academic Adviser to the Department of Social Work, Hong Kong Baptist University.

Loretta Pyles is Professor at the State University of New York, Albany. Her practice and research experience has been in the areas of violence against women, poverty/welfare, racial justice, disasters, and integrative/holistic pedagogy and practice. She has worked in, researched and written about disasters in the US and globally and is co-author of the book (with Juliana Svistova), *Production of disaster and recovery in post-earthquake Haiti* (2018). She is the author of *Healing justice: Holistic self-care for change makers* (2018), *Progressive community organizing: Reflective practice in a globalizing world* (2nd edition, 2013), co-editor with Gwendolyn Adam of *Holistic engagement: Transformative social work education in the 21st century* (2016), and the author of more than 40 articles and book chapters.

Satu Ranta-Tyrkkö is Senior Lecturer, University of Jyväskylä, Finland. She became interested in voluntary and popular social work in India in the 1990s, acquainting herself first with Gandhian social work, and later socially committed theatre as social work, as well as environmental issues in social work. Her PhD thesis is entitled: *At the intersection of theatre and social work in Orissa, India* (Tampere University Press, 2010), while her postdoctoral research (Academy of Finland, 2014–17) explored the ramifications of mineral extraction in Northern Finland and Northern Odisha. She has also published on international, postcolonial and ethical issues in social work.

Lynda Shevellar is a lecturer in Community Development in the School of Social Science at The University of Queensland, Australia. She is influenced by 25 years of experience and study in community development, organisational psychology, the disability sector, mental health and education, looking at how to effect positive social change. Her current research explores the contribution of community development to the field of mental health.

Peter Westoby is Associate Professor in Social Science and Community Development at Queensland University of Technology, Australia; and a visiting professor at the Centre for Development Support, University of Free State, South Africa. He teaches and researches on community development theory and practice, dialogue studies and forced migration studies. He is known for monographs such as *Participatory development practice* (2018, Practical Action Press), *Dialogical community development* (2013, Routledge), *Soul, community and social change* (2016, Ashgate/Routledge) and *The sociality of refugee healing* (2009, Common Ground).

PART 1

The ethico-political context

ONE

Ethics, equity and community development: mapping the terrain

Sarah Banks

Introduction

Rationale for the book

This book is part of the *Rethinking Community Development* series. As such, it offers a range of critical perspectives, both cross-disciplinary and international, on the place and meaning of ethics and the nature of ethical practice in community development work. The first two books in the series, *Politics, power and community development* (Meade et al, 2016) and *Class, inequality and community development* (Shaw and Mayo, 2016), had a primary focus on the structural context in which community development operates. *Ethics, equity and community development* takes account of context, but its focal point is the 'micro-ethics' of daily practice, often neglected in the literature which focuses on the broader political climate and how to develop equitable social policy to tackle disadvantage and inequity. In this book we are concerned with the *ethical agency* of the people practising community development, and the *dilemmas and difficulties* they face in their *everyday work* as they strive towards ethical practice and equitable outcomes. We are also interested in how micro-level or 'everyday ethics' interacts with the macro-level ethics of social and institutional policies in the community development field (see Banks, 2016 for the concept of 'everyday ethics'; Truog et al, 2015, for 'micro- and macro-ethics').

Example of everyday ethics

To illustrate what is meant by 'everyday ethics', I will give an example from Chapter Five of the book. Here we are given an account of an ethically challenging situation faced by practitioners working for an NGO in India with a focus on participatory practice. In evaluating the effectiveness of interventions aiming to empower sex worker collectives, some of the sex workers felt the collective had made major achievements in ending false arrests and harassment by the police. They felt this indicated that the collective should be categorised as 'vibrant', which indicated sustainability and a high level of functioning. However, the NGO workers and some other members of the collective questioned this claim, as the reduction in false arrests had been achieved through threatening to inform the families of police officers who were clients of the sex workers. This was not regarded as a sustainable outcome (one of the criteria of 'vibrancy') by the NGO staff, nor was it ethically acceptable to use threats to achieve goals, according to mainstream standards of morality. This created a dilemma for the NGO workers: should they accept and value the coping mechanisms adopted by some members of the sex workers' collective, who are stigmatised and marginalised by wider society and find it hard to assert their rights, or should they stick with their own standards of sustainability and ethics?

The book is concerned with questions like this. Recognising the issues calls for a high degree of ethical sensitivity, as well as political awareness, on the part of community development practitioners, while making responses and taking action may require courage and compassion, alongside ethical reasoning. One of the aims of this book is make more visible the ethical dimensions of community development practice and hence enhance the ethical literacy and competence of practitioners.

Outline of this chapter

This chapter introduces the reader to ethics as a topic of study and considers the nature of the ethical issues and challenges inherent in community development work as a prelude to the following chapters, which focus on specific topics and themes. The chapter first discusses and problematises the key concepts of the book, 'ethics', 'equity' and 'community development', before considering the role of ethics in community development work, the relationship between ethics and politics and different theoretical approaches to ethics. The ambivalence of community development workers towards professionalisation is raised in the context of recent trends towards the development of national and international practice standards and several examples of codes of ethics. As a counterweight to a view of 'ethics as regulation', an argument is made for 'everyday ethics', an approach to the study and practice of ethics as relational, embedded and embodied in community development work, based on the 'ethics work' that practitioners do in their day-to-day interactions and relationships. An argument is made for the importance of an ethics that is both politicised (rather than individualised) and embedded in (rather than abstracted from) practice. The chapter ends by drawing out a selection of themes from the book chapters relating to: practising ethically in an unethical world; working out roles and boundaries; negotiating community consent; and alternative relational paradigms for ethical being and action.

Key concepts in the book

Before proceeding further, I will offer a brief discussion of each of the key concepts in the title of the book.

Ethics

Our understanding of ethics is as a topic that covers questions relating to what actions are right and wrong, what qualities of character people should develop, what kinds of lives people should lead, what counts as a good society and what responsibilities humans have for each other and the ecosystem. On this view, ethical issues are ever-present in community development work. However, relatively little community development literature explicitly discusses ethical issues per se, identifying 'ethics' as a specific topic linked with ethical theories in philosophy or models of professionalism and professional ethics. This book is designed to go some way towards filling that gap.

Some philosophers and theorists distinguish 'morality' (as socially accepted norms) and 'ethics' (as the study of those norms, or people's own personally considered norms; see Banks, 2012: 4–7). In everyday English language, however, these terms, along with the associated adjectives 'moral' and 'ethical', are generally used interchangeably. In this book we use the terms interchangeably, unless stated otherwise.

Equity

Equity is about finding a fair distribution of goods (such as power, health, social well-being or material resources) among individuals and social groups. While in ordinary language the terms 'equity' and 'equality' are often used interchangeably, they do have different meanings. 'Equality' entails each person having the same amount of a particular good (such as income or access to healthcare); equity is about people having the 'right amount' of certain goods to enable them to live decent lives according to norms of fairness and human rights (however we may define these). Equity requires recognition of people's different life circumstances and needs, and ensuring they get the goods required, which will be different for each person. As Son (2011: 1) says: 'equity is about putting things right' – at least those things that can be remedied by human intervention, such as poverty-related ill health, poor educational outcomes or low salaries due to ethnic and/or gender bias. The World Health Organization offers a succinct description of equity as: 'the absence of avoidable or remediable differences among groups of people' (WHO, 2018).

In the community development literature 'equality' is often stated as a core value, and equity in the sense described here is subsumed within it as 'equality of outcome' (as distinct from other types of equality – 'equality of treatment' and 'equality of opportunity'). We have highlighted 'equity' in the title of the book as we believe it encapsulates a core purpose of community development, which is often subsumed within the more commonly espoused values of social justice, equality and human rights. It also provides a bridge between the traditional politics and ideological values of community development and the ethical challenges of everyday practice.

Community development

There are many definitions of community development available in textbooks and mission statements, which are usually fairly abstract and use slightly different forms of words. Given this book has a global reach, we will take as a starting point the definition agreed by the International Association for Community Development (IACD) in 2016:

> Community development is a practice-based profession and an academic discipline that promotes participative democracy, sustainable development, rights, economic opportunity, equality and social justice, through the organisation, education and empowerment of people within their communities, whether these be of locality, identity or interest, in urban and rural settings. (IACD, 2018: 8)

This definition, of course, is not uncontested, not least its characterisation of community development as a profession and academic discipline. However, it is perhaps an indicator of recent trends in some parts of the world towards professionalisation and a desire for greater recognition of community development work, which also bring matters of ethics and professional conduct to the fore.

It is important to note that the term 'community development' is sometimes used in a narrow sense, with a focus on self-help and citizen participation, to refer to one approach to community work (see Thomas, 1983: 108–17; Banks, 2011a: 166–70). Other approaches include community service and planning (developing community-based services and policies) and community action and organising (issue-based campaigning). However, in much literature, including the IACD documentation, the term 'community development work' is used in a broader sense, to encompass a whole range of approaches to work in and with communities, and is often regarded as synonymous with 'community work'. We are using the term in a broad sense in this book, noting that it encompasses various approaches, models and traditions, which are underpinned by a range of ideological positions from conservative and social conformist, through democratic consensual and reformist, to more radical and conflict oriented (see Gilchrist, 2004: 23–5; Westoby, 2014: 41–53; Popple, 2015: 57–72).

The contested nature of community development

The term 'community development' is used, rather confusingly, to refer to several different types of activity, which relate to people acting collectively in communities of place, interest or identity to achieve transformative social change. For now, let us take communities to be collectivities of people with some, but not necessarily all, characteristics in common, who may sometimes come together (perhaps for only a short time) for perceived, mutual benefit (Banks et al, 2018). In this context, the term 'community development' may be used in several different ways to refer to:

1. A *process* of community formation and movement towards change, regardless of whether the people involved consciously see themselves as engaged in community development.
2. A *practice* undertaken by people, paid or unpaid, who consciously engage in a purposeful process, which they recognise as community development and can locate within a tradition.
3. An *occupation*, that is, a field of work based on recognised sets of knowledge, skills and values, which may involve paid or unpaid work and may or may not be regarded as a profession.
4. An *academic discipline* or subject of study, which is based on a body of knowledge and literature.
5. A *social movement* (in addition to being a process, practice or occupation that underpins or supports social movements),

advocating for community development approaches at local, national and international level.

In this book the term 'community development' is used in all five senses, although the main focus of attention is on community development as a practice and an occupation, in effect what is often called 'community development work'. Community development work supports the process of community development and is a major part of the subject matter of the academic discipline of community development. Community development workers and academics are also the driving force behind community development as a social movement, campaigning for greater community participation or respect for human rights through bodies such as the IACD (www. iacdglobal.org) or European Community Development Network (http://eucdn.net), for example.

If we return to the IACD's definition of community development quoted in the introduction to this chapter, we see that it encompasses community development as a practice, occupation ('profession') and academic discipline, although not explicitly as a process or a social movement. It also boldly uses the term 'profession' (rather than 'occupation'), although softening this by prefacing it with 'practice-based'. The description 'practice-based' seems somewhat redundant (as all professions involve people practising their values, knowledge and skills). However, it was possibly added for political reasons, given the long-standing resistance of community development work to professionalisation.

As already outlined, the topic of ethics includes matters relating to respecting and promoting rights and responsibilities, distribution of harms and benefits and cultivation of virtues leading to human and ecological flourishing. If this is what ethics comprises, then clearly ethical issues are embedded in, and raised by, community development in all of the senses in the fivefold list outlined earlier. However, the ethical dimensions are most evident in community development as a practice and occupation. Here they are brought into being through self-reflection by practitioners, and critical analysis by observers, relating to the implicit or explicit norms, values, ethical principles and character traits relevant to community development.

Community development as 'value-based'

While there may be a gap in the mainstream community development literature in the field of 'ethics', there is no shortage of accounts of the values of community development work. 'Values' (beliefs about what is regarded as worthy or valuable) are regarded as vitally important in community development work and feature frequently in professional and academic literature. The occupation and practice are often characterised as 'value-based', with underpinning values listed as variations on human rights, social justice, democracy, equality and solidarity. There are many accounts of the values of community development work, all framed slightly differently, but with much in common. They often comprise very broad headings such as 'social justice' or 'empowerment', followed by brief descriptions of what these mean and sometimes examples of how they might be put into practice. Table 1.1 shows some examples of different configurations of values found in a small selection of the available literature, with the values listed in the order in which they appear in the source documents. These values are contested, overlapping and open to interpretation, but the lists are remarkably similar. It is noteworthy that 'equity' does not feature separately in any of the headings. This may be partly because its meaning is subsumed within 'social justice' and 'equality', or perhaps because it also implies a commitment that is quite radical for key stakeholders in community development (distribution of goods according to need to create equality of outcome).

These lists of values are both useful and problematic. They are useful because they offer a framework within which community development practitioners can conceptualise and justify their practice. They signify

Table 1.1: Community development values

International Association for Community Development (IACD, 2018)	European Community Development Network (EuCDN, 2014)	National Occupational Standards for Community Development, UK (NOS, 2015)	All Ireland Endorsement Body for Community Work Education and Training (AIEB, 2016)
• rights • solidarity • democracy • equality • environmental and social justice	• collective learning • empowerment • meaningful participation • collective action for collective outcomes • equality	• social justice and equality • anti-discrimination • community empowerment • collective action • working and learning together	• collectivity • community empowerment • social justice and sustainable development • human rights, equality and anti-discrimination • participation

that community development is not just a set of techniques and skills that can be deployed for a range of ends in any way that is effective. Rather, community development requires a commitment on the part of its practitioners to work towards a world that is fairer and more participatory, and to practise in ways that are respectful of diversity, challenge unjust differences and encourage a culture of collective learning and action, for example. A statement of values helps generate a sense of identity among practitioners and encourages debate and discussion about the meaning of those values and how they can or should be put into practice. Given they are relatively generic and abstract, people from very diverse backgrounds can sign up to them.

However, the generic nature of these values is also one of their weaknesses. The list of values given by the IACD is probably the most generic of those in Table 1.1, and is unusual in that no further description or discussion is offered about each value. It reads like a list of values that might be espoused in any democratic society and, presented without any discussion, raises a number of critical questions. What does it mean to subscribe to the value of 'rights', for example? While eschewing the more specific 'human rights' in order to include environmental rights may mean more people buy into the value, this also makes it relatively meaningless. Whose rights are we talking about, what kinds of rights, in what circumstances are the rights to be respected and whose responsibility is it to honour them?

Some of the values in the lists have a more radical edge to them – with headings like 'empowerment', 'anti-discrimination' and 'collective action'. Taken literally, they signal a belief in a radically different kind of society and world from the one we currently inhabit. However, while displaying fine ideals, are they any more than empty rhetoric that makes community development workers feel good about themselves? The extent to which community development can achieve these transformative ideals is a matter of debate, and certainly there are plenty of examples of community development work that is engaged in propping up the status quo, focusing attention on 'problem' people and places and being co-opted by the local or national state and private business, as many of the chapters in this book show (see especially Chapters Five and Seven on work with sex worker collectives and mining communities in India).

The first step to making these values meaningful and useful is, of course, to unravel what they might mean, how they might be implemented in practice and how workers can recognise and handle the inevitable conflicts and contradictions between them (achieving social justice outcomes versus democratic involvement of all parties, for example). While there is no one definitive set of values, I offer here a selection that seems to encapsulate the sentiments of those listed in Table 1.1.

- *Respect and promote human rights and capabilities* – recognition that all human beings have dignity and worth qua humans, with rights to make choices, to cultivate their human capabilities and live decent lives in accordance with United Nations Declarations and Statements.
- *Promote social justice, equality and equity* – working for a fair distribution of material and social goods in society according to people's needs, acknowledging harmful differences that can be remedied, respecting diversity of cultures, religions and lifestyles, and challenging oppressive power structures and discriminatory treatment.
- *Work towards environmental justice and sustainable communities* – respecting the well-being and habitats of non-human creatures and promoting a flourishing ecosystem as a good in itself, as well as out of consideration for humans whose livelihoods depend on a well-functioning ecosystem.
- *Respect and encourage solidarity between people and groups* – encouraging people experiencing similar problems to stand together and support each other, as well as engaging other people to take a stand alongside them.
- *Promote and support collective action* – bringing diverse people and groups together to identify their common concerns and interests and take action for positive social change.
- *Promote individual, group and community empowerment* – supporting people to mobilise, create or draw out their own power to make decisions and take actions on issues that concern them.
- *Promote and support democratic participation* – ensuring that people who are often invisible or unheard take part in community activities, decision making and actions about matters affecting their lives.
- *Facilitate people in processes of learning together* – valuing mutual learning and growth among people engaging in community development and fostering critical knowledge, confidence and skills of individuals and groups.

These values may not always be shared or well understood by employers of community development workers or by many other people encountered in daily work. They may also conflict with each other, hence creating ethical problems and dilemmas for workers in deciding what actions to take – for example, which community or group to support, whose rights have priority, how to respect diversity while also challenging racism, or how to balance multiple accountabilities (for a more detailed discussion see Banks, 2013). It is at this point that questions of ethics become relevant – when workers reflect on what kind of society they wish to live in and promote, what values they hold personally and as workers, how they prioritise their commitments, what kinds of people they want to be, how to develop good and trusting relationships and engage in fair tactics for achieving positive social change.

These kinds of issues are frequently raised in the community development literature, where we find no shortage of references to 'contestation', 'contradictions' and 'complexity', along with 'dilemmas', dialogue' and 'dialectic' (see, for example, Hoggett, 1997; Kenny, 2002; Hoggett et al, 2008; DeFilippis et al, 2010; Westoby and Dowling, 2014; Shevellar et al, 2015; Cameron et al, 2016; Shevellar and Barringham, 2016). However, they are less often named as relating to 'ethics' and there are few texts that explore the topics of ethics in community development in any depth. Arguably, framing these contradictions and dilemmas in terms of ethics adds an extra and important dimension to the understanding and practice of community development work. It enables us to connect the personal and political and draw on a rich body of literature from moral philosophy.

The 'ethics gap' and the 'ethics boom'

The 'ethics gap' in the community development literature is particularly surprising given the 'ethics boom' in many areas of public and academic life in recent decades (Davis, 1999; Banks, 2014). The growth of interest in, and concern about, ethics can be seen at the macro level in the arena of public debate and policy making, including increasing concern about the implications of human-engendered ecological damage, the use of new technologies (from social media to genetic engineering), or the rights of migrants and asylum seekers, for example. It is also apparent in the context of public and private corporations, with questions being raised over growing inequalities in pay, corporate greed and the personal conduct of politicians. In the professions (including academia and research) there is a growth of regulatory bodies, increasingly long codes of ethics and a concern with right conduct and professional integrity at a micro level.

These concerns are about the allocation of rights, responsibilities, harms and benefits; the nature of human and inter-species relationships; and what kind of society and planet we wish to inhabit and leave to future generations. They are generating public and private deliberation and debate, policies and laws, and systems of regulation. They are also impacting on the everyday lives and practices of people, groups, communities, professional practitioners and other workers.

In many fields of study and occupations this has generated a growth in academic and professional literature, practice guides, rules and regulations under the guise of ethics. We can see this in the fields of science (biomedicine, for instance), as well as social work and youth work. In the field of community development, however, ethics as a topic is only just beginning to emerge. We see the beginnings of a concern about ethics in the creation of several codes of ethics (such as ACWA, 2017; CLDSCS, 2017), often linked to the professionalisation and/or regulation of community development as an occupation.

While there is little or no coverage of ethics per se in mainstream community development textbooks, ethics is featuring more in some of the philosophically inclined literature, especially that promoting alternative economic, ecological and feminist paradigms, as discussed in Part 3 of this book. For example, Pyles (Chapter Eight) advocates a feminist approach to community organising based on relational ethics and healing justice (see also Pyles, 2014, 2018), while Hill and Diprose (Chapter Nine) describe a Community Economies perspective for ethical community development drawing on Gibson-Graham et al (2013). Westoby (Chapter Ten) concludes with a holistic and ecological philosophy of community development construed as an ethical space of hospitality, dialogue and responsibility, drawing on the ethical philosophies of Levinas (1999) and Derrida (1997), among others. Indeed, being invited to write a chapter for this book has perhaps encouraged authors to view their work through an ethical lens.

Ethics and politics

In spite of this boom in ethical concerns happening around the field of community development, why is there as yet so little coverage in mainstream textbooks and the work of occupational networks and professional associations for community development? One of the answers, as already intimated, is that many community development workers self-identify as being engaged in a political practice and hence many of the ethical dilemmas and issues are named as political and ideological rather than ethical. The reluctance to name 'the ethical' may link to a view of ethics as pertaining to matters of personal conduct, individual responsibility and blame. Such versions of ethics can easily be co-opted by neo-liberal and new managerial agendas (see

Banks, 2014) and used to control community development workers and activists, emphasising their ethical agency and responsibility for what are essentially structural problems beyond their control.

Tony Taylor, writing in a UK youth and community work context from a radical standpoint, expresses precisely these fears (Taylor and Banks, 2015). His concern is that the growth of interest in ethics in youth work (with new textbooks and a code of ethics) marks a retreat from politics and 'public issues', towards a focus on the individual and 'private troubles'. Here he echoes the distinction made by C. Wright Mills between troubles and issues. Mills (1970: 14–15) characterises troubles as occurring 'within the character of the individual and within the range of his [or her] immediate relations with others ... A trouble is a private matter'. On the other hand, issues have to do with 'matters that transcend these local environments of the individual and the range of his [or her] inner life... An issue is a public matter'.

These kinds of concerns can also be picked up in the community development field, and arise partly because of a particular view about the nature of 'ethics'. First, ethics tends to focus attention on individuals, their choices and decisions, paying less attention to the bigger picture, including structural constraints and the location of power. Second, 'ethics' is often associated with 'morality' (indeed, in ordinary English language we tend to use the terms interchangeably), which in some contexts has a more specific meaning, referring to prevailing social norms. Those taking a more radical perspective may recall Karl Marx's dismissal of morality as a 'bourgeois illusion' (Marx and Engels, 1848/1969: 60, 68) designed to encourage responsibility, conformity and an illusion of free choice. This version of ethics sits uneasily with radical practice, not only from a Marxist viewpoint, but also feminist, anti-oppressive and other progressive, transformative and liberatory approaches that are commonly espoused in community development work.

However, while this critique may apply to particular versions of ethics, does it provide grounds for dismissing ethics altogether? Are there versions of ethics that are not about individual conformity to social norms? The answer must surely be 'yes'. In the next section I will discuss different approaches to ethics and the inextricable link between ethics and politics.

Approaches to ethics

I have already characterised ethics earlier as a topic covering a number of themes, which can be identified as follows (Banks, 2014: 5):

- *Conduct* – what actions are regarded as right and wrong? (promise-keeping and lying).
- *Character* – what moral qualities are regarded as good and bad? (trustworthiness and deceitfulness; altruism and selfishness).
- *Relationships* – what responsibilities attach to people's relationships with each other, individually and in groups? (the responsibility of a parent towards a child; responsibility of a community towards its vulnerable members).
- *The good society* – in what kind of society do we want to live? (a society in which all living beings flourish in harmony with the natural environment; a society in which all human beings are free to enjoy the fruits of their labour).

This is a deliberately broad characterisation of ethics, in contrast to some that focus largely on one area, or regard one as the starting point or foundation of ethics. I will now outline briefly some different theoretical approaches to ethics and their relationship to the themes listed here.

Principle-based ethics, with a focus on conduct

The dominant ethical theories in modern times in the global North tend to centre on conduct, with the aim of answering the question 'what should I do?'. These tend to be principle-based theories, taking as a starting point abstract, universal principles, valid for all people in all places and times, from which more specific action guidance can be deduced by a process of impartial, rational inquiry. The two most common ethical theories of this kind are Kantian and utilitarian ethics, which have very different starting points, but are both principle-based. In Kantian ethics (Kant, 1785/1964) the ultimate principle is 'respect for persons' as rational and self-determining beings. This leads to a moral philosophy that stresses the dignity and worth of individual human beings, their rights to make their own decisions and choices and an imperative that people should never be treated as means to the ends of other people. For a Kantian, lying, manipulation and cheating would always be wrong, regardless of the consequences. Utilitarianism, on the other hand, is a consequentialist theory, based on the premise that the right action is that which produces the greatest amount of good for the greatest number of people (Mill, 1863/1972). In professional ethics, as conceived and practised in the global North, there tends to be a focus on conduct, with codes of ethics echoing Kantian principles predominantly (focusing on the rights of clients/

service users/participants) alongside some more utilitarian principles about promoting human welfare.

Character and relationship-based ethics, taking account of the 'good society'

Dissatisfaction with the impartial, principle-based approaches to ethics, which neglect the motives, intentions and character of the people whose conduct is being judged, has led to a revival of interest in character-based ethics, the most common version of which is known as 'virtue ethics', associated with the ancient Greek philosopher, Aristotle (350 BCE/1954). This is beginning to be influential in professional ethics, in which a concern with the development of practitioners of 'good character' (who are honest, reliable, compassionate, courageous) is felt to be as important as ensuring people simply do the right action by following the rules (Oakley and Cocking, 2001; Banks and Gallagher, 2009). This version of ethics could be described as 'situated', as it takes account not only of the character, motivations, intentions and emotions of the people who are moral actors, but also the particularities of each situation and the professional wisdom required for professionals to discern what to do in the particular circumstances they face (Banks, 2018).

Similarly, what might be called relationship-based or relational ethics is also situated (as opposed to abstracted from context) and has a focus on the relationships between people and the roles and responsibilities they have towards each other (which may be as loving parents, trusting colleagues, caring partners or professionals). One of the most well-known relationship-based approaches to ethics is the ethics of care, which stresses the importance of caring relationships between people. Often associated with feminist ethics, it has developed significantly in recent years from its early beginnings in the work of psychologist Gilligan (1982), educationalist Noddings (1984) and political theorist Tronto (1993, 2012) who developed a political ethics of care. The ethics of care also has resonances with the ethics of proximity, drawing on the work of Levinas (1989), Løgstrup (1997) and Buber (1937), for example, which takes as an ontological starting point the response we each have to make to the call or demand of the other person. Relationships are also at the heart of communitarian ethics, where the focus is less on the individual and more on the 'community', seeking solidarity, harmony and the common good (Kuczewski, 1997; Gyekye, 2010), some features of which are outlined in Chapter Ten of this volume.

While some may categorise character- and relationship-based approaches as ethical theories, generally their proponents do not wish to build systematic, large-scale theories to rival Kantianism and utilitarianism, hence it might be more accurate to call them theoretical approaches. Virtue ethics, the ethics of care and communitarian ethics do not attempt to articulate universal abstract principles that apply to all people in all places, at all times. Rather they adopt a more situated (contextual) approach to ethics, starting from the realities of everyday life, as opposed to applying abstract principles. They regard emotions as an important feature of ethics, arguing that empathy and compassion, for example, are essential to ethical being and acting. These relational approaches, particularly communitarian ethics, are much closer to those commonly found in the global South and Indigenous communities in the global North, where the individual is defined in relationship with others, as outlined in Chapter Six of this book (see also Li, 1994; Gbadegesin, 2005; Keown, 2005; Chuwa, 2014).

There are many other approaches to ethics, including existential ethics (focusing on action in the here and now of each unique situation), case-based ethics (or 'casuistry', which works by comparing particular cases) and narrative ethics (based on stories and accounts of what matters to people). All of these take a more situated, particularistic approach to considering ethical questions and may be regarded as much as methodologies for tackling ethical problems and issues as theories or theoretical approaches.

Ethico-politics

While Kantianism and utilitarianism focus more on the form of ethical judgements and are criticised for not giving a substantive account of the 'good society', virtue, care and communitarian ethics are premised on a vision of what counts as human flourishing – a society in which the virtues are practised or one in which caring and communal relationships are valued and promoted. As already stated, some might argue that questions about the nature of the good society are questions of politics, rather than ethics. However, arguably this is the point where ethics and politics meet, and questions about the nature of human and ecological flourishing might be regarded as 'ethico-political'. While a distinction is often made between political matters (how to organise government) and ethical matters (how people should conduct their lives), there is clearly a large degree of overlap, as recognised by ancient Greek philosophers Plato and Aristotle, who maintain that personal morality, good citizenship and the best way to organise a state, all fit together (Hughes, 2001: 13). As Critchley (2007: 132) comments: 'Politics is an ethical practice that is driven by a response to situated injustices and wrongs'. Indeed, Critchley suggests that ethics is needed to decide how to act in a political situation (120), concluding that 'if ethics without politics is empty, then politics without ethics is blind' (148).

It is in this domain of ethics (or ethico-politics) that arguably community development as an academic discipline, occupation and practice has much to say, at least in its more radical incarnation. For the values of community development are firmly located in a social justice and participatory paradigm and demand that practitioners take both a political and ethical stance.

The political element of the work, and the call for workers to align themselves on the side of those who are powerless, marginalised and impoverished, is one reason why community development as an occupation has been reluctant to professionalise. Another related reason is that professionalisation tends to demarcate between employed and volunteer community workers and activists, hence creating divisions within the field of work. Yet, the closeness and commitment of community development workers to the people with whom they work, and the lack of clear boundaries between employed worker and activist, also bring challenges of over-involvement, 'boundary violations' and misuse of power (see Chapter Three in this volume). These are used as arguments for creating forms of professional organisation, codes of ethics and standards for competent and ethical practice. In the next section I discuss the implications of moves towards professionalisation in community development work.

Professionalisation and codes of ethics

Community development workers have traditionally had an uneasy relationship with the idea of professionalisation, tending to associate professions with elitism, exclusivity and the creation of distance from the people with whom they work (Banks, 2004: 32–3; Ife, 2016: 360–2). While there is no one model of what counts as a 'profession', and the concept and practice of professionalism has changed over time and varies between countries, usually a process of professionalisation is linked with all or some of: the development of a specialised body of knowledge and skills; the introduction of qualifying education; the development of codes of ethics; and creation of systems of licensing and regulation of practitioners (Banks, 2004: 17–46). At various times in different countries, the 'professionalisation debate' has come to the fore, as moves have been made to raise the profile of community development work by developing more formal associations or institutes, qualifying educational programmes and national or international standards for practice.

While professional associations have existed for many years (for example, the IACD was founded in 1953; Association of Community Workers in the UK in 1968: Australian Community Workers Association in 1969), it is only in recent years that some of these bodies have begun to introduce 'standards' for community development practice or have supported other bodies to do so. In 2018, IACD published international standards (IACD, 2018), building on the work done in other countries to create national occupational standards (for example, AIEB, 2016; NOS, 2015). The extent to which the production of standards is viewed as part of the professionalisation project depends on how professionalism is regarded, the reasons standards are produced and what kinds of bodies validate, monitor and use the standards. In the UK, where the first national occupational standards for community work (now called community development) were produced in 1995 (FCWTG and Mainframe, 1995), the instigator was the then Federation of Community Work Training Groups (a national grassroots body that no longer exists). The aim was to create a means to give national recognition to community activists and people who could not access higher education, by validating their learning from experience (Banks, 1990). However, this was achieved as part of a government-led initiative to standardise vocational qualifications in the UK. Hence, community work in effect bought into a state-sponsored system, albeit one that engaged the field in the development and periodic revision of the standards. The standards are used in the validation of university-level courses, as well as serving as benchmarks for employers.

Building on the development of occupational standards, recently we have seen the emergence of several codes of ethics for community development work. The Community Learning and Development Standards Council Scotland (described as the 'professional body' for community learning and development (CLD), funded by the Scottish government) adopted a code in 2011, now in a revised edition (CLDSCS, 2017). The Australian Community Workers Association (ACWA), a membership organisation that promotes and supports community work and accredits higher education programmes in Human Services (which includes community development) has also created a code of ethics (ACWA, 2017). The stated purpose of these codes is to guide and regulate the conduct of community development workers as 'professional' practitioners, ensuring accountable practice within clear boundaries of the professional role and respectful and fair treatment of the people with whom they work (called 'constituents' in the CLD code and 'clients' in the ACWA code). The codes of ethics fit within a framework of professional values and standards (or 'competences') expected of qualified workers. According to the CLD Standards Council, the code provides a clear statement about standards of professional behaviour expected of qualified workers, wherever they practise, and a means of 'systematically relating the values and principles to practice' (CLDSCS, 2015: 5). The CLD document is a fairly short set of 12 statements, including some value statements ('equity' and 'empowerment') alongside statements about the nature of relationships with 'constituents' ('duty of care', 'transparency', 'confidentiality' and 'boundaries') and ways of working with colleagues and looking after oneself ('cooperation', 'professional learning' and 'self-care'). The ACWA code (2017: 3–4) follows a more traditional format with the following headings:

- Principles underlying the code of ethics
- Responsibility to clients
- Responsibility to employers
- Responsibility to colleagues
- Protecting the reputation of the profession

While codes of ethics are certainly designed to protect the people with whom community development practitioners work, and may provide useful guidance for practitioners, they also serve to reinforce professional status and credibility and foster a sense of identity in the occupational group. Furthermore, they exemplify a particular notion of ethics in professional life as being about rule-following and compliance, and can play a role in professional regulation through use by employers in disciplinary hearings.

In the community development field the occupation is generally not regulated by the national or local state, as is the case in other 'professional' occupations in some countries where state-sponsored regulatory bodies can strike people off a professional register. However, recent debates in South Africa about professionalisation do relate to proposals involving state regulation (see Chile, 2012; Westoby and Shevellar, 2014), adding a further dimension to the professionalisation debate, namely the advantages of (apparently) increased professional status and credibility versus reticence about state control. This goes beyond the fears of self-serving exclusivity that were current in the last century when professions were regarded as self-governing elites, exemplifying how the nature of professionalism (and the debates associated with it) changes over time.

The model of professionalism most suited to community development work would be that of the 'new' or 'democratic professionalism' (Dzur, 2008; Banks, 2012: 106). This entails less emphasis on professional expertise and distance and more on power-sharing – seeing the people with whom professionals work as fellow citizens (rather than 'participants'/'service users'/'clients') and working from and valuing their experiences, expertise and interests. However, with deprofessionalising trends at work and increasing emphasis on state regulation of occupations, the scope for this more progressive model of professionalism seems narrower now than when it was first mooted in social work in the 1970s/1980s (Jordan, 1975; BASW, 1980). Cribb and Gerwitz (2015: 40), in their overview of professionalism in health and social care, address two concerns about professionalism in the current climate: first that 'constructions of professionalism evolve' and many views people hold about professionalism may no longer be relevant (for example, that professions are self-governing, trust-based occupations); and second, the environments required to support meaningful professionalism (including democratic professionalism) are not available for many workers. This is very apparent in the accounts from Australian practitioners in Chapter Three, which present a picture of an organisational climate that often treats community development workers as technicians.

Everyday ethics and ethics work

While it is important that people practising community development work engage in ethical conduct, and it is the case that codes, rules and regulations may assist in this, it is equally important that ethical conduct and rules are not seen as the whole of what ethics in community development is about. We need to be aware of the dangers of 'new managerial ethics' (Banks, 2011b, 2018), which works to instrumental utilitarian principles and reduces the scope for independent ethical agency, discretion and meaningful human interaction in the context of particular relationships and situations. The concept of 'everyday ethics', which I have developed in relation to social work and the social professions (see Banks, 2016, 2018), is an alternative way of looking at ethics in professional (or work) life that is situated in practice, as opposed to derived from abstract principles, and draws on character- and relationship-based approaches to ethics (virtue, care and communitarian ethics). It stresses the fact that 'ethics' is ever-present in all aspects of life, not just when people face dilemmas or difficult decisions have to be made or rules in the code of ethics are infringed. Ethics is also about how people comport themselves and look at each other, for example. It involves emotions as well as reason; our bodies as well as our minds; and stories as well as rulebooks.

Everyday ethics is about developing a particular type of ethical and political sensitivity; cultivating qualities such as care, courage and trustworthiness; and a willingness to be flexible, cope with complexity, contradictions and dilemmas. In short it requires a certain kind of moral labour, or what I call 'ethics work', which refers to: 'the effort people put into seeing ethically salient aspects of situations, developing themselves as good practitioners, working out the right course of action and justifying who they are and what they have done' (Banks, 2016: 35). It requires an ability to reflect on the ethical stances and attitudes of oneself and others, recognise responsibilities, see possible and actual actions, and exercise a high degree of reflexivity – seeing oneself and situations in a larger political context, in the light of power relations and inequities.

Drawing on accounts of ethical challenges from social welfare practitioners, I have developed an account of ethics work in terms of several different, but interrelated, elements or dimensions as follows (taken from Banks, 2016: 37):

1. *Framing work* – identifying and focusing on the ethically salient features of a situation; placing oneself and the situations encountered in political and social contexts; negotiating/co-constructing frames with others (including service users and colleagues).
2. *Role work* – playing a role in relation to others (advocate, carer, critic); taking a position (partial/impartial; close/distant); negotiating roles; responding to role expectations.
3. *Emotion work* – being caring, compassionate and empathic; managing emotions; building trust; responding to emotions of others.
4. *Identity work* – working on one's ethical self; creating an identity as an ethically good professional; negotiating professional identity; maintaining professional integrity.
5. *Reason work* – making and justifying moral judgements and decisions; deliberation with others on ethical

evaluations and tactics; working out strategies for ethical action.

6. *Relationship work* – engaging in dialogue with others; working on relationships through emotion, identity and reason work (dialogue work).

7. *Performance work* – making visible aspects of this work to others; demonstrating oneself at work (accountability work).

Many of the chapters in the book include case studies from practice or extracts from interviews with practitioners. Some of these include reflections from practitioners about what they felt, what they did and reasons for their feelings and actions in particular situations. It is here that we can see some aspects of ethics work in action. In the next section I explore just some of the themes raised by the book chapters, with the concept of ethics work in mind.

Ethics at work: exploring key themes in the book

Practising ethically in an unethical world?

The theme of how community development workers can practise ethically in a profoundly inequitable world is one that recurs in many chapters. In Chapter Two, Popple outlines the current context for community development work in many parts of the world, within a neo-liberal global economy, with increasingly tight resources and growing inequalities of wealth and power. While the challenges of working 'in and against the state' are well rehearsed in community development work, new forms of governance and governmentality of workers and citizen-activists are co-opting and controlling the work, based on managerial agendas and economic values. Popple offers the example of an action group campaigning to save trees in Sheffield, UK, placing this in the context of global economic interests, paralleling the environmental destruction taking place in many other parts of the world. Although Popple does not give details of the activists' motivations and reasonings, we can envisage that one of their key tasks will be to work on the framing of the issue as one of social and environmental justice, with both political and ethical import – seeing it in terms of power structures in local government, the interests of private corporations and the marginalisation of the interests and needs of local citizens. While Popple talks in terms of 'inequalities', his broad use of the term is very much focused on 'inequities' (avoidable or remediable differences among groups of people) and the role of community development in identifying and challenging these.

This theme of economic imperatives and environmental destruction is taken further by Ranta-Tyrkkö and Jojo in Chapter Seven. They offer a case study from a mining region in India, which demonstrates how the power of private companies rides roughshod over the local ecosystem and livelihoods of its inhabitants (many of whom are Indigenous Adivasis), offering token recompense in the form of corporate social responsibility (CSR) programmes. These programmes seem to provide piecemeal welfare and health services, with no overall planning for a sustainable future nor meaningful engagement of local people. While CSR programmes may be regarded as community development initiatives, and sometimes employ community development workers (see Owen and Kemp, 2012; Martínez Domínguez and Scandrett, 2016), in this case community development values and approaches were absent. Ranta-Tyrkkö and Jojo advocate for meaningful community development involving local people, while noting pessimistically that the dependence of the inhabitants on mining jobs compromises their willingness to organise and engage in making demands for better working conditions. Any community development workers practising in this area will be faced with myriad ethical dilemmas at both macro and micro level in dealing with the power of large corporations and well as intra-community tensions and the extreme marginalisation of the Indigenous people. The creative and courageous ethics work called for might include some of the approaches outlined in Chapter Six on working with Indigenous communities in Australia.

Working out roles and boundaries: ethics work in action

In Chapter Three, Shevellar and Barringham directly address many of the micro challenges facing community workers in their daily work, drawing on a focus group discussion and interviews with community workers practising in Brisbane, Australia. They discuss participants' views about the impossibility and undesirability of drawing clear boundaries between the roles of paid workers, volunteers and citizen-activists. In community development work, which often takes place in public and informal settings, 'dual relationships' (involving workers being friends or family of those with whom they work, for example) are commonplace, and apparently are handled with reference to personal ethics rather than codes or regulations. Workers discuss the challenges of working within layers of accountability (to self, profession, organisation and community members) and the blurred boundaries between personal and professional life in a practice that may be regarded more as a vocation than a career. Quotations from some workers show them giving accounts of themselves as doing many aspects of ethics work. We hear about them working on their identities as people as much as professionals and employees, and engaging in relationship work through 'sitting with people' and 'discovering what it is they are yearning for'. Through their framing work, they see themselves and their practice against the backdrop of larger political, policy and organisational contexts and a world that is in many respects unjust.

Chapter Five, about community development and participatory research with sex workers in Indi,a is written with a similar sensitivity to political and social context, as Narayanan and Bharadwaj give an account of the many dilemmas faced by themselves and their organisation. One of the challenging issues with which they struggled ethically relates to the question of whose values and norms should be used to judge the pathways to positive development of sex worker collectives. As a group facing serious stigmatisation in wider Indian society, their demands for rights to safe working conditions are in opposition to some of the hidden, or not so hidden, agendas of government and NGOs, which often regard quitting sex work and prevention of the spread of HIV as positive outcomes of community development interventions. This tension between the values and norms of sex worker communities and societal norms (also echoed in the values and norms of some NGOs) is reflected in the chapter title: 'Whose ethics count?' This is a challenging question for community development workers on the ground to consider. While they do not wish further to stigmatise or blame sex workers for freely choosing their livelihoods, neither do they wish to regard sex workers merely as victims of sexual exploitation.

Community consent: a constant process of renegotiation

How community workers obtain consent to work on particular issues in communities is an issue directly raised in both Chapter Four on neighbourhood-based work (Gradener and de Kreek) and Chapter Five. According to Gradener and de Kreek in Chapter Four, gaining consent in a community work context entails recognition of communities as sources of diversity, made up of people and interest groups holding different opinions and priorities, which may also clash with those of community workers or community leaders. They give two examples (from the US and the Netherlands) of occasions when consent was not initially obtained by community workers. They argue that working towards consent is a slow and delicate process, requiring practical wisdom (*phronesis*) on the part of all involved. They emphasise the importance of community workers' involvement being regarded as legitimate, suggesting signs of legitimacy that can guide them through the phases of gaining consent. These include an inconspicuous but deliberate presence on the part of community workers, leading to community engagement with the issues at stake and finally the future embeddedness of the community workers in local structures and community visions. Gradener and de Kreek recommend humility, and the use of generative questions in the 'subjunctive voice' (as in, 'might we consider this?') as ways of proceeding.

The examples and arguments in Chapter Four demonstrate the sensitive ethics work required in the practice of community development – including the capacity to undertake relationship work through recognising and valuing different interests and opinions, while also being prepared to challenge received ideas and vested interests (through the work of reframing). Gradener and de Kreek briefly mention the work of Paulo Freire in connection with the idea of 'generative themes'. Clearly the critical pedagogy approach for which Freire (1972, 1993, 2001) advocates provides an important way of starting with the concerns and themes of members of a community, while developing a critical consciousness of sources of power, oppression and vested interests. In this sense, building on the analysis of Gradener and de Kreek, community development could be regarded as a constant process of negotiating and *re*negotiating consent – with workers, activists, leaders and community members being prepared to reframe their work, seeing new issues and changing views and tactics as they go along.

The idea of renegotiating is also implicit in Chapter Five, where consent emerges explicitly towards the end. 'Consent letters' were presented to members of a sex worker collective by an NGO in India planning to undertake monitoring and evaluation research on the community development programmes with which it had been involved. These letters, explaining the purpose of the research and asking individual sex workers to agree to participate, were part of the recognised requirements for conducting 'ethical' research and are commonly asked for by research ethics committees or institutional review boards. However, the sex workers dismissed these letters, turning the tables on the NGO workers (Narayanan and Bharadwaj, the chapter authors) by demanding that they, the sex workers, should set the terms of reference. Narayanan and Bharadwaj note their own discomfort as power shifted from themselves towards members of the sex worker collective. They were called on to undertake the ethics work of reframing the situation to foreground community rights rather than worker responsibilities, along with handling emotions and renegotiating their identities as co-researchers.

This example in Chapter Five shows how the situation moved from a case of the community workers/researchers *obtaining consent* from community members to undertake work defined by the NGO, to community members setting the terms of reference for the work that could be done and *making demands* of the community workers/ researchers and NGO. Arguably this was a positive outcome, showing how the earlier community development work undertaken by the NGO, Praxis, was effective in enabling the sex workers to take power and organise themselves as collectives. Meanwhile, Praxis has now developed processes for community-led ethical review. In writing this chapter, Narayanan and Bharadwaj show themselves doing reason work, and performing as ethically reflexive and sensitive practitioners.

Alternative paradigms for ethical being and action: relational approaches

Chapter Six, on working with Indigenous Australian communities, takes a very different form (a conversation between three people, Buchanan, Collard and Palmer) and uses different language from the previous two chapters. However, the questions it considers are similar: how do community development workers, as outsiders, enter a community, understand its culture and norms, and engage respectfully? Nevertheless, the difference between 'insiders' and 'outsiders' is probably greater in the case of Indigenous communities than in the examples given in Chapters Four and Five. In Chapter Six we find references not just to distinctive experiences and knowledges, but 'ontologies' (what exists). This chapter, which focuses on the *Noongar* people and country of south-western Australia, gives two related messages. The first concerns how non-Indigenous people should approach community development work in this area, by respecting Indigenous beliefs, customs and ways of being. The second message is about what community development practitioners can learn from indigenous ways of working that makes for good community development practice in general.

With regard to the second message, this chapter is, in effect, offering an alternative paradigm for community development practice, based on a deep connection with place, people, ancestors and the natural world. Its use of *Noongar* language is particularly evocative, providing many metaphors for the careful, sensitive and relational 'ethics work' of the community development worker. The section on *birniny* (digging and scratching) affirms the embodied nature of the work, emphasising the way we hold ourselves and how we move, 'constantly looking out for prickly things', 'always on the lookout, attentive to what might lie just out of the corner of the eye, and always prepared to adjust to what we see and do'. As Len Collard comments here (p 128): '*Birniny* is a philosophical way of being. A way of doing things and holding yourself. And I think an approach to community development too.'

The final three chapters of the book (Eight, Nine and Ten) also engage more philosophically with practices and visions that offer alternatives to the prevailing neo-liberal paradigm outlined by Popple in Chapter Two. Pyles sets Chapter Eight in 'the neo-liberal US context', where she critically explores different models of community organising. She argues for a re-evaluation of the traditional conflict-oriented approach pioneered by Saul Alinsky (1969, 1989), with its utilitarian focus on instrumental tactics for achieving desired ends. Pyles presents a model of transformative organising, which pays as much attention to processes as outcomes, based on a relational ethics, stressing the importance of self-care and healing justice. She is nevertheless aware of the need for community organisers to have constantly in mind the balance between engaging with healing work and action for social change. She calls for community organisers to do both the inner and outer work of transformation, giving the example of Hunter's (2015) work around promoting a movement to end racialised mass incarceration, which combines organisation and movement building with provision of material and social support to incarcerated people and families of victims. She also stresses the value of transnational work, intergenerationality and intersectionality (the interrelationships between ethnicity, gender and so on in exacerbating oppression), drawing on immigrant labour organising in the US. Pyles challenges the traditional model of professionalism, which imposes boundaries between personal and work life and between community organisers and people with whom they work, suggesting they need to be aware of, and use, their own identities as people of colour, immigrants and so on, which are shared with the people living in the communities where they work.

Diprose and Hill in Chapter Nine also advocate an alternative paradigm. They take a Community Economies (CE) perspective as developed by Gibson-Graham (2013) and others, in which 'ethical questions around care and "economic being-in-common" are central', with a focus on the everyday work people do to care for each other and the 'more-than-human'. Following Negri (2003) they describe ethics as 'responsibility for the common' and focus their chapter on the question: 'How do we encounter others as we seek to survive well?' A CE approach challenges the dominant assumptions that the economy has to be both capitalist and separate from the ecosystem. They offer case examples of CE approaches in a post-industrial neighbourhood in Canada and a storm-devastated area in the Philippines, showing how the history of places is important and how the creation of cultural capital maps and pooling of individual funding for collective social enterprises can enable community survival and flourishing. Here the work of ethically framing and reimagining economic futures in community terms is very important.

Finally, in Chapter Ten, Westoby draws together the philosophical insights of earlier chapters, along with his own theorising of community development practice (Westoby, 2014, 2016; Westoby and Dowling, 2014), arguing for community as an ethical space – of hospitality, dialogue, solidarity and ecological sensibility – where people come together and may act collectively. He insists, however, that our vision of community should be non-essentialist in its understanding of commonality, and that community development workers see themselves not as making interventions or achieving prescribed outcomes, but rather as part of the fabric of community – nudging, inviting, responding, holding and sometimes simply 'being with' or 'walking alongside' people and groups in solidarity. He highlights the importance of the ethics work undertaken by practitioners as part of the dialogical process of community development work.

Concluding comments: "laden with the sweat of community workers"

Community development work is not easy. In Chapter Six (p 126), Dave Palmer asks his *Noongar* co-author a question: "Len, could we then conclude that an ethical practice with *Noongar* community would have to be laden with the sweat of community workers?" Len replies: "Both literally and metaphorically." Sweat has a special significance for *Noongar*, as it reveals who people are, what they have been doing and their intentions. It 'speaks'. In all cultures sweat also signifies hard work and effort. This metaphor seems relevant for community development in all contexts, not just with *Noongar*. For community development work requires not just knowledge and skills, but also commitment to a set of idealistic values, an ability to handle inevitable contradictions and dilemmas, to be creative and empathic and engage in the constant, but often hidden, labour of ethics work in highly politicised contexts in which inequities are endemic and entrenched. We, the editors and authors, hope this book may prove both stimulating and inspiring for practitioners, students and academics as they sweat on their own community development journeys.

References

ACWA (Australian Community Workers Association) (2017) *Australian community workers ethics and good practice guide*, Melbourne: Australian Community Workers Association. Available at: www.acwa.org.au/resources/ACWA-Ethics-and-good-practice-guide.pdf

AIEB (All Ireland Endorsement Body for Community Work Education and Training) (2016) *All Ireland endorsement standards for community work*, Galway: Community Work Ireland. Available at: http://communityworkireland.ie/wp-content/uploads/2015/12/All-Ireland-Standards-for-Community-Work.pdf

Alinsky, S. (1969) *Reveille for radicals*, New York: Vintage Books.

Alinsky, S. (1989) *Rules for radicals*, New York: Vintage Books.

Aristotle (350 BCE/1954) *The Nichomachean ethics of Aristotle*, translated by Sir David Ross, London: Oxford University Press.

Banks, S. (1990) 'Accrediting prior learning: Implications for education and training in youth and community work', *Youth and Policy*, 31: 8–16.

Banks, S. (2004) *Ethics, accountability and the social professions*, Basingstoke: Palgrave Macmillan.

Banks, S. (2011a) 'Re-gilding the ghetto: Community work and community development in 21st-century Britain', in M. Lavalette (ed), *Radical social work today: Social work at the crossroads*, Bristol: Policy Press, pp 165–85.

Banks, S. (2011b) 'Ethics in an age of austerity: Social work and the evolving New Public Management', *Journal of Social Intervention: Theory and Practice*, 20(2): 5–23.

Banks, S. (2012) *Ethics and values in social work* (4th edn), Basingstoke: Palgrave Macmillan.

Banks, S. (2013) 'Negotiating values, power and responsibility: Ethical challenges for managers', in S. Banks, H. Butcher, A. Orton and J. Robertson (eds) *Mananging Community Practice: Principles, Policies and Programmes* (2nd edn), Bristol: Policy Press, pp 99–122.

Banks, S. (2014) 'Reclaiming social work ethics: Challenging the new public management', in I. Ferguson and M. Lavalette (eds) *Ethics*, Bristol: Policy Press, pp 1–23.

Banks, S. (2016) 'Everyday ethics in professional life: Social work as ethics work', *Ethics and Social Welfare*, 10(1): 35–52.

Banks, S. (2018) 'Practising professional ethical wisdom: The role of "ethics work" in the social welfare field', in D. Carr (ed), *Cultivating moral character and virtue in professional practices*, Abingdon: Routledge, pp 55–69.

Banks, S. and Gallagher, A. (2009) *Ethics in professional life: Virtues for health and social care*, Basingstoke: Palgrave Macmillan.

Banks, S., Hart, A., Pahl, K. and Ward, P. (2018) 'Co-producing research: A community development approach', in S. Banks, A. Hart, K. Pahl and P. Ward (eds) *Co-producing research: A community development approach*, Bristol: Policy Press, pp 1–18.

BASW (British Association of Social Workers) (1980) *Clients are fellow citizens*, Birmingham: Britsh Association of Social Workers.

Buber, M. (1937) *I and Thou*, trans R. Gregor Smith, Edinburgh: T. and T. Clark.

Cameron, J., Hodge, P., Howard, A. and Stuart, G. (2016) 'Navigating dilemmas of community development: Practitioner reflections on working with Aboriginal communities', *Community Development*, 47(4): 546–61.

Chile, L. (2012) 'International experience of community development professionalization: Indicators for South Africa', *Africanus*, 42(2): 42–54.

Chuwa, L.T. (2014) *African Indigenous ethics in global bioethics: Interpreting Ubuntu*, New York: Springer.

CLDSCS (Community Learning and Development Standards Council Scotland) (2015) *A code of ethics for CLD: Learning resource*, Glasgow: Community Learning and Development Standards Council Scotland. Available at: http://cldstandardscouncil.org.uk/wp-content/uploads/Ethics_Learning_Resource__Complete_ednote.pdf

CLDSCS (Community Learning and Development Standards Council Scotland) (2017) *A code of ethics for community learning and development (CLD)*, Glasgow: Community Learning and Development Standards Council Scotland. Available at: http://cldstandardscouncil.org.uk/wp-content/uploads/Code_of_Ethics_2017.pdf

Cribb, A. and Gewirtz, S. (2015) *Professionalism*, Cambridge: Polity Press.

Critchley, S. (2007) *Infinitely demanding: Ethics of commitment, politics of resistance*, London: Verso.

Davis, M. (1999) *Ethics and the university*, London: Routledge.

DeFilippis, J., Fisher, R. and Shragge, E. (2010) *Contesting community: The limits and potential of local organizing*, New Brunswick, NJ: Rutgers University Press.

Derrida, J. (1997) *Politics of friendship*, London: Verso.

Dzur, A. (2008) *Democratic professionalism, citizen participation and the reconstruction of professional identity, ethics and practice*, Philadelphia: Pennsylvannia State University Press.

EuCDN (European Community Development Network) (2014) *Community Development in Europe: Towards a Common Framework and Understanding*, European Community Development Network. Available at: http://eucdn.net/wp-content/uploads/2014/10/2014-24-09-EuCDN-Publication-FINAL.pdf

FCWTG (Federation of Community Work Training Groups) and Mainframe Research and Consultancy Services (1995) *Community work S/NVQ project: National occupational standards and proposed award specifications*, Sheffield: FWCTG and Mainframe.

Freire, P. (1972) *The pedagogy of the oppressed*, London: Penguin.

Freire, P. (1993) *Education for critical consciousness*, New York: Continuum.

Freire, P. (2001) *Pegagogy of freedom: Ethics, democracy and civic courage*, Lanham, MD: Rowman and Littlefield.

Gbadegesin, S. (2005) 'Origins of African ethics', in W. Schweiker (ed), *The Blackwell companion to religious ethics*, Oxford: Blackwell, pp 413–22.

Gibson-Graham, J.K., Cameron, J. and Healy, S. (2013) *Take back the economy: An ethical guide for transforming our communities*, Minneapolis: University of Minnesota Press.

Gilchrist, A. (2004) *The well connected community: A networking approach to community development*, Bristol: Policy Press.

Gilligan, C. (1982) *In a different voice: Psychological theory and women's development*, Cambridge, MA: Harvard University Press.

Gyekye, K. (2010) 'African ethics', *Stanford Encyclopedia of Philosophy*. Available at: http://plato.stanford.edu/entries/african-ethics/

Hoggett, P. (1997) 'Contested communities', in P. Hoggett (ed), *Contested communities: Experiences, struggles, policies*, Bristol: Policy Press, pp 3–16.

Hoggett, P., Mayo, M. and Miller, C. (2008) *The dilemmas of development work: Ethical challenges in regeneration*, Bristol: Policy Press.

Hughes, G. (2001) *Aristotle on ethics*, London: Routledge.

Hunter, D. (2015) *Building a movement to end the new Jim Crow: An organizing guide*, Denver, CO: Veterans of Hope Project.

IACD (International Association for Community Development) (2018) *Towards shared international standards for community development practice*, Glasgow: IACD. Available at: www.iacdglobal.org/wp-content/uploads/2018/06/IACD-Standards-Guidance-May-2018_Web-1.pdf

Ife, J. (2016) *Community development in an uncertain world: Vision, analysis and practice* (2nd edn), Cambridge: Cambridge University Press.

Jordan, B. (1975) 'Is the client a fellow citizen?', *Social Work Today*, 6(15): 471–5.

Kant, I. (1785/1964) *Groundwork of the metaphysics of morals*, trans H. Paton, New York: Harper and Row.

Kenny, S. (2002) 'Tensions and dilemmas in community development: New discourses, New Trojans?', *Community Development Journal*, 37(4): 284–99.

Keown, D. (2005) 'Origins of Buddhist ethics', in W. Schweiker (ed), *The Blackwell companion to religious ethics*, Oxford: Blackwell, pp 286–96.

Kuczewski, M. (1997) *Fragmentation and consensus: Communitarian and casuist bioethics*, Washington, DC: Georgetown University Press.

Levinas, E. (1989) 'Ethics as first philosophy', trans S. Hand, in S. Hand (ed), *The Levinas Reader*, Oxford: Blackwell, pp 75–87.

Levinas, E. (1999) *Alterity and transcendence*, London: Athlone Press.

Li, C. (1994) 'The Confucian concept of *Jen* and the feminist ethics of care: A comparative study', *Hypatia: A Journal of Feminist Philosophy*, 9(1): 70–89.

Løgstrup, K.E. (1997) *The ethical demand*, Notre Dame, IN: University of Notre Dame Press.

Martínez Domínguez, M.T. and Scandrett, E. (2016) 'The politics of environmental justice: Community development in Ecuadorial and Peruvian Amazonia', in R. Meade, M. Shaw and S. Banks (eds) *Politics, power and community development*, Bristol: Policy Press, pp 159–77.

Marx, K. and Engels, F. (1848/1969) 'Manifesto of the Communist Party', in L. Feuer (ed), *Marx and Engels: Basic writings on politics and philosophy*, Glasgow: Collins/Fontana, pp 43–82.

Meade, R., Shaw, M. and Banks, S. (eds) (2016) *Politics, power and community development*, Bristol: Policy Press.

Mill, J.S. (1863/1972) 'Utilitarianism', in *Utilitarianism, on liberty, and considerations on representative government*, London: Dent.

Mills, C.W. (1970) *The sociological imagination*, Harmondsworth: Pelican.

Negri, A. (2003) *Time for revolution*, London: Continuum.

Noddings, N. (1984) *Caring: A feminine approach to ethics and moral education*, Berkeley: University of California Press.

NOS (National Occupational Standards) (2015) *Community development national occupational standards UK*, Wath-upon-Dearne: UK Commission for Employment and Skills. Available at: http://cldstandardscouncil. org.uk/wp-content/uploads/CDNOStandards2015.pdf

Oakley, J. and Cocking, D. (2001) *Virtue ethics and professional roles*, Cambridge: Cambridge University Press.

Owen, J. and Kemp, D. (2012) 'Assets, capitals and resources: Frameworks for corporate community development in mining', *Business and Society*, 51(3): 382–408.

Popple, K. (2015) *Analysing community work: Theory and practice* (2nd edn), Maidenhead: Open University Press.

Pyles, L. (2014) *Progressive community organising: Reflective practice in a globalizing world* (2nd edn), New York: Routledge.

Pyles, L. (2018) *Healing justice: Holistic self-care for change makers*, New York: Oxford University Press.

Shaw, M. and Mayo, M. (eds) (2016) *Class, inequality and community development*, Bristol: Policy Press.

Shevellar, L. and Barringham, N. (2016) 'Working in complexity: Ethics and boundaries in community work and mental health', *Australian Social Work*, 69(2): 181–93.

Shevellar, L., Westoby, P. and Connor, M. (2015) 'Flirting with danger: Practice dilemmas for community development in disaster recovery', *Community Development*, 46(1): 26–42.

Son, H.H. (2011) *Equity and well-being: Measurement and policy practice*, Abingdon: Routledge.

Taylor, T. and Banks, S. (2015) 'Ethics in youth work: A retreat from politics', *Concept*, 6(2): 14. Available at: http://concept.lib.ed.ac.uk/article/view/2411

Thomas, D. (1983) *The making of community work*, London: Allen and Unwin.

Tronto, J. (1993) *Moral boundaries: A political argument for an ethic of care*, London: Routledge.

Tronto, J. (2012) 'Partiality based on relational responsibilities: Another approach to global ethics', *Ethics and Social Welfare*, 6(3): 301–16.

Truog, R., Brown, S., Browning, D., Hundert, E., Rider, E., Bell, S. and Meyer, E. (2015) 'Microethics: The ethics of everyday clinical practice', *The Hastings Center Report*, 45(1): 11–17.

Westoby, P. (2014) *Theorising the practice of community development: A South African perspective*, Farnham: Ashgate.

Westoby, P. (2016) *Soul, community and social change: Theorising a soul perspective on community practice*, Farnham: Ashgate.

Westoby, P. and Dowling, G. (2014) *Theory and practice of dialogical community development: International perspectives*, Abingdon: Routledge.

Westoby, P. and Shevellar, L. (2014) 'Beware the trojan horse of professionalization: A response to De Beer et al. (2012), *Africanus*, 42(2)', *Africanus*, 44(1): 80–7.

WHO (World Health Organization) (2018) 'Equity', Geneva: WHO. Available at: www.who.int/healthsystems/topics/equity/en/

TWO

Community development in an unequal world: challenging neo-liberal values

Keith Popple

This is a very weird time in the world; we've sort of lost faith in our political system, we've lost faith in our leaders, we're not quite sure of our values, and I just hope that my winning the Nobel Prize contributes something that engenders goodwill and peace. It reminds us of how international the world is, and we have to contribute things from our different corners of the world.

(The British author Kazuo Ishiguro on hearing he was the winner of the 2017 Nobel in Literature, quoted in Ellis-Peterson and Flood, 2017: 1)

We're in the middle of a global struggle between liberal democracy and authoritarianism.

(Hillary Clinton, former US Democratic presidential candidate, speaking at the Cheltenham Literary Festival, England, October 2017, quoted in Wintour, 2017: 4)

Introduction

This chapter offers an overview of the rapidly changing social, economic and political context for community development practice globally and locally, highlighting the growing challenge to neo-liberalism as a credible economic and political strategy that offers stability and growth. I will consider the indicators of rising income and wealth inequality internationally and the resultant polarisation of societies, which are creating considerable risks to sound and secure global activity. The chapter discusses the drift of power away from the state and into the hands of unelected corporations, which presently receive vast sums of taxpayers' money for delivering what previously was public sector managed provision. The fast-changing milieu has created a situation where, particularly in the global North, people feel left behind and not listened to. I will look at the resultant rise in nationalism, and the demands for regional self-determination, all of which are reactions to circumstances with which people feel unable to identify.

The chapter refers to the core values of community development, and discusses the role the activity can play in challenging the risks of this new world through collective action in contexts that are local, national and international. I consider community development values in an environmental sustainability scenario and see how a community-led project has made connections between what is happening in local streets with the power and influence of a multinational corporation funded with public money.

The challenge to the credibility of neo-liberalism

We are presently witnessing unprecedented international social, economic and political change and challenge, the magnitude of which we have yet to fully understand. The change is so fast and deep that it can prove testing to capture both the current situation and the direction of travel in which this shift is moving. However, there are several aspects of these movements that have now crystallised, which give some measure of the challenge we will need to consider for the future direction of community development and the activity's significant values and ethical practice.

The impact of neo-liberal globalised finance capitalism has come to preoccupy populations in all societies. Importantly, neo-liberalism as both a theory and a practice is now undergoing a significant reassessment as to its credibility among millions of individuals and communities and by leading economists and commentators (Hall et al, 2013; Srnicek, 2016). The failure of the international established order to deliver on the promise of growth and stability has led communities and individuals globally experiencing inequality and insecurity to join a growing political consensus that is pressing for more economically viable, socially just, democratic, and socially and ecologically desirable alternatives.

To recap, neo-liberalism in different forms emerged as the dominant economic and political ideology in most 'developed' and 'developing' countries during the early 1980s (Bullock and Trombley,

1999; Piketty, 2014). The view was that neo-liberalism could better address persistent economic problems, which it was claimed were a symptom of many years of an over-reliance on state funded and state supported economic activity. For example, soaring levels of inflation, high levels of taxation on companies and individuals, and the action of powerful trade unions, were believed to be discouraging enterprise and preventing the necessary liberalisation of economies. The advocates of neo-liberalism, supported by the writings of the US economist and Nobel Prize winner Milton Friedman (1962, 1993; Friedman and Friedman, 1980), and Professor Friedrich von Hayek (1944, 1948, 1978) the Austrian-British economist and philosopher known for his criticisms of the Keynesian welfare state, argued that future rising prosperity and increased employment in a free market economy could best take place by privatising state assets. This would, according to the neo-liberal economists, policy makers and politicians, remove what were thought to be penal tax rates, and curb the power of trade unions and their right to free collective bargaining. Neo-liberals wanted to see easy access to markets and vital resources, and advocated that governments should strengthen internal security and contain alternatives to the status quo. The mantra of the time was that people should be required to 'stand on their own two feet' and encouraged to purchase their own and their families' housing, health, social care and education.

The push to 'roll back the state' and impose neo-liberal policies attracted responses from a number of key critics, including the renowned linguist Noam Chomsky who argued that global free trade damaged the livelihoods of people in the global North as well as driving 'developing' countries further into debt. In his view, the outcome for both the 'developed' and the 'developing' world has been the reduction and closure of public services while economies are restructured to suit Euro-American elites and corporations (Chomsky, 1998, 2003, 2017).

In his extensive writings Chomsky argues that neo-liberalism has seriously damaged 'developing' countries that the global North has claimed to assist through global finance. Chomsky presents evidence that negotiated loans to 'developing' countries actually add to a country's level of debt; that trade liberalisation makes the balance of payments worse by replacing domestic production with increased imports; and the International Monetary Fund (IMF) structural adjustment programme fails to promote growth in debtor nations. Instead these countries must pay back their debt through exports before they can focus on domestic growth.

The state gives way to the market

Over time, global North governments, in their pursuit of low personal taxation and the expansion of the market into the welfare state, such as health and education, have relinquished direct responsibilities for their citizens' welfare. Arguing that 'choice' should be central in economic and political affairs, they have hived off critical services normally provided by the state into a mix of state-corporate systems, which being hybrid arrangements are protected from challenge in areas such as commercial confidentiality, civil law and property rights. The outcome has seen vast sums of public money being channelled into the private sector, but without the protection usually associated with democratic organisations. In the UK this was most clearly seen in Private Finance Initiatives (PFIs), an approach which originated in Australia and which is now used extensively in many countries, particularly in the global North. PFIs are a method by which private companies provide the up-front funds for major public capital investments. These companies then receive payments from the public purse for the capital they invested. In many cases the private companies are responsible for operating the public facilities, sometimes using former public sector staff that have had their employment contracts transferred to the private sector. Individual PFIs, which usually run from between 25 to 30 years, have been deployed by British governments since 1992, and have been used in a range of public services including in the National Health Service, London Underground, school building programmes, social housing, defence contracts, prisons and road improvements.[1]

There is little doubt that PFIs have proved controversial. Those who are in favour of PFIs argue that the private sector is superior to the public sector at managing investment projects, creating overall cost efficiencies as well as bringing much needed up-front finance that the public sector could only achieve by raising taxes and instituting higher borrowing. The advocates also argue that the private sector can bring about innovation in a way the public sector cannot; it has higher specifications in regard to the delivery of projects; and it is able to lower maintenance costs.

However, critics of PFIs point to the significant debt incurred by governments when taking this route. UK government figures, for example, indicate that a £1 billion debt can cost £1.7 billion to clear (see website in note 1). There has also been concern that long contracts can be difficult and costly to change and overall can be poor value for money. Further, the cost of financing the debt prevents money going to front-line services (Pollock et al, 2002).

The 2008 international financial crash, austerity and the impact on communities

The international financial crash of 2008 and the ensuing fiscal crisis showed how globalised the world is and how closely tied countries are to each other. The crisis started in the US with banks lending to hundreds of thousands of homebuyers with poor credit histories, usually termed 'sub-prime lending'. The loans were then packaged into portfolios and with other bonds and assets were sold to investors worldwide. However, hikes in US bank interest rates led to large numbers of homebuyers defaulting on their mortgages as they could no longer afford the increasing monthly payments. As a result the American housing market slumped with properties having large loan-to-value mortgages and becoming worth less than the purchase price. As a consequence, the loans that had been sold to international investors significantly dropped in value. The outcome was a massive shortage of credit in the international financial system as banks became wary of lending to each other. In turn, investment banks around the world suffered significant financial losses leading to banks in the UK, Iceland and France being taken into government ownership to prevent them from collapsing (Mason, 2009). In the UK, the bailout of banks was estimated to have cost the government £141 billion (Oxfam, 2013).

The financial crash had a massive impact on economies worldwide, with high levels of indebtedness in countries such as Greece, Ireland and Portugal, the economies of which shrank while their level of indebtedness rose. Governments in many countries introduced 'austerity measures', which led to hundreds of millions of people globally experiencing stagnant wages and rising living costs alongside greater work insecurity. This is at a time when countries' welfare systems and public services were being reduced and in some cases disbanded, putting individuals, families and communities under increasing pressure (Varoufakis, 2017, 2018). Commentators such as the American economist and Nobel Prize winner Paul Krugman (2012) have argued that the real purpose of the introduction of 'austerity measures' by governments has been political rather than economic. It was, in his opinion, an opportunity for neo-liberal governments to reduce state expenditure and activity, and in particular to diminish the scope of social welfare, while maintaining the power of dominant classes and groups.

The impact of the financial crash on communities has resulted in an increasing lack of confidence in the present form of capitalism (that is, neo-liberal globalised finance capitalism) (Mason, 2012, 2015). One of the results of this lack of confidence in finance capitalism was the parallel lack of confidence in both the electoral system and the role of politicians, blamed by many voters for their financial insecurity. When neo-liberalism was introduced it quickly became considered the 'common sense' and 'taken-for-granted' response to previous economic failures. The individual was celebrated over the collective. However, as the virtues of the free market became critically questioned, it has waned in popularity as people felt the practical downside of the ideology. In the UK in 2016, for example, millions of voters who thought they had no natural political home for their despair, anger and sense of insecurity, voted in a referendum for the country to leave the European Union (Peston, 2017). In the British general election the following year, voters registered their opposition to the austerity policies of the Conservative government, which although returned as the largest party in Parliament, did so with a substantially reduced parliamentary majority and have since had to operate with support from the right-wing Northern Irish Democratic Unionist Party.

A legacy of the financial crash and the resultant lack of confidence in the established order has been increased pressure for the neo-liberal ideology to change and adjust. The demand for a major change had emerged in the early years of the twenty-first century when it was becoming clearer that the neo-liberal ideology was failing, with slower economic growth, greater inequality among huge swathes of the world's population, and more frequent financial crises (Chang, 2015). The Green movement had made this point much earlier, arguing that neo-liberalism needed a complete re-evaluation and extensive change if it was to regain the trust of populations worldwide (Woodin and Lucas, 2004). Others such as Mendoza (2015) argue that there is a need to abandon altogether neo-liberal economics and refute those economists that advocate the policies:

> Such economists use models to forecast economic performance that do not even include debt, money or time as factors. They contributed to the financial crisis by endorsing the behaviour of the financial services industry and of the governments that deregulated that industry. They not only failed to foresee the financial crisis, but actually said that it was an impossibility. To continue to seek answers from this community when they have so clearly been proven wrong, is utter folly. (Mendoza, 2015: 189)

There is also an increasing awareness of the impact of neo-liberalism on environmental sustainability, which we will consider later. In the US, for example, despite the protestations of climate change deniers, including President Donald Trump, there is now recognition of the connection between climate breakdown and the economy (see www.weforum.org/agenda). It is anticipated that in places like Florida (where Trump has a holiday home), the impact of rising sea levels together with the increased prevalence of hurricanes could lead to a slump in coastal property prices. This will have a knock-on effect on real estate mortgages, which could extend through banks, insurers and other industries in a manner not dissimilar to that experienced in the global financial crash of 2008 (Monbiot, 2017).

Growing inequality

One of the major criticisms of neo-liberalism has been its contribution to the increase in economic inequality – a cornerstone of its ideology and practice. The neo-liberal ideology is based on a belief that the 'market is the best arbiter in the creation of wealth and distribution of income' (Popple, 2015: 3) and according to the Organisation for Economic Co-operation and Development (OECD) has led to rising inequality in nearly every country on the planet. OECD (2015) research indicates that in most countries, the gap between rich and poor is at its highest level for 30 years. In OECD countries, the richest 10% of the population earn 9.6 times the income of the poorest 10%, whereas in the 1980s, this ratio stood at 7:1, rising to 8:1 in the 1990s, and 9:1 in the 2000s. In several emerging economies, particularly in Latin America, income inequality has narrowed, but income gaps remain generally higher than in OECD countries. While inequality has fallen in Turkey, Chile and Mexico, in the latter two countries the incomes of the richest remain more than 25 times those of the poorest. Emerging economies including China and India have enjoyed recurrent periods of strong economic growth, which has helped lift millions of their citizens out of poverty. However, OECD research has found that the benefits of this economic growth have not been evenly distributed and high levels of inequality have risen further.

Inequality is the focus of an influential report by Oxfam (2018), which reveals how the global economy enables the wealthy elite to accumulate vast fortunes while hundreds of millions of people are struggling to survive on poverty pay. The report outlines the key factors that are driving up rewards for shareholders and corporate employers at the expense of workers' pay and conditions. These include the excessive power of big business over government policy-making; the erosion of workers' rights; and the unabated drive by corporations to minimise costs in order to maximise returns to shareholders. The Oxfam report presents the following two powerful comments on the impact of inequality and injustice in the international garment-making and -selling industry: 'In 2016, annual share dividends from the parent company fashion chain Zara to the world's fourth richest man, Amancio Ortega, were worth approximately €1.3bn' (Oxfam, 2018: 8). And 'Anju works sewing clothes in Bangladesh for export. She often works 12 hours a day, until late at night. She often has to skip meals because she has not earned enough money. She earns just over $900 dollars [sic] a year' (Oxfam, 2018: 8).

Forbes (2017) reveals that in 2017 there was the biggest increase in the number of billionaires worldwide, who themselves experienced a huge increase in their wealth. Oxfam (2018: 8) claims that the wealth of these billionaires would end extreme poverty seven times over, with 82% of all the growth in global wealth going to the top 1%, whereas the bottom 50% had no increase at all. The Oxfam figures are supported by those from Credit Suisse (2017), whose research shows that 42 people own the same wealth as the poorest half of the world's population.

To understand this phenomenon I turn to the work of the French economist Thomas Piketty (2014). Piketty has produced findings from his extensive, groundbreaking research on the historical dynamics of wealth and income, which show, he argues, that a market economy has a principal destabilising force because:

> the private rate of return on capital ... can be significantly higher for long periods of time than the rate of growth of income and output ... the inequality ... implies that wealth accumulated in the past grows more rapidly than output and wages. This inequality expresses a fundamental logical contradiction. The entrepreneur inevitably tends to become a rentier, more and more dominant over those who own nothing but their labor. Once constituted, capital reproduces itself faster than output increases. The past devours the future. (Piketty, 2014: 746)

Piketty's revealing findings are based on research that analysed long-term trends in wealth distribution in 'developed' economies since the eighteenth century, and in particular the UK, Sweden, France, the US and Germany, where sufficient detailed data are available. Piketty explains how the accumulation of wealth creates further wealth, although after the Second World War there was what he calls 'convergence' with countries rebuilding economies and repairing the damage caused by the numerous bankruptcies of the 1930s depression. In the period from 1945 to the early 1980s, the nationalising of key industries and the strength of the trade union movement internationally helped reduce inequality. However, since then, there has been a return to a long-term trend of the accumulation of capital among the richest in societies which consistently outstrips economic growth rates. What this means is that the wealthiest individuals internationally who accumulated their wealth in previous decades have seen their fortunes continuing to grow faster than those gaining their wealth only from income. So counter to the capitalist edict that entrepreneurship and hard work is rewarded with greater wealth, the reality is that this is far outstripped by those with substantial inherited wealth, who do little in the way of paid employment. Piketty argues this state of affairs will lead to increased social conflict and disharmony and urgently needs to be addressed by radical means, particularly redistribution through a progressive global tax on wealth.

Internationally, inequality disparity, however, does not only reside in measurements of income and wealth. Evidence shows, for example, that those living in low-income countries such as Bangladesh, Nepal and large areas of eastern, western and sub-Saharan Africa dominated by agricultural economies, suffer from poor health outcomes. These countries suffer from inadequate health facilities, have homes and buildings that lack proper sanitation, and contain rivers and water supplies that are heavily polluted, leading to the risk of individuals and communities contracting diseases and infections. Moreover they are likely to suffer from famine and starvation as well as malnutrition which reduce individuals' ability to effectively fight illness and disease. All this reduces life expectancy.[2]

The polarisation of income and wealth, as well as other forms of inequality, is negatively impacting on communities globally. Rising nationalism is now commonplace in emerging markets like India, Turkey and the Philippines, as well as resonating in countries such as Hungary, Russia, Poland and the US. The US saw the election in 2016 of President Donald Trump, whose populist campaign emphasised protectionist and nationalist policies in order to capture the parts of the country that had been badly affected by globalisation. Heralding that he would 'Make America Great Again' Trump in office has turned his back on the poorest, many of whom voted for him as their saviour.

Instead Trump has reduced income tax rates, disproportionally assisting the richest, while removing regulation on businesses.

There is now proven data from established and respected international organisations that inequality damages economic growth and harms opportunities. For example the report by the OECD (2015) reveals the impact that growing and higher inequality has on both social cohesion and long-term economic growth. The report argues that the main transmission mechanism between inequality and growth is human capital investment. While there is always a gap in education outcomes across individuals with different socio-economic backgrounds, the difference widens in countries with high inequality as those from disadvantaged households struggle to access quality education. The outcome is a significant loss in people's potential and consequent lower social mobility. To overcome rising inequality the OECD is advocating a number of measures, including encouraging countries to focus on early years education; providing the appropriate skills for young people to participate in the labour market; and bringing businesses and unions together to promote the continuous upgrading of skills during a person's working life. The OECD also advocates wealthier individuals and multinational corporations paying their fair share of the tax burden. At the same time, the OECD report argues that low-income groups should be able to benefit from well-designed income-support policies.

Research by Dorling (2015, 2017a, 2017b) makes an important contribution to the thesis that inequality is not inevitable. Dorling's incisive arguments, supported with solid statistical evidence and research, show the steps that can be taken to reduce the impact of inequality and ways in which we can move towards greater equality that benefits everyone. This argument is similarly made by Wilkinson and Pickett, who present extensive evidence from a range of international sources that greater equality is possible and would create a 'qualitatively better and more sociable society for all' (2010: 272).

The reaction

One of the disturbing reactions to increasing inequality and the attendant changing circumstances has been the growth in the influence of anti-immigrant and anti-globalisation parties in European countries. In the 2017 German general election, the far-right Alternative for Germany party secured 20% of the votes cast in eastern Germany. Similarly during recent years there has been a rise in the popularity of the far-right National Front in France, while the far-right Freedom Party in Austria used the October 2017 general election to present messages that reflected hostility towards elites and outsiders, and campaigns centred mainly on immigration and fears of radical Islam.

The 2016 Brexit vote in the UK, too, had an element of nationalism where the pro-leaving EU campaign spearheaded by the United Kingdom Independence Party (UKIP), the right-wing of the Conservative Party, and some Labour Party MPs highlighted the demand to tightly regulate immigration in order to improve economic conditions for British workers. While there has been increasing nationalism, which has tested countries throughout the world, we have also seen communities and regions demanding the right to self-determination, a right which is written into Article 1 of the Charter of the United Nations.[3] For example, in Spain there has been a struggle in the Catalonia region for the right to claim its own identity separate from that of the national Spanish government based in Madrid. At the same time, in Italy people living in the northern regions of Lombardy and Veneto are demanding the right for self-determination and perceive many of their needs at odds with the priorities of the national government located in Rome. Meanwhile, although the Scottish Nationalist Party has experienced setbacks in recent elections, there remains a groundswell of opinion in Scotland that advocates for a different arrangement with the EU when the UK eventually leaves. According to Mason (2017) austerity, corruption and the failure of centralist governments to adapt and change have all contributed to the demands for self-determination. Mason argues that the need for self-determination is driven by the call to maintain and nurture cultural identity, as well as to attract financial investment into the regions which benefit the people living there rather than the countries and central governments within which they are presently located. According to Mason the issue of self-determination is about social justice.

The demand for self-determination is documented by Walker (2018), who provides examples of movements internationally. For example, he notes the protests in Sudan over the price of bread following a move to double it after IMF intervention. The Sudanese government ended subsidies for bread as part of an IMF-supported economic programme. In Iran there were protests in December 2017 and January 2018, with demonstrations which commenced by focusing on economic problems and expanded to include opposition to the government. The Iranian government described them as 'riots' and responded by censoring the internet.

The role for community development

The chapter moves now to consider the roles community development can play in addressing the considerable challenges and changes presently impacting on the international, national and local scene. To undertake this I will focus on the key area of environmental sustainability that will help us judge the possibilities of community development playing a part in the changing world at this time. I present a case study that shows how people have responded in their thousands in the city of Sheffield, England to threats to their local environment, demanding to be informed and consulted on an issue they consider of vital importance to their own well-being and that of the local environment.

In my previous work I have referred to the core values of community development, which inform practice and provide the basis for the ethically informed action that is possible in this unequal world (Popple, 2015). These centre on notions of social justice, equality and anti-discrimination, collective action, community empowerment, and working and learning together (see Banks, 2013; also Chapter One of this volume). In the following case study the motivations for community action are based on people's beliefs in social and environmental justice and their commitment to working together collectively to challenge established power structures and interests.

Environmental sustainability and community development

The concept of environmental sustainability has been around for a number of years. Recently it has become much more prominent in the international political arena, which is also reflected in its more prominent place in accounts of the values and purpose of community development (see Chapter One in this volume). A central argument is that globalisation has led to destroying the environment and what is needed is economic localisation to address issues of poverty, democracy and inequality. Scientists, environmental groups, campaigners, researchers and political parties have for many years alerted us to the impact of global warming, overpopulation, air and water pollution, resource depletion, food shortages, genetically modified crops, increasing consumerism, and the problems associated with the production of different forms of energy, including nuclear power and shale gas.

The importance here for community development is that the concept of environmental sustainability, although arguably not having a precise definition, exists to guide politicians in solving challenges at the global, national, and regional and community levels. What community development excels at is making the link between wider social, economic and political forces and the local and community.

Sheffield Tree Action Groups (STAG)

A recent illustration of community development in the UK and its relationship to environmental sustainability can be found in the work of the Sheffield Tree Action Groups (STAG), as outlined in the following case example. I offer this example as it meets with the broad definition of community development offered by Gilchrist and Taylor that the activity 'is primarily concerned with supporting communities around issues that they identify for themselves' (2016: 27). It is also in line with the IACD definition of community development, which acknowledges that: 'the strategies and tactics that communities choose to adopt (and that are most likely to enable them to achieve positive change) vary greatly, under the influence of different political, economic environmental, social and cultural contexts' (2018: 16).

Case example: STAG, 2012–18

STAG is a non-party political umbrella grouping that arose to oppose the threat to trees being felled in the city of Sheffield's streets. The tree felling came about due to Sheffield City Council (SCC) signing a 25-year £2.2 billion PFI contract with Amey plc, a subsidiary of a huge multinational company Ferrovial, which has its headquarters in Spain. As noted earlier, PFI contracts are not subject to the transparency rules that govern public sector organisations and have at their heart the ideology of neo-liberalism – using taxpayers' money to underwrite project financing that is arranged by the private sector. The argument is that PFIs use taxpayers' money more efficiently than if the projects were delivered by the public sector. In this case the contractor, Amey plc, was contracted to fell up to 6,000 trees in Sheffield as part of a 'Street Ahead' highway renewal programme that was launched in 2012. SCC's rationale for tree felling is given here by a local councillor: 'Tree replacement is always a last resort and happens only if a tree is dead, dying, diseased, dangerous or damaging' (Councillor Bryan Lodge, Cabinet member for environment and street scene, SCC, letter to *The Guardian*, 27 October, 2017).

SCC's main argument is that the trees need to be felled because of the root damage to the streets, pavements and kerbs. However STAG has substantial evidence, including written statements from residents and accompanying photographs as presented on their website (www.savesheffieldtrees.org.uk) that suggest otherwise. The view from STAG is that a large mature tree provides considerably more environmental benefits than the small trees that are replacing them. The STAG website claims that it would 'take 60 replacement trees to replace overall the volume of one mature tree'. They also claim that there is a high expected failure rate of new planting and it will take many decades before a replacement tree comes close to fulfilling the same role as the tree being felled. Photographs on the website show pictures of newly planted trees that are themselves causing damage to pavements with raised paving slabs. Finally, the STAG website lists the top ten benefits of having trees in the street, which the group says improves 'our health, our communities and our climate'.

STAG has had its case discussed on regional and national radio and TV programmes (including on the nationally broadcast prime-time television programme *The One Show*, BBC1, 4 January, 2017), they have a dedicated busy Twitter account and in 2017 there was almost daily coverage of the stand-off between SCC and the group covered in regional and national newspapers and magazines (Bramley, 2018).

STAG members state they do not object to the removal of dead, dying, dangerous or significantly diseased trees and they do not want to prevent highway tree stock renewal. However, they claim that the present tree-felling practice is far too drastic and believe that some of the trees being removed have over 100 years of safe and useful life expectancy. STAG is demanding a halt to all non-essential tree felling operations and asking SCC to undertake a robust evidence-based Highway Tree Strategy, similar to those undertaken in other UK cities. They also want SCC to carry out a cost–benefit analysis that acknowledges the value of street trees in Sheffield. Their view is that:

> Sheffielders are being expected to foot the bill for the removal of healthy, albeit 'damaging' or 'discriminatory' trees, when felling is more expensive than repairing the kerb or pavement. It does not take a huge leap of imagination to conclude that Amey's profit-motive is the deciding factor, and that this is written into the sections of the 'Streets Ahead' contract that the public are not allowed to see. (www.savesheffieldtrees.org.uk, accessed 28 October 2017)

STAG is a community-led group engaging in community action and campaigning for social and environmental justice purposes. With a focus on a single issue, and tactics of mobilising broad-based support, STAG is adopting many of the recognisable strategies of community organising (see Pyles in Chapter Eight of this volume). STAG members are drawn from communities that are affected across the city – people who are involved in 'local tree groups' and who have used a variety of methods to raise their concerns. The action by STAG is to be applauded on a number of levels. First, we know from research and practice accounts (for example, Warburton, 1998; Ledwith, 2005; Popple, 2015; Gilchrist and Taylor, 2016) that successful community development intervention commences with people's everyday experiences and becomes collectivised in a dynamic form when people learn from and engage with each other. The sharing of experiences and the accompanying human inquiry encourages and assists the process of making critical connections between personal experiences and the oppressive structures that impact on them. As Ledwith comments: 'Community development always focuses on the stories of the people as the basis of action and reflection ... Without an analytical commentary linking the personal to the political, stories remain subjective and without criticality' (Ledwith, 2005: 67).

This is clearly happening in the Sheffield experience where the STAG website provides both accounts of people's experience and a critical appraisal of the PFI that has enabled this tree felling to take place. It also offers a critique of other PFIs and the harm they can do in terms of democracy, while providing evidence of them being poor value for money.

Second, the actions taken by STAG and its local tree groups are challenging the top-down approach to solutions. STAG members argue that they want a dialogue between themselves and SCC, as relations are proving to be unsatisfactory. Community development values highlight and support community-led collective action, participatory democracy, empowerment and collaboration. While STAG is democratic and empowers its members through collaboration, it is being faced with a hybrid arrangement that defends capital and corporate profits at the expense of democracy. If anyone wants to experience and understand the downside of neo-liberalism then this situation in Sheffield is an example.

The stand-off between STAG and SCC as presented here provides us with a case study of both the best of community development values and ethical practice and the worst of neo-liberal economic policies as practised locally on communities, adding to the unpopularity of neo-liberalism. It also highlights the calls to find alternatives that are focused on the needs of local communities rather than those of private corporations and investors. There is overwhelming scientific evidence that globally our environment is deteriorating and the work of STAG is an example of how citizens of one city have worked collectively, collaboratively and democratically to propose an alternative to the mass street tree felling. The work of STAG shows the importance of values-based community development that is focused on local action and change, while maintaining an understanding of the wider economic and political environment that is opposed to these alternatives.

The implications for community development

As we move through the twenty-first century the challenges facing community development as a process, a practice and an occupation are considerable. The widening gap between the rich and the poor in terms of income, health and life chances, together with the increasing massive accumulation of wealth of the global super-rich, are placing an enormous strain on the credibility of the neo-liberal doctrine and practice which many governments are entrenching even further. Meanwhile, these same governments have failed to properly respond to the environmental crisis and climate change which are posing a real threat to the future of sustainable life on earth.

The disproportionate impact of 'austerity measures' on people's life chances, living standards and incomes alongside swingeing cuts in public services, and in particular welfare services, in the pursuit of addressing the financial crisis in many countries is leading people everywhere to look seriously at just, socially equitable and democratic alternatives. Hence we are seeing demands for self-determination and nationalism in some areas, sometimes alongside groups and political parties calling for a halt to immigration.

It was in the period after the Second World War that community development emerged as a force: a period during which wealth and income was slowly and modestly redistributed and the state intervened in addressing social ills and establishing social rights. The situation now is different. Globalisation and neo-liberalism have clawed back many of the gains made by the working class as the market was moved centrally into people's lives. If the state financially supports community development it does so with goals more aligned to the needs of neo-liberalism than the ideals of social democracy.

The outcome is that community development has to find a new and dynamic role for itself. This role is based on its core values, providing a voice for those damaged by the excessive power of corporations, the interests of a privileged class that benefits from their rapid accumulation of wealth at the expense of the poor and who lack any real understanding of the needs and lives of 'ordinary people'. At the same time, community development needs to reflect and address the complex class, gender and racial divisions. These divisions are often used to exploit and divide people from each other. However, these same differences can be used as a source of strength in driving protest movements, campaigns and local projects.

In these uncertain and difficult days community development, with its roots in localities impacted by the many negative aspects of neo-liberalism, has an important role in its theory and practice to counter the ideology of individualism, the pursuit of instant gratification, the frequent disregard for moral standards, and the acceptance of massive inequalities. Never have the values of community development been more urgent and significant.

Concluding comments

This chapter has provided an overview of the rapidly changing context that community development presently occupies. We have noted the challenge to the credibility of neo-liberal economic policies, which have failed thousands of communities and millions of people worldwide who are experiencing growing inequality and insecurity due to their governments' policies and the resultant economic and social polarisation. At the same time, governments in the global North have removed themselves from the delivery of certain services to citizens and instead have channelled enormous amounts of taxpayers' money into projects such as PFIs which have proved controversial and have been shown to be undemocratic and poor value for money.

One of the reactions to people feeling left behind, together with their negative experience of austerity, has been growing nationalism. In certain regions, too, there have been demands for self-determination as people feel their national governments have failed satisfactorily to change and respond to their particular needs.

It is in this dynamic and rapidly changing context that community development needs to dig deep into its values and respond to the significant challenges that confront communities. We have seen in the example of action taken by residents in Sheffield that it is possible both to practise in a way that reflects community development values, while challenging the local authority whose PFI contract has led to action being taken by the contractor that is contrary to people's wishes and to environmental sustainability.

Evidence points to neo-liberal globalised finance capitalism being to blame for growing inequality both between and within countries. At the same time there has been a movement away from power residing with elected governments, workers and citizens, and a growth in the power and influence of private corporations and investors creating risks to stable and secure global activity. Community development has a role to play in proposing an alternative to systems that polarise societies and damage communities. One way it can engage is to be certain of its values, which are fundamental to achieving progressive democratic, socially and economically just ways of operating where the needs of people and communities are put before the needs of private capital.

Notes

[1] See: www.gov.uk/government/publications/private-finance-initiative-and-private-finance-2-projects-2015-summary-data

[2] See: www.who.int/sdhconference/background/news/facts/en/

[3] See: www.un.org/en/sections/un-charter/chapter-i/index/

References

Banks, S. (2013) 'Negotiating values, power and responsibility: Ethical challenges for managers', in S. Banks, H. Butcher, A. Orton and J. Robertson (eds) *Managing community practice: Principles, policies and programmes* (2nd edn), Bristol: Policy Press, pp 99–122.

Bramley, E.V. (2018) 'The roots of resistance', *The Guardian*, 28 February: 8–9.

Bullock, A. and Trombley, S. (eds) (1999) *The new Fontana dictionary of modern thought*, London: Harper Collins.

Chang, H.-J. (2015) 'The failure of neoliberalism and the future of capitalism', in S. Fujii (ed) *Beyond global capitalism*, Tokyo: Springer, pp 19–34.

Chomsky, N. (1998) *Profit over people: Neoliberalism and the global order*, New York: Seven Stories Press.

Chomsky, N. (2003) *Understanding power: The indispensable Chomsky*, London: Vintage.

Chomsky, N. (2017) *Who rules the world?* London: Hamish Hamilton.

Credit Suisse (2017) *Global wealth report 2017*, Zurich: Credit Suisse. Available at: www.credit-suisse.com/corporate/en/research/research-institute/global-wealth-report.html

Dorling, D. (2015) *Injustice: Why social inequality persists*, Bristol: Policy Press

Dorling, D. (2017a) *The equality effect: Improving life for everyone*, Oxford: New Internationalist.

Dorling, D. (2017b) *Do we need economic inequality?* Cambridge: Polity Press.

Ellis-Peterson, H. and Flood, A. (2017) 'Kazuo Ishiguro wins the Nobel Prize in literature 2107', *The Guardian*, 6 October: 1.

Forbes (2017) 'The world's billionaires, 2017 ranking'. Available at: www.forbes.com/billionaires/list/

Friedman, M. (1962) *Capitalism and freedom*, Chicago: University of Chicago.

Friedman, M. (1993) *Why government is the problem*, Stanford, CA: Hoover Institution Press.

Friedman, M. and Friedman, R. (1980) *Freedom to choose: A personal statement*, San Diego, CA: Harcourt.

Gilchrist, A. and Taylor, M. (2016) *The short guide to community development* (2nd edn), Bristol: Policy Press.

Hall, S., Massey, D. and Rustin, M. (2013) 'After neoliberalism: Analysing the future', *Soundings*, 53: 8–25.

Hayek, F.A. (1944) *The road to serfdom*, Chicago: University of Chicago Press.

Hayek, F.A. (1948) *Individualism and economic order*, London: Routledge.

Hayek, F.A. (1978) *The constitution of liberty*, Chicago: University of Chicago Press.

IACD (International Association for Community Development) (2018) *Towards Shared International Standards for Community Development Practice*, Glasgow: IACD. Available at: www.iacdglobal.org/wp-content/uploads/2018/06/IACD-Standards-Guidance-May-2018_Web-1.pdf

Krugman, P. (2012) *End this depression now!* New York: W.W. Norton.

Ledwith, M. (2005) *Community development: a critical approach* (2nd edn), Bristol: Policy Press.

Mason, P. (2009) *Meltdown: The end of the age of greed*, London: Verso.

Mason, P. (2012) *Why it's kicking off everywhere: The new global revolutions*, London: Verso.

Mason, P. (2015) *Postcapitalism: A guide to our future*, London: Verso.

Mason, P. (2017) 'Catalonia, Lombardy, Flanders … why are regions around Europe striving for self-determination now?' *The Guardian*, 23 October. Available at: www.theguardian.com/commentisfree/2017/oct/23/we-need-to-understand-why-catalonia-lombardy-scotland-are-reposing-question-of-self-determination

Mendoza, K.-A. (2015) *Austerity: The demolition of the welfare state and the rise of the zombie economy*, Oxford: New Internationalist.

Monbiot, G. (2017) 'Capitalism can't save the planet – it can only destroy it', *The Guardian*, 13 September. Available at: www. theguardian.com/commentisfree/2017/sep/13/hurricane-irma-capitalism-growth-economics-environment-financial-crisis

OECD (Organisation for Economic Co-operation and Development) (2015) *In it together: Why less inequality benefits all*, Paris: OECD.

Oxfam (2013) *Truth and lies about poverty: Ending comfortable myths about poverty*, Cardiff: Oxfam Cymru.

Oxfam (2018) *Reward work, not wealth*, Oxford: Oxfam. Available at: www.oxfam.org/en/research/reward-work-not-wealth

Peston, R. (2017) *WTF?* London: Hodder & Stoughton.

Piketty, T. (2014) *Capital in the twenty-first century*, London: The Belknap Press of Harvard University Press.

Pollock, A.M., Shaoul, J. and Vickers, N. (2002) 'Private finance and "value for money" in NHS hospitals: A policy in search of rationale?' *British Medical Journal*, 324(7347): 1205–9.

Popple, K. (2015) *Analysing community work: Theory and practice* (2nd edn), Maidenhead: Open University Press.

Srnicek, N. (2016) 'What comes after neoliberalism?', film of talk at the launch of Economic and Social Research Aotearoa. Available at: www.esra.nz/what-comes-after-neoliberalism

Varoufakis, Y. (2017) *And the weak suffer what they must? Europe, austerity and the threat to global stability*, London: Vintage.

Varoufakis, Y. (2018) *Adults in the room: My battle with Europe's deep establishment*, London: Vintage.

Walker, T. (2018) 'News from movements around the world', *Red Pepper*, February/March: 6–7.

Warburton, D. (ed) (1998) *Community and sustainable development: Participation in the future*, London: Earthscan.

Wilkinson, R. and Pickett, K. (2010) *The spirit level: Why equality is better for everyone*, London: Penguin.

Wintour, P. (2017) 'Clinton tours Britain to condemn Brexit, Putin and Weinstein', *The Guardian*, 16 October: 4.

Woodin, M. and Lucas, C. (2004) *Green alternatives to globalisation: A manifesto*, London: Pluto Press.

PART 2

Everyday ethics in community development practice

THREE

Negotiating roles and boundaries: ethical challenges in community work

Lynda Shevellar and Neil Barringham

Introduction

In recent times, Professor Susan Kenny called for 'an unsettled and edgy community development' that went beyond 'social maintenance and defensive active citizenship' (2011: i7). Such edgy community work demands critical, proactive, visionary, cosmopolitan and active citizens who are prepared to challenge existing structures, values and power relations (p i7). But what do workers do when being edgy and being employed are increasingly at odds with one another? Tensions such as this exemplify the deep and uncomfortable ethical questions facing community workers described in this chapter. In this discussion we listen to the reflections of workers who are currently engaged at the front-line of 'unsettled and edgy' community work.

Many community workers hold an aspiration for paid employment. A formal role and (albeit modest) income in the field that they have trained in enables people to pursue the work they want to do, seemingly with the luxury of more resources and time. At least in Australia, where our work is located, there is often a real struggle between people's initial vision for the work and the reality of their work context. Workers initially enter the field driven by their desire to work with and support people and find themselves unprepared for a world of competitive tendering, financial and staff management concerns, audit cultures, market-based welfare systems and outcomes evaluation. Such a world is often at odds with a worker's personal values (Rosenman, 2000). As a number of social work commentators have noted, the reconstruction of people as customers, the prioritisation of financial over personal relationships, and the moral authoritarianism reflected in, for example, the scapegoating of young people and asylum seekers, all create dissonance with the motivations that bring people into human services work in the first place to be a potential basis for change (Butler and Drakeford, 2001; Ferguson and Lavalette, 2006). Thus the environments that workers experience can create a strong incongruity between the values found in policy mandates and organisational mission statements, and the values workers find themselves inhabiting through their actions and inactions (Argyris and Schön,1974).

Professional community workers may have different accountabilities to employers, to funders, to professional bodies and accreditors, to the people with whom they are working and to different community-based interest groups. Workers may wrestle with dual relationships; needing to manage being in a professional paid role while also being a neighbour, friend, relative and/or colleague. And there are also contested loyalties, which influence ways of working. How can a paid worker be an activist at the same time? What does it mean to hold a desire for radical social change while working within the context of a politically or socially conservative organisation? In this chapter we name some of the ethical tensions that community workers encounter and explore what it means to work ethically in community work.

Background

We have deliberately used the term 'community work' to encompass a range of job titles (discussed further later). We argue that what is central is not the title but the practice. We see the key element of this work as recognition that community is not simply the site in which activities take place – but the means by which change occurs (Burkett, 2001). This kind of work, at least in its normative sense, assists citizens to band together and to utilise their collective power to effect change in the matters that affect their lives. This banding together can emerge *organically*, with people finding one another within their existing networks, or alternatively, it can happen *purposefully* with someone (paid or unpaid) taking the role of networking and inviting people to come together (Westoby and Shevellar, 2012). Underpinning this kind of work is a shared belief in the fundamental *good* of working for positive change in the lives of people and society. Shaw (1997: 61) provides a useful starting place for discussion: 'Community work is essentially a moral activity, concerned with the creation of a better and fairer world. Its curriculum should emerge from the social reality of those we work with at the grassroots and should seek to locate personal experience in collective forms of reflection and action.'

At the same time, this notion of moral activity to create 'a better and fairer world' creates a tension for workers as they wrestle with what constitutes ethical behaviour. Who determines the fairer world, and in what ways is it better for whom? This ethical complexity is captured by Kelly and Westoby (2018: 14) who argue that:

> The study of people-centred development involves an exploration of human values and beliefs, and an examination of theory and practice wisdom that shapes helpful, purposeful action. It is not a study that involves only objective knowledge, hard facts and scientific rationales. It is a study of the human capacity for change and transformation and as such it can be complex, confusing, frustrating and/ or rewarding.

In this way we argue that ethics cannot be separated from the practice of community work, but is an intrinsic part of it.

Many workers would be familiar with the conceptual model of ethics as working at multiple levels. Traditional sociological approaches recognise three 'levels' of inquiry in which practice may be observed and understood: micro, meso and macro (Austin et al, 2005, 2016). For example, at the micro level, workers consider their own conduct and the rights of individual participants. Concern is with the level of individual actors within organisations. At the meso level workers are required to think about the expectations of their given profession and thus concern is located in the intermediate level of organisations. Finally, at the macro level, a worker needs to consider her or his duty to, and the expectations of, society, and thus concerns are at the level of social institutions. Models such as this have tended to be adopted by a range of fields, such as social work, nursing, engineering and business. Tensions between micro and macro levels of practice have long been acknowledged. In social work in particular, micro and macro levels of practice have increasingly become separate fields of work with their own professional identities. Workers see themselves as working either with individuals in clinical settings or working in community settings, with an often-divisive tone between the two (Austin et al, 2005). However, what we argue here is that this traditional sociological approach has been largely unhelpful to community workers and has led to greater rather than less confusion. We suggest that there are ethical implications at all levels for the worker who is often required to hold competing and contradictory ethical demands at once.

In this chapter we explore the 'complex, confusing, frustrating and/ or rewarding' work that Kelly and Westoby characterise, and in doing so, explore what constitutes ethical behaviour in the mind of the community worker, to better understand how decisions are made about the best way to act.

In undertaking this writing we acknowledge that as authors and researchers we, too, are engaging with ethical frontiers. Previously, we have named this kind of research and writing as a 'risky conversation' (Shevellar and Barringham, 2016: 181). To speak honestly about how we work requires us to move beyond the glib patter and reassuring facade of detached, theoretical and professional discussion. Such a task interrogates what people think and what they actually do, and thus requires extraordinary candour, potentially making people vulnerable to the scrutiny of the field. It means articulating practices that may directly contravene organisational edicts and even contradict conventional wisdom of good practice. But we argue this work is vital if we are to tread the delicate line between safety and growth for our practice. And it is this work that will take us in this discussion into a place where we can respond to Kenny's call for 'an unsettled and edgy' kind of work that goes beyond social maintenance.

Community work as a moral activity

In considering the challenge inherent in Shaw's thinking, quoted earlier, it is tempting to respond that it is 'the community' itself that determines the better and fairer world. Such a response however is both idealistic and simplistic. Numerous interrogations of community participation have demonstrated its limitations and shown how participatory practices can be co-opted to serve various masters and ultimately undermine rather than assist the communities for which they are apparently designed (see for example, Guijt and Shah, 1998; Cornwall, 2008; MacLeod and Emejulu, 2014; Penderis, 2014; Thomas and Van de Fliert, 2015). The simple top-down/bottom-up binary is an inadequate determiner for judging the worthiness of the work, and workers require a more sophisticated ethical framework to guide their practice.

A framework is a means of synthesising complex sources of knowledge, skills and values, to assist workers to navigate the work (O'Connor et al, 2008). This section of the chapter provides an overview of the literature on how community workers typically build an ethical framework for themselves. We identify four layers to this framework that give direction to the decisions workers make. We offer a limited discussion of these four layers, and later will draw from the reflections of community workers about the relative value of these layers to their work. These four layers can be understood as professional ethics, organisational ethics, personal ethics and situational ethics.

Professional ethics

The first, perhaps most obvious ethical layer is adherence to external regulations, standards and professional codes of conduct, established by a national or global professional accrediting body. Perhaps the best example is the International Federation of Social Workers (IFSW), which has developed global standards for the education and training of the social work profession, which then flow into national regulatory bodies.

One of the challenges of the work is that community workers are no more homogenous than the communities they serve. They may be employed in a professional capacity, work as volunteers, or they may act in their citizen role. As such they may have highly formal qualifications based on education and training in community work or a related field of practice, some training, or none whatsoever. Backgrounds of community workers are equally diverse. Alongside qualifications in community work may be training in human services, welfare, social work, psychology, social and town planning, social science, arts and cultural work, government sector work, international relations, development and foreign aid, or theological studies – just to name a few. As already indicated, some workers, such as psychologists and social workers, are part of a professional body and sign up to professional codes of conduct. However, in Australia and many other countries, there is no single training or educational background, and there is no compulsory professional regulatory body for community workers. Although there is an Australian Community Workers Association (ACWA), which covers human services, it is a voluntary organisation and workers in Australia do not require ACWA registration to gain employment and many of the educational backgrounds of community workers mentioned here are not recognised.

Added to this is the complexity that many community workers are not situated in formally named community work or community development roles, but rather, will operate in developmental, people-oriented roles under the guise of other titles such as 'project officer', 'resource officer', 'consultant', 'inclusion worker' or even 'support worker'.

Professional standards for community development practice are currently being developed on the international stage (IACD, 2018). Yet, already within Australia there are resistant voices to these attempts (Lathouras, 2017). There is frustration over a perceived preoccupation with paid roles, and a discussion that fails to adequately recognise volunteer and citizen-led community work, and that subsequently reduces community development to a professional project. We see this chapter as potentially contributing to this discussion by acknowledging that professionalism can sometimes increase complexity, rather than automatically reduce it.

Organisational ethics

The second ethical layer focuses on people connected to an organisation through paid or volunteer community roles. Ethical behaviour is prescribed by job descriptions detailed in organisational codes of conduct, and reinforced through training and supervision.

One of the unpopular truths of the community sector is that the roles of paid professional community workers are usually different from and much more ethically complex than those of volunteers and community activists. Employees may be surprised to find themselves with less, rather than greater, clarity – despite the well-written job descriptions. People may come to their work with very clear spiritual and professional dreams, but then find themselves disappointed in the role. For example, a worker may understand their role as dedicated to community inclusion. They may see that inviting a person they work with to a community group in which they both share an interest, or introducing a person they work with to others in their life with similar interests, as an act of hospitality and deliberate community inclusion. However, the employing organisation may have strict views on personal boundaries and forbid the sharing of networks and the socialising of workers and the people with whom they are working (see Shevellar and Barringham, 2016).

Further, there is often a real struggle between people's initial vision for the work and the reality of their work context. This reality is increasingly shaped by the dynamics of new public management, public austerity, market-based welfare systems, and audit cultures (Power, 1994; Shore and Wright, 2015). As Banks observes, in such an environment the danger is that practice becomes dominated by 'employer-designed protocols, government-demanded outcomes and marketised measures of efficiency' (Banks, 2013: 597), with the consequence that professional ethics can be pulled too far into the new accountability paradigm – what Banks (2013: 597) calls 'the managerialisation of professional ethics'. Far from providing support and guidance to community workers as they grapple with complex settings, organisational frameworks tend to promote increasing levels of mistrust, as professional judgement is replaced by formal systems of auditing and inspection. Comments from workers later in this discussion will illustrate this point clearly.

Personal ethics

The third ethical layer is that of the individual themselves and their own personal practice framework that helps to guide their way of working. Kelly sees frameworks as useful in enabling workers to become more conscious of the way they work, helping to order the work and ensuring safe, predictable ways of managing dilemmas as they emerge (Kelly, cited in Westoby and Ingamells, 2012: 385). Additionally, as Kelly and Westoby (2018: 8) point out:

> Because people are so different, those differences make the work complex, interesting and varied, and of course sometimes very difficult. The reality is that workers cannot deal with all the issues that such diversity brings. In participatory development work, creating order from this complexity does not come from organizational authority, but from a range of frameworks.

Kelly and Westoby advocate the purposeful articulation of frameworks to help workers navigate the chaos of practice (2018: 7). However, even where such an explicit exercise has not taken place, people still operate through frameworks, albeit implicit and perhaps unconscious, constructed through their cultural upbringing, socialisation in dominant institutions, and personal experiences over their lifespan – the accumulation of what they know and what they believe.

This idea of frameworks sits alongside, and perhaps is part of, what Banks (2013: 598) refers to as 'professional wisdom'. By this she means:

> sensitivity to and the ability to perceive the ethically salient features of a situation; empathy with the feelings, values, desires and perspectives of the people involved and the ability to exercise moral imagination; the ability to reflect on and deliberate over what is the right course of action; and the ability to give reasons for actions.

So, whereas frameworks would determine how a worker might engage with a community to undertake the necessary work, professional wisdom enriches this with a sense of what the 'right' work might be.

Situational ethics

In thinking about the context of community work, three unique challenges for workers emerge. First, the nature of the work itself often requires multilayered and embedded relationships. This means that what we call dual relationships, where people are known in multiple roles, are much more likely. Community workers, grounded in community life, are not only workers, but at any time may be neighbours, colleagues, fellow citizens and members of a group, team, congregation or even a family. This layering is what allows them to appreciate the complexities and assets of the community, enabling them to do the work well; but it also means the worker is not afforded the luxury of a single bounded professional persona. Dual roles – so often denounced by ethical counsel – may be a greater risk in community work, but they may also strengthen and deepen the work.

The second challenge is that community work occurs in any range of settings: in a cafe, on a park bench, in a meeting room, over a fence, in a hall, in a supermarket, in someone's home, on the street or in any other community setting. There may be no doors to close, desks to sit behind, telephones to hang up or superiors to keep an eye on proceedings. Additionally, time may be more opportunistic and happenstance, working despite – rather than because of – careful planning and organisation. This means that there may not be clear 'appointment times' with indicators to suggest when the allotted time is over. In practice, this means that much of community work is spatially and temporally unbounded. In community work the boundaries tend to be less clear, leaving many workers confused about whether it is appropriate to develop deeper relationships, participate in social activities, serve on community boards, provide one's home phone number, accept goods and services, discuss religious or political beliefs, or how and whether physical touch is permitted. This accords with the work of Jayaratne et al (1997) in social work who observed that situations for workers are rarely clear. And this makes boundary crossing far more likely.

Third, the nature of the work means that the worker is often not in control of the context. As Kelly and Westoby (2018: 7) observe:

Many jobs are structured and organized such that the workers are given a fixed set of priorities, an established order of implementation, and control over the resources to complete the work. This level of control is rarely possible in participatory development work, for community members are not staff over whom the worker has authority, nor are the issues that they face simple enough to respond to mechanistically and with production line type answers. Working in, and with, communities in a participatory way is a complex activity with many variables beyond the control of the worker.

These three factors make community work more ethically challenging than many other so-called 'helping professions', lending support for what Banks (2016: 36) calls 'ethics work' – by which she means that workers need to be understood as moral agents 'in context' (see also Chapter One in this volume). Importantly Banks proposes what she calls a 'situated ethics' by which she means that dilemmas and decisions are placed in a broader social, political and cultural context, and responsibility is located beyond the isolated individual decision maker in a wider, more relational sense. Such thinking demonstrates the limitations of professional and organisational ethics, as well as the limits of the ethics training that workers may receive. How, after all, does one train for contexts as diverse as these?

We have presented these four ethical influences as layers of an ethical framework that each worker needs to negotiate and construct for themselves. And while it would be ideal if all four layers integrated seamlessly, we suspect that the experience of workers is nowhere as neat and balanced as this idea. As will become evident from the ensuing discussion, professional, personal, organisational and situational ethics can pull workers in different directions with little space of overlap (see Figure 3.1). How then do workers navigate their ethical worlds? In the next section we give an account of a small piece of research with Australian community workers that explored their self-identified ethical challenges.

Collecting stories from practice: methodology

A workshop was held with community workers in Brisbane to probe the nature of ethical challenges in community work. We were keen to ensure stories came from not one particular sector but from a range

Figure 3.1: Building an ethical framework for community work

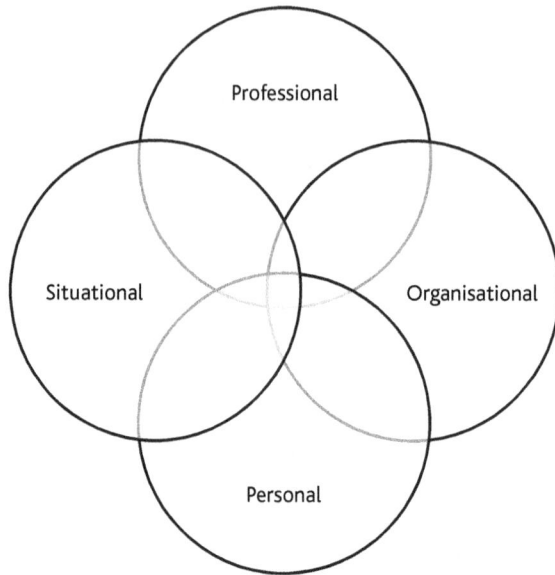

of practice contexts. We identified 17 different practice contexts and sent invitations to community workers in each of these types of organisations which contained an earlier version of the abstract for this chapter, inviting people to come and comment on how they were experiencing the ethical challenges of their work. Ten people accepted the invitation, with nine able to attend the focus group on the day. The workers were drawn from the following practice contexts: community neighbourhood centres, a community garden, mental health work, community inclusion work, local government, domestic violence, disability, work with migrants, work with people who are homeless, and work with refugees and asylum seekers. Workers were located in a number of different roles: all were engaged directly in community work, but some were also managers. Most workers spoke from both a paid and unpaid context – meaning they undertook community work in a paid role, but also undertook some form of community volunteer work in addition to this. We also conducted follow-up interviews with two additional participants to enable us to pursue particular issues raised in greater depth. Of the participants, seven were female and four were male.

The workshop utilised the spiral model of facilitation (see Arnold et al, 1991: 48), which is illustrated in Figure 3.2. The spiral model encompasses five steps: (1) The process begins by inviting participants

Figure 3.2: The spiral model

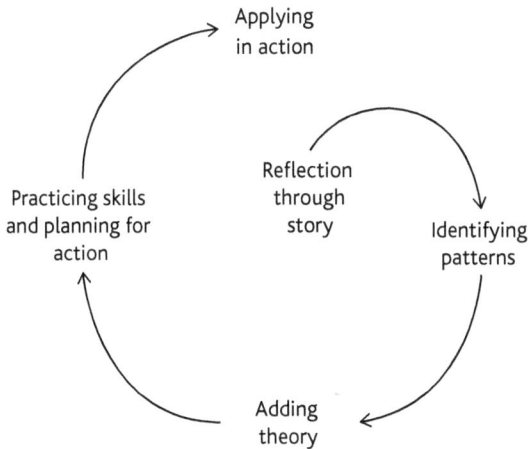

Applying
in action

Reflection
through
story

Identifying
patterns

Practicing skills
and planning for
action

Adding
theory

Source: Arnold et al, 1991: 48

to reflect on their experiences by asking, 'What is the greatest tension for you in trying to do good community work?' and then asking them to illustrate that tension by telling a story from their practice. (2) Identifying patterns: after all the stories were told, participants were asked to think across the stories to identify places of connection as well as disconnection. Ideas were clustered and themes emerged from these clusters. (3) New theory and information was added by the facilitators, drawing from their previous research into ethics and community work. (4) Participants were invited to consider frameworks or ideas they found helpful in navigating tensions within their work and to plan for further engagement with this tension. (5) Participants then moved from planning into action.

The two authors facilitated the process, and also both took extensive notes. Narratives were transcribed and copies sent back to participants after the workshop for verification, clarification or change. The project received ethical clearance from the University of Queensland.

Stories from practice: findings

How do community workers describe the primary ethical challenges in their practice? What common threads and patterns are there across their stories and experiences?

What frameworks assist workers to make ethical decisions? To answer these questions we now describe some of the themes emerging from our discussions. We have utilised the ethical framework presented earlier, to order the findings of our research and to speak through and back to the literature on ethics.

The danger of professional standards

The first and clearest finding was that for the community workers with whom we met, there was no direct reference to external bodies or professional standards. For all the reasons outlined earlier, this was not surprising. For example, one community worker we spoke with who worked as an 'inclusion worker' had no formal community work training, had worked in retail and in construction and came to the work by being "around the place" and "knowing lots of people". His entry into paid community work was when people receiving support from an organisation asked if he would be willing to join the organisation to assist them. This was a trajectory for a number of people who had befriended or advocated for people who were vulnerable: they were friends first and were invited to receive payment for particular work that they were undertaking with a community organisation. In practice, this meant that many of the questions asked in the name of ethical challenges were met with perplexity.

Conventional wisdom on ethics sees dual relationships – relationships where a professional inhabits a number of roles, for example as a worker and as a friend – as problematic because the abuse of power is more likely to occur. When the professional relationship becomes a dual relationship the exercising of power is not checked by the rules of professional conduct (Kagle and Giebelhausen, 1994). This is not necessarily a conscious or deliberately malevolent transgression, there is collusion by both members of the relationship, and both may be under the false illusion that power is being more equally shared. However, the idea of mutuality makes this explanation much more problematic, as it introduces ideas of connection, relationship and agency. One of the participants in the workshop, Rosa (real names have been changed), referred to this as being "a human professional":

> 'The thing I hear most from the people we work with is that the thing they HATED most … was the fact that it was an us-and-them situation. And they were lorded over and they still have fear of doctors and police people. Like, people are people and when they see that you are just the same – with weaknesses and strengths in exactly the same way, it enhances the relationship.'

Other workers shared a similar viewpoint. When asked directly about his view of professional ethics, one worker, Chris, reflected, "When I think of the word 'professional', it's distinct from amateur. Yet the people I work alongside knew me before I was paid to work with them". Later he observed that making a distinction between what is professional work and what is amateur or community work was unhelpful: "I've never drawn a line between what's professional and what's not. It's not how I think about things … it just encourages the 'us' and the 'them'. The more we teach professional boundaries and stuff the more we end up in a more and more segregated world".

Several workers saw the dual relationship they inhabit as worker and fellow community member as a means of enhancing rather than diminishing their role in a person's life. Such ethical challenges were understood not within the framework of any professional code of conduct – but in the frame of the relationship.

Rosa, already quoted, saw the dual relationship she inhabits, as worker and fellow community member, as a means of enhancing rather than diminishing her role in a community member's life. What immediately became apparent in talking to Rosa is the importance of what she called "value alignment" between herself and the organisation she works for. Reflecting on why she chose to work for that particular organisation, Rosa explained, "Just from Day One I felt at home. [There is] a freedom to live and work as myself rather than the way an organisation would believe you should work". The importance of value congruence is clear in the following anecdote:

> 'I used to volunteer on the cancer wards at the [Hospital]. And one of the number one rules was that you weren't allowed to touch the person and you weren't allowed to pray with them. I judged every person and every situation for what was needed. And if I felt they needed my hand on their hand, or if they needed a hug, if they asked me to pray for them, if I sensed that – then I did it.'

At first this story suggests the privileging of the personal over the professional and what appears to be the flaunting of rebellion against organisational rules. However, when asked to explain how she knew this was the 'right' thing to do, the worker shared the following reflection:

> '[T]he man I was being asked to work with had certain struggles [with women]. But I never felt threatened.

Although I'm a very demonstrative, affectionate person, I never offered those sorts of things because it wouldn't have helped him in any way. So that's how I often I judge my boundaries, by asking, is this going to help a person?'

In this sense Rosa is pursuing 'the right balance between closeness and distance, passion and rationality, empathic relationships and measurable social outcomes' (Banks 2013: 587), actively engaging in what Banks refers to as professional wisdom.

These workers show that for them, determining right action is not about adherence to externally taught or imposed professional standards. They argue that there are many times when such standards are dangerous, serving to decrease our humanity, encouraging separation and segregation, and making the world a poorer place. Yet these workers are at the same time able to accommodate the different worlds of community member and paid professional – somehow juxtaposing these roles through the lens of relationship, shared humanity and empathy – somehow drawing from what we have already named here as 'professional wisdom' – an ethic and a practice which is deeper and more internal than 'professional standards'.

We protect people from our organisations

The second layer suggested by our ethical framework, constructed by the organisation in which people's paid work was located, was even more problematic for the community workers with whom we spoke. Rather than provide leadership and clarity in ethical issues, organisations were seen as a key site and cause of ethical dilemmas. One worker, Rachel, commented:

'I've grown careful of sharing the successes as I find the organisation appropriates them for their own use and the person or project is reduced to a Public Relations piece: "That's a good story for our quarterly report!" The marketing people and policy people all say: "We don't just want numbers – we want stories" – but it's all a farce because it's about promoting the organisation. It just turns people into a commodity.'

In listening to Rachel's story we were reminded of the work of Martin Buber (1923/2010) and his reflections on the difference between an I–thou relationship (which captures the search for connection between two people) and an I–it relationship (in which one connects to another person so as to use them for some purpose). For workers such as these, the ethical challenge is not about the maintenance of boundaries between workers and the community members they work for and with, but the protection of boundaries between community members and the organisational *machine* that was seen to capture people as possessions or extensions of itself. Another worker in the health field, Emma, reflected, "There is a jarring of values every time I go to work. I love the people but the work and the way the work reduces people to a diagnosis and numbers and different data sets does my head in."

A similar challenge was recognised in the grey space in which community members became formal 'volunteers' for an organisation. Whereas volunteerism has historically been seen as a citizen role, in the modern organisational context, volunteers are now reduced to an organisational role; Ben shared how:

> 'There are volunteers: people in the community, people who want to be involved; but technically they need to sign up under sector quality standards – volunteers are needing to sign privacy agreements, agree to codes of conduct (for example, "I will not give my phone number", "I won't invite a person home") and position descriptions. Yet the very nature of what we are trying to do in this work is the exact opposite of this. I'm trying to create real connections between people. I want them to be in the kind of relationship where people exchange phone numbers and share their homes and lives. The organisation wants volunteers to develop and support these wholesome and informal relationships but the very presence of the organisation and its formal approach to volunteers undermines the exact work we seek to do.'

For the worker in this context, the ethical challenge is less about the preservation of clear boundaries between people, but an ongoing challenge to *reduce* boundaries to help relationships flourish for vulnerable people. As another worker, Kat, explained,

> 'The ethical conversation is about what do you believe, and in carving out that space to what extent is it possible for the external system to come in without compromising it. What can you live with? The system is fundamentally compromised; so what strategies can I use to protect the work?'

"Work is not the most important part of our life"

What seemed to be of greater importance to people than professional standards or organisational requirements was the role of personal ethics and what we referred to earlier as a practice framework. As Chris reflected, "I don't see my work as only my unpaid work – I don't draw a line between what's work and what's not." Workers constantly emphasised the importance of alignment between their personal values and how well their workplaces and work roles enabled them to enact those values. Chris shared how:

> 'I try to develop my moral compass generally in all areas of my life: the fact that I recycle, or that I'm vegetarian. I've thought through things and I'm willing to defend those things and talk about them, rather than follow someone else's rules ... Your moral compass isn't just something you turn on when you clock into work. That doesn't resonate with me.'

For a fortunate few, the organisations in which they were located, afforded them congruency between what they believed and how they could act. Other workers were not so lucky, as David commented: "I work in an organisation that says one thing and does another [but] I have to pay my bills and support my family – so I stay."

Numerous workers also spoke of the difficulty of wanting to advocate for change, but feeling unable to do so because of the political positioning or funding threat to the organisations they worked for. According to Jonas, "I often find myself in a moral dilemma as I am employed to advocate on behalf of a very vulnerable population, but I am funded by the very system I am advocating to. This forces me to walk a very fine line." In contrast, workers like Chris felt they were able to live out their values by ensuring they were not beholden to any one organisation. He was able to use the part-time nature of his employment to his advantage. Reflecting on his activism he explained, "Many things I do are unpaid – I couldn't do them if I was paid ... Work is not the most important part of our life."

Moral agents in context

The final layer in the ethical framework for community workers was that of situated ethics. The idea of the community worker as a moral agent 'in context' – to use Banks' phrasing – was apparent throughout all of our discussions. As one of the managers (Steve) in the focus group explained:

> '[The work we do] is about relationships, it is about handling paradox and being fluid, not just being binary right/wrong, in/out, professional/amateur or professional/ community member. So this is entering that whole different space, which is managing tensions, paradoxes, dilemmas, and saying that different parts of life can augment each other and that this is good community work. It is a risk to the work, but if done well, it can strengthen the work.'

Numerous stories and conversations revealed that workers were constantly grappling with ethical issues throughout their work. The ethical dilemmas that workers faced were embedded in relationships. The relationship always occurred in context and this context helped construct the ethics of the situation as Rosa commented: "It just depends on the person and the circumstance, everything … you judge every situation, every moment, and the person."

However, the challenge for workers was that the situation in which they found themselves often had multiple layers and was rarely straightforward. A number of workers articulated that while they see the work they are doing is valuable and effective, there are ethical and emotional tensions for them in seeing the systemic issues around their work with individuals. As one worker, Jesse, explained:

> 'The greatest tension for me is being mindful towards the sacredness of the micro level work and the uniqueness of individual, and being mindful of the macro level problems and the systemic issues that hold people back. I want to honour the one-on-one work, but it sometimes feels like you are bailing out a ship with a thimble. I can positively frame what I'm doing, but I can see the despair of what macroeconomic policy is creating. A lot of my work feels like rescue work – we need structural and political change.'

And this brings us to what might be regarded as a higher layer of practice knowledge and skill that we have not yet discussed: the ability to situate and negotiate ethics in multiple contexts at once.

Holding the whole

The vast majority of texts and edicts on professional conduct and ethical behaviour are focused at the micro level, to ensure workers engage in an appropriate level of care, diligence and skill to maintain safe and competent practice, to do good work, and in short, to be able to answer the question, 'What's the right thing to do in this situation?' Also known as 'micromorality' this approach concerns the professional conduct of a worker and the person or people they seek to assist.

However, what is often missing from conversations about professional ethics is macromorality – which is a far more abstract attitude. It refers to the ethical disposition required when engaging with a larger group, community, public or even world composed of individuals whom one does not – and indeed, cannot – know personally. It involves reflecting on the nature of the roles one inhabits and the responsibilities of the role to the larger context, such as the responsibility of the student to the school or of the citizen to the community (Rest et al, 1999; Gardner, 2012). It is the capacity to look beyond self-interest to a wider, more abstract consideration of the effect of one's actions on a wider, often distant, community or public. Clayton and Opotow (2003: 96) refer to the difference between micro- and macromorality as personal versus transpersonal morality.

Weaving together two earlier points, we observed that for many people in so-called 'helping professions' the ethical identity of a profession is woven into a worker's own moral framework. We observed at the beginning of this chapter that the majority of workers interviewed engaged in volunteer community work alongside their own paid role.

This suggests that for the majority of people, the work they do is a vocation rather than a career. It is an extension of who they are and how they need to live. Perhaps it is also for this reason that people spoke of themselves as 'workers', grounded in their life's work – rather than the more erudite term of 'practitioners'. And it is for this reason that consideration of roles and boundaries and the various ethical dilemmas that community workers face become more complex as workers revealed the intermingled nature of their work. They did not separate the ethical conduct and procedure of a paid professional role from the morals of how best to live one's life as a citizen in the world. Rachel, quoted earlier, explained, "The ethical conversation is about what do you believe". The ethics of the work is seen not as a professional component, but as deeply personal, needing to align with each person's own moral code.

The overarching theme across all our discussions is that workers see significant tensions, and even contradictions, between their micro work on the ground with individuals and groups, and the macro level of political, structural and legal contexts. While some workers place limits on how far they would push a line because of obligations to family and fear of unemployment, others would and indeed had pushed back against the law and even had spent time in jail. They see ethical tension between the stated mission and values of the organisations they work for and the policies through which their work is funded that serve to place limitations on their practice. They try to work ethically on the ground with, for example, Indigenous people or refugees, but believe the laws are fundamentally immoral and unjust. And they struggle daily to reconcile these positions. And as the following quote from Amanj illustrates, they see they are in a fundamentally compromised position: "When I entered this work I thought I'd be just hanging out with people. Instead what I do is put out spot fires for the government every time they make a policy announcement. We are puppets of the government. We justify our inaction through our organisational values."

And this means that workers see their action – and inaction – emerging from the violence of the systems they are located within. Consequently, the issues that workers raise are not about ethical challenges they face in relation to the people they work alongside – issues of boundaries and challenges of dual roles – but about how can they work ethically, when the contexts they are in are so unjust and – for them – immoral. As Kat said:

> 'I feel that there's a lot of harm that can be done to the people who we are working with. I was harassed to perform. Two things come to mind: Gandhi's observation that "busyness is violence" – the pressure is put on workers to do more and more in the same amount of time. It's violence to us as workers and violence to the people we are working with. It doesn't allow for true empowerment.'

Workers are trying to enact situated ethics, guided by their personal practice frameworks. They choose to stay in the work, hoping their actions may make a difference; however, the situations in which they find themselves, within organisations, within sectors, and within global political and economic systems, leads to guilt, anger and despair, as Jesse commented: "The sector is fucked – it's a self-serving beast – and I don't know how to reconcile this."

Argyris and Schön (1974) have observed that the more incongruence that exists between a person's espoused values and values in action, the more stressed the person will become. This is often seen in workers who assume a cynical victim role, with its potential for burnout. Once a person is made aware of this incongruence they can move to resolve the tension between espoused values and values in action. For this resolution to occur one of two things must happen: they must change what they do, or they must change what they believe. What we are arguing here is that in the progressively professionalised world of community, micro- and macromorality are sitting in increasing tension, making neither option palatable.

Ife (1997) contends that the value base of community work is not widely shared throughout society, but is seen as increasingly deviant and even dangerous to economic development. Writing over 20 years ago, Ife remarks that community workers should not be surprised at finding themselves at this point of crisis (1997: 7). The inherent values within community and the espoused values of many workers, 'that people matter', stand at odds with the global neo-liberal welfare regime that privileges economics over people (see also Chapters One and Two in this volume).

Conclusion

We began this discussion by listening to Susan Kenny's call for 'an unsettled and edgy community development' that went beyond 'social maintenance and defensive active citizenship' (2011: i7). This is an edgy community work that demands critical, proactive, visionary, cosmopolitan and active citizens who are prepared to challenge existing structures, values and power relations (2011: i7). Indeed, is this not exactly where we have travelled in this discussion? We honour the bravery, honesty, fortitude and resilience of activated, visionary, ethical and thoughtful workers as represented here in this discussion. We honour their quest to remain true to the people they serve as they negotiate such multiple levels of complexity in and around their work. Their somewhat disturbing and uncomfortable insights have reminded us that:

- There is potential danger, alongside the possible usefulness, of professional standards.
- Far from offering protection from risk, some organisations actually pose a far greater risk to the communities that they are intended to serve.

- Many community workers see their work beyond their paid role, and that their paid role is integrated into a larger, deeply reflective and continually evolving moral system.
- Community workers are moral agents not in context – but in contexts.
- We need to see the whole to judge what it means to behave ethically.

However, this is not a bleak space. In hearing people's struggles with ethics, we heard the 'second story' (Denborough, 2012): the reason people stay in systems they named as ethically compromised and unjust, as Jesse explained:

> 'I spent a lot of time thinking that if I was politically active with the organisation, the system and the sector then I would make a difference. It's bullshit. The work is political, but if you're going to invest in the political discourse then why not just start with the people because it's easier and nicer! So the work has become about just sitting with people: to discover what is it they are yearning for and how can we make that happen, and how can we join with others to make it happen. We believe in the innate capacity of people.'

In reflections such as these, what becomes evident is that the core source of hope and enrichment for workers to enable them to negotiate the enormous and sometimes debilitating ethical and political dilemmas they face is the very method and approach that drew them to community work in the first place. As Mae Shaw suggested, this is at the grassroots, working with people's social reality to locate personal experience in collective forms of reflection and action. As Rachel succinctly summarised: "I am hopeful because what I know about the community process still rings true, when I sit with people and talk about possible futures it is possible to move from oppressive and hopeless to hopeful, And while I might not have the answers, collectively we can find the answers."

Acknowledgement

This chapter is part of a larger body of work examining the role of ethical challenges for workers. We wish to acknowledge the many workers who continue to inform our thinking and have taken the risk of speaking openly and honestly about the challenges of the work they do. The names of participants have been changed to preserve anonymity.

References

Argyris, C. and Schön, D.A. (1974) *Theory in practice: Increasing professional effectiveness*, London: Jossey-Bass.

Arnold, R., Burke, B. James, C., Martin, D. and Thomas, B. (1991) *Educating for a change*, Toronto: Doris Marshall Institute for Education and Action.

Austin, M., Anthony, E., Knee, R. and Mathias, J. (2016) 'Revisiting the relationship between micro and macro social work practice', *Families in Society*, 97(4): 270–7.

Austin, M.J., Coombs, M. and Barr, B. (2005) 'Community-centered clinical practice: Is the integration of micro and macro social work practice possible?', *Journal of Community Practice*, 13(4): 9–30.

Banks, S. (2013) 'Negotiating personal engagement and professional accountability: Professional wisdom and ethics work', *European Journal of Social Work*, 16(5): 587–604.

Banks, S. (2016) 'Everyday ethics in professional life: Social work as ethics work', *Ethics and Social Welfare*, 10(1): 35–52.

Buber, M. (1923/2010) *I and thou*, Eastford, CT: Martino Publishing.

Burkett, I. (2001) 'Traversing the swampy terrain of postmodern communities: Towards theoretical revisionings of community development', *European Journal of Social Work*, 4(3): 223–46.

Butler, I. and Drakeford, M. (2001) 'Which Blair project? Communitarianism, social authoritarianism and social work', *British Journal of Social Work*, 1(1): 7–19.

Clayton, S.D. and Opotow, S. (2003) *Identity and the natural environment: The psychological significance of nature*, Cambridge, MA: MIT Press.

Cornwall, A. (2008) 'Unpacking "participation": Models, meanings and practices', *Community Development Journal*, 43(3): 269–83.

Denborough, D. (2012). 'Visiting memories together: the use of collective narrative memory in Srebrenica', in P. Westoby and L. Shevellar (eds), *Learning and mobilising for community development: A radical tradition of community-based education and training*, Farnham: Ashgate, pp 149–61.

Ferguson, I. and Lavalette, M. (2006) 'Globalization and global justice: Towards a social work of resistance', *International Social Work*, 49(3): 309–18.

Gardner, H. (2012) *Truth, beauty, and goodness reframed: Educating for the virtues in the age of truthiness and Twitter*, New York: Basic Books.

Guijt, I. and Shah, M.K. (1998) 'Waking up to power, conflict and process', in I. Guijt and M.K. Shah (eds) *The myth of community: Gender issues in participatory development*, Bourton-on-Dunsmore: ITDG Publishing, pp 1–23.

IACD (International Association for Community Development) (2018) *Towards Shared International Standards for Community Development Practice*, Glasgow: IACD. Available at: www.iacdglobal.org/wp-content/uploads/2018/06/IACD-Standards-Guidance-May-2018_Web-1.pdf

Ife, J. (1997) 'The changing role of the state in the provision of human services in Australia', *Asia Pacific Journal of Social Work*, 7(1): 6–18.

Jayaratne, S., Croxton, T. and Mattison, D. (1997) 'Social work professional standards: An exploratory study', *Social Work*, 42(2): 187–99.

Kagle, J.D. and Giebelhausen, P.N. (1994) 'Dual relationships and professional boundaries', *Social Work*, 39(2): 213–20.

Kelly, T. and Westoby, P. (2018) *Participatory development practice: Using traditional and contemporary frameworks*, Rugby: Practical Action Publishing.

Kenny, S. (2011) 'Towards unsettling community development', *Community Development Journal*, 46(5): i7–i19.

Lathouras, T. (2017) 'Our strength is in our connectedness', *New Community*, 15(1/2): 57–8.

MacLeod, M.A. and Emejulu, A. (2014) 'Neoliberalism with a community face? A critical analysis of asset-based community development in Scotland', *Journal of Community Practice*, 22(4): 430–50.

O'Connor, I., Wilson, J., Setterlund, D. and Hughes, M. (2008) *Social work and human service practice* (5th edn), Melbourne, Australia: Pearson Longman Education.

Penderis, S. (2012) 'Theorizing participation: From tyranny to emancipation', *The Journal of African and Asian Local Government Studies*, 1(3): 1–28.

Power, M. (1994) *The audit explosion*, London: Demos. Available at: www.demos.co.uk/files/theauditexplosion.pdf

Rest, J.R., Narvaez, D., Bebeau, M.J. and Thoma, S.J. (1999) *Postconventional moral thinking: A neo-Kohlbergian approach*, Mahwah, NJ: Lawrence Erlbaum.

Rosenman, L. (2000) 'Turning threats into challenges: A positive perspective on the future', in I. O'Connor, P. Smyth and J. Warburton (eds) *Contemporary perspectives on social work and the human services: challenges and change*, Melbourne: Longman, pp 190–7.

Shaw, M. (1997) 'Community work: Towards a radical paradigm for practice', *The Scottish Journal of Community Work and Development*, 2: 61–72.

Shevellar, L. and Barringham, N. (2016) 'Working in complexity: Ethics and boundaries in community work and mental health', *Australian Social Work*, 69(2): 181–93.

Shore, C. and Wright, S. (2015) 'Audit culture revisited: Rankings, ratings, and the reassembling of society', *Current Anthropology*, 56(3): 421–44.

Thomas, P.N. and van de Fliert, E. (2015) *Interrogating the theory and practice of communication for social change*, Palgrave Studies in Communication for Social Change, London: Palgrave Macmillan.

Westoby, P. and Ingamells, A. (2012) 'Teaching community development personal practice frameworks', *Social Work Education*, 31(3): 383–96.

Westoby, P. and Shevellar, L. (eds) (2012) *Learning and development for community development: A radical tradition of community based education and training*, Farnham: Ashgate.

FOUR

Negotiating consent in neighbourhood-based community development work

Jeroen Gradener and Mike de Kreek

Introduction

This chapter discusses the efforts of community workers to obtain consent in local communities as a basis for taking action on issues that are affecting local people's lives. Crucial here is that community workers resist the initial urge to settle for consensus and as a consequence limit the possibilities for creativity, exploration and interpersonal development. Drawing on two case studies, one from Amsterdam (the Netherlands) and one from Chelsea (US), the requirements and process of acquiring consent are outlined. Consent in general refers to a form of permission to act or take action. In this chapter we consider it as a sense of approval by neighbourhood community members to engage in a collective course of action. Community workers often play a crucial part in the acquisition of community consent as they support the process of recognition of the diversity of interests, opinions and values that characterises local life. Consent is necessary for creating sustainable local initiatives, incorporating, instead of eliminating, conflicting positions. This acknowledgement of diversity can be seen as an ethical requirement in community development practice, but also as a strategic issue for community workers. After all, without being able to obtain legitimacy for their engagement with local issues, effective community development work is impossible.

This chapter focuses on neighbourhood-based community development work in geographical communities. However, similar principles apply in all forms of community development, including work with communities of interest and identity. We use the term 'community worker' to refer to someone who takes on a facilitating and coordinating role with members of communities to build community capacity and/or bring about social change. Such workers may be paid and professionally qualified, or unpaid volunteers and activists. They may live in the communities where they work/are active, or reside outside these areas. These circumstances influence the legitimacy of their interventions, as well as how consent is gained and consensus reached.

The importance of consent in community development work

One of the key concerns for community workers is the creation and maintenance of consent. Ultimately, consent for community development work exists when there is mutual recognition among local people who have become collectively engaged around specific issues in their lives, often to do with the perceived fairness and desirability of community action over time.

However, community consent is not something that is established easily. On the contrary, it is a result of an active process of aligning the concerns of local people and the intentions of the community workers. Ideally, this process of alignment should result in a mutual commitment to become, and stay engaged, in community development activities.

Besides aligning the intentions of local people and community workers, there is another, even more profound challenge in creating consent. This is linked to transcending the initial urge of people who become engaged around local issues to focus on reaching *consensus* when confronted with a specific goal. As we will address in this chapter, consensus can be a crucial, albeit temporary, element in determining community development strategies where all members of a group need to agree to all aspects of a decision (Beck and Eichler, 2000). But consent is far more 'normative' and far-reaching than consensus: it binds everyone concerned to specific ways of action or rules of conduct based on a deeply felt or – as Baerveldt and Voestermans (2005) call it – 'embodied' commitment, even though there is no complete unanimity. In other words, while creating *consensus* reflects the *thoughtful and patient elimination of conflicting positions*, *consent* reflects *the acknowledgement of the variety and fluctuation of options, interests and values*. In our view a focus on consent offers a more sustainable strategy to address the diverse, and sometimes incremental and fluid nature of community life (Harfield, 1997). Consequently, the development and continuity of consent demands that community workers are able to establish at a local level a sense of community that is able to deal with the variety of opinions and ambitions as a basis for collective action.

The recognition of diversity over uniformity in local community life relates to a tradition of thinking about communities that is rooted in in number of key notions. For example, philosopher Hannah Arendt (2005) highlights the ability to deal with diverse opinions as an opportunity for personal development, and the anthropologist Claude Lévi-Strauss (1955) focuses on multiculturalism as a condition for social resilience. More recently, sociologist Richard Sennett argues in *Together* (2012) for the power, as well as the inherent challenges, of human cooperation.

Thinking along those lines, of community as a source of diversity, building community consent requires that community workers are well aware of the variety and fluctuation over time of the interests, values and entitlements of different community members. But key here is that they are also aware of their *own* intentions as people who have not necessarily always been intrinsically part of the local community with which they are currently engaged. After all, community workers not only have to initiate and support the emergence of new collective efforts that generate a strong enough appeal to be sustainable over time, but also obtain consent about their involvement in these efforts. This refers to what scholars such as Berger and Luckmann (1991) theorise as the issue of 'legitimacy'. For community workers to be able to become, and stay, engaged over time, they require what Suchman (1995: 574) defined as: 'a generalized perception or assumption that the actions of an entity [for instance a community worker] are desirable, proper, or appropriate within some socially constructed system of norms, values, beliefs, and definitions'.

In this chapter we will also discuss the ability of community workers to obtain consent by creating legitimacy for their own engagement with local development issues, in relation to the concept of 'applied *phronesis*' (Flyvbjerg et al, 2012). This nurtures knowledge of active community members that can 'challenge power not in theory but in ways that inform real efforts to produce change' (Schram, 2012: 20). It is the everyday experience of local people that, no matter how diverse and sometimes conflicting, it is important to foster a common sense of direction based on consent. By making themselves instrumental to these challenging, yet change-producing endeavours, the involvement of community development workers will eventually be seen as a natural component of the local community development processes (Gradener, 2016).

Consequently, one could say that obtaining consent is a key practical issue, and legitimacy is a corresponding strategic challenge to be able to act ethically in community work, for instance to secure the variety of different interests and opinions. In this chapter, we illustrate empirically not only *what* consent entails in practice, but also *how* community workers tend to address this ethical and strategic challenge. Legitimacy concerns the rights of community workers to be present and engage in and with the local community; consent concerns the agreement of 'the community' for community workers to engage in specific activities with them/on their behalf.

Case studies from practice

To illustrate *what* 'community consent' entails, and *how* it is negotiated and maintained in practice, we use two case studies. Some of the theories and concepts used are drawn from a doctoral research project (Gradener, 2016) on legitimation strategies of community workers. This research project, which finished in 2016, involved a comparative case study based on three ethnographic studies, each of three months, of community development practices in the US (May–July 2012), the Netherlands (October 2013–January 2014) and South Africa (January 2014–April 2014). In total 31 individual interviews and eight focus-group interviews were conducted. In order to contextualise, additional observational data and documents were collected. The presented case from the United States focuses on the efforts of Claire (a pseudonym), a community worker from Chelsea (US), in creating consent among local residents to tackle the construction of an environmentally hazardous salt storage pile close to a residential area. The focus of the analysis is on some of the critical incidents Claire experienced in that process.

The other case is situated in a 14-year-old community group in Amsterdam East (Netherlands) that collects local, personal memories on a website called the Memory of East. It builds on the results of de Kreek's doctoral research on the relation between group and collective levels of empowerment within this community, both off- and online (de Kreek, 2017). Since early 2016, the community of volunteers has been organised as an association, with a board, an editorial group that edits and publishes memories online, and an activity group that organises workshops for new and present participants. Finding a balance in this new configuration and reaching decisions that include both group and community interests have seen some of the participants taking on roles that could be regarded as volunteer community workers.

A taxonomy of community consent

In the two case studies, we discerned three phases or what we call 'intensities of consent'. In reality, these phases tend to emerge simultaneously in everyday practice, but to enable a closer view of how community workers obtain community consent it is instructive to delineate them, however artificial the division might be in practice.

In phase one, consent on an individual level legitimises the community worker's presence and involvement with people's concerns. Individuals or small groups of people, often implicitly, give the worker permission to have conversations with them about their daily lives and well-being. If there is a latent community issue, some people might acknowledge it and others might ignore it. Although it does not look like it on the face of it, these conversations and the various opinions form a necessary step towards building community consensus (Beck and Eichler, 2000) – that is, agreement or unanimity on an issue.

In phase two, the community worker, to a certain degree, receives the consent to organise dialogues among local groups of people with diverse standpoints. The exchange of arguments with adequate guidance can slowly lead to crystallising of consensus *within* the parts of the community for action.

In phase three, the worker elicits further consent by scrutinising the emerging consensus in terms of its implications for the community as a whole. This way a new consensus *between* the community worker and local people emerges. This consensus is not only a mutual agreement on the goal and direction of common action, but also on the modus operandi of the collective community worker–community effort. In this process consent develops for the worker's actions and for future cooperation.

In this creation and maintenance of consent, the perspectives on direction and modus operandi have to be negotiated and from time to time renegotiated between the sometimes highly variable and versatile interests, morals and knowledge of the community and the interests, values and knowledge of the community worker. Obviously, ethical aspects, such as the acknowledgement of diversity, are crucial parts of every phase in the process towards community consent.

According to Berger and Luckmann (1991), such negotiation is a form of legitimation in the sense that negotiating consent legitimises the ongoing collaborative work between community members and the community worker. To legitimise this collaboration, a new shared framework has to be developed that acknowledges and clarifies the interests of the community members as well as the interests of the community worker's engagement with the local community as it evolves over time. This common framework as a legitimation for collective action has been termed a 'symbolic universe' by Berger and Luckmann. It is made up of ideas and beliefs that makes the collaboration plausible, 'makes sense' for the people involved and gives every action its 'right place' as this framework 'locates all collective events in a cohesive unity that includes past, present and future' (p 120). As such, by working towards a new symbolic universe, the community worker creates consent for collective action by enabling the recognitions of people's experiences in the past, their current ideas and their ambitions for the future. Such a symbolic universe for collective action founds consent for collective community action but at the same also legitimises the involvement of the community worker with the local community issues. Furthermore, the development of such a symbolic universe of mutually recognised experiences and interests is the cornerstone of consent, and provides the community workers with a sense of legitimacy that helps them steer through the different phases of consent and consensus.

With the brief introduction of the three phases overleaf, we will introduce two cases that illustrate challenges community workers face when working towards consent going through these phases.

The challenge of obtaining consent

Case 1: The salt pile in Chelsea, US

Claire is employed in the role of community organiser by a local grassroots community development organisation in Chelsea, an industrial town near Boston. The community development organisation focuses on initiating local community campaigns on, for instance, improving the position of migrants, workers and tenants. Furthermore, until 2017, the organisation hosted the Chelsea Green Space and Recreation Committee, a strong local environmental justice coalition. A long-time Chelsea resident herself, over the years, Claire has initiated a great many successful health and sustainability campaigns that are now an integral part of Chelsea life. For instance, she was able to engage the community to develop plans for the local Chelsea Creek, and co-design parks and recreational spots in Chelsea. Central in her work as community organiser is raising local awareness about social issues that can negatively affect the community, mobilising community members around these issues and supporting them to become able speak out on their own behalf.

One day, Claire found out about the plan of a local businessman to create a salt pile in front of the Chelsea waterfront. She saw grounds for local resistance, because for the area, plagued by environmental burdens due to polluting industrial activities, the salt pile would be hazardous. She was angry and was anticipating taking a radical adversary position herself.

Unfortunately, the reasons for her anger were not recognised by the majority of residents who could be potentially affected by the salt pile. While some of them raised concerns, a significant number of the local people had no complaints about a future restriction of the view of the river. Besides, the owner of the storage business was a local, which provided him with preliminary goodwill. Still, Claire decided nevertheless to proceed with raising the hazards of the construction activities with the local environmental protection agencies. However, she received resistance from the residents, and complaints about taking matters too far and in too serious a way.

This case example reveals three crucial aspects about consent in working with communities.

First of all, Claire did not act on a local issue that was already acknowledged as urgent, but on what *she* as a local community worker considered as a legitimate case for mobilising the community. The ground for this decision was that the construction of the salt pile could become an environmental hazard. There was no initial consensus about the desirability of local action, but, for her, it had to be created. Second, Claire was, along the way, confronted with different opinions in the community – those in favour of granting the corporation permission for the salt pile construction, those against it and those yet undecided. Third – and as we will address later in this chapter – she was confronted with the challenge of how to deal with the different positions, values and interests in the community as part of the organising process, being aware that local consensus about whether or not the salt pile should be allowed would not be a realistic perspective. In other words, she had to look for a basis on which she could initiate collective community action by searching for consent for her initial involvement.

We now consider another example to contrast what happens when consent develops in spite of a bad start, as illustrated in Case 2.

Case 2: Memory of East in Amsterdam, the Netherlands

This case is about a community group in Amsterdam that collects memories of the area and organises activities relating to this work. The group is run by volunteers who are in effect volunteer community workers, who are also engaged in building membership and developing and supporting community activities.

In this story a key member of the Memory of East activity group responsible for regular Friday afternoon workshops withdrew. This person's withdrawal meant that the board of the Memory of East was faced with a challenge. The Friday workshops that were a crucial part of the organisation's work had largely depended on this person. Consequently, just before the summer holidays, the board decided to change the workshops from what had been a rather loosely organised set of meetings into a more structured format, with workshops planned for every two weeks. When the regular Friday afternoon participants were informed about this they resisted the plans proposed by the board despite the good intentions, because they wanted to think about the programming too. At the same time, they expressed the distance they experienced from the board and its members. The chair was surprised about this. In her eyes the board was rather informal. But she embraced their worries and decided immediately to stop the proposed plans for the new workshops. The urgency to communicate in the neighbourhood about the Friday afternoons led the chair to use the phrase "an ad hoc and improvised programming until December". Everyone at the table agreed enthusiastically with this proposal and started to share ideas. At the end, everyone promised to be involved in organising one of the afternoons.

Both examples feature the contributions of people in community worker roles (Claire and a board member) in obtaining consent. They had to have the unwritten and informal permission of the community members to facilitate, question and be part of the collective actions of a community in the phase of becoming or remaining engaged. Our hypothesis is that by being ethically involved in the development of the consensual domain of a group or a community, community workers, whether working professionally or voluntarily, can obtain consent.

We consider working towards consensus and achieving consent as categorical imperatives for community work. After all, consensus and consent are not only of practical use, but are also ends in themselves as processes of collaborative and participatory learning (Beck and Eichler, 2000). This dual characteristic of community work also emerges in Claire's conclusion about why her efforts to organise local resistance against the salt pile failed. She first of all acknowledged: "A community organiser should not act on her own, but only on behalf of the community." She later added: "Because there was no clear agreement in the community, there was no basis for action." Here the categorical imperative of creating consent and consensus surface. It derives its ethical nature by its perpetual reference to the aspirations and interests of the local community as they evolve over time.

However, this process is fragile, and acting 'ethically' implies here at the outset being sensitive to the tensions between the interests, morals and knowledge in the community and between the community and the community development worker. But more critically in this process, is the success with which the community worker is able to translate these tensions into questions and remarks that are seen as legitimate by the engaged community members.

In the case of the salt pile, there was a lack of a minimal mutual agreement between the organiser and her constituency and also within the community itself – the local community. This led to an implosion of momentum to resist the construction of the hazardous mountain of salt. In the Memory of East case, the explicitly expressed discontent towards the chair, for one-sidedly changing the character of the Friday meetings without consent, was rooted in the consensus within the activity group about wanting to be involved in the changes. The chair tapped into this consensus by throwing her initial plans aside, which made it possible to achieve consent for an 'ad hoc programme'.

In short, in initiating and creating support, in creating continuity and credibility for the community organising process, a community worker has two simultaneously emerging challenges: (1) creating consent for their engagement with the community; and (2) creating consent and, where necessary, consensus within a group of active community members about the goals and directions of community action. Both challenges demand that community workers create legitimacy for their choices, considerations and actions in relation to the community. In the next section this legitimacy issue is elaborated in more detail.

The interplay between consent and legitimacy

In this section, we explore the 'sense of legitimacy' community workers experience in their engagement with local people that can function as a steering wheel to create consent for collective community actions. Central here is the assumption that the community workers' actions are crucial in this consent-creating process. For this process, the community workers' involvement has, at the outset, at least to possess a form of local legitimacy. Gradener (2016), for instance, demonstrated how in different areas of the world community development workers in all stages of community engagement are intuitively searching for an affirmation that their involvement is being accepted by local people. This affirmation of acceptance is derived from a number of signs, supporting community workers to connect to the various opinions and interests in the community. Initially, community development workers will already have to have a sense of legitimacy for their local engagement. For example, in the first case, when Claire initiated the campaign against the salt pile, without any doubt she did so with deep considerations for the health of the local residents. She had a sense of legitimacy about the issue. As she explains: "The company toxicologist said it's a very solid form of salt and doesn't break apart. Nobody had done a study to show the magnitude of [pollution and what it would do if] exposed to the rain and the sun, wind, 24 hours a day, every single day of the year."

Claire's statement reveals that she explicitly took the interests of the residents to heart, and one could say that this would be, among community development workers, an ethically defensible position. In this sense, there was ethical legitimacy for her stance. Yet, looking back, she nevertheless acknowledges her actions were neither *perceived nor experienced* as in the interests of (all) the local residents. She realised that her legitimacy as an organiser was at stake here. In a similar, but more positive vein, in the Memory of East case, the chair and the board, based on their roles, possessed a certain legitimacy to think about the future of the Friday afternoon programming. However, the group of Friday afternoon participants did not consent to the board's ideas and, maybe more importantly, the way they were developed without them. Once the chair realised this had been unethical, the thinking about the programming restarted with everyone involved. Once the 'ad hoc' programme emerged, with everyone's consensual agreement, the group gave their consent to the chair and in turn the chair and board had regained legitimacy in the collaboration.

As outlined earlier in this chapter, intrinsically related to this 'sense of legitimacy' of the community workers is the development and acknowledgement of that 'symbolic universe' of collectively shared notions about what is desirable and useful. In our two cases, the norms, values, beliefs and definitions of the community workers needed to be tuned into the norms, values, beliefs and definitions of the local communities. In Claire's case, no consent emerged about collective action against the salt pile, as she was not able to attune her own perspective to the variety of perspectives of the local people. In contrast, by facilitating everyone's involvement in the ad hoc programme, the chair and board of Memory of East did create a basis for consent.

Having explained the interplay between consent and legitimacy on the background of the challenges of obtaining consent in the two cases, we can now return to the three phases of consent. In the next section we explore in more depth what we have come to name 'the signs towards consent' for each phase.

The legitimacy signs towards consent

In this section we introduce three crucial signs of legitimacy for community workers that can steer them through each of the three phases of intensity of consent. In doing so, we come to a deeper understanding how legitimacy and consent are interdependent sides of the same coin.

Sign 1: inconspicuous but deliberate presence

The first sign of legitimate engagement for the community workers is what one could call 'inconspicuous but deliberate presence'. This sign provides them with an initial 'sense of legitimacy' of their intentions to become engaged with the local community. Usually, this is relevant in the first encounters with local people, when the 'shared symbolic universe' is not yet established. As we outlined earlier in this chapter this is the first phase of building consent, as the community worker spots a potential opportunity for collective community actions, but that opportunity is not yet fully fledged, recognised or felt as urgent. It is like a precarious flame that needs to expand in size and intensity. As with such vulnerable flames, community workers need to balance their initial presence: not too obvious (or the weak flame will be extinguished), but also not without intention (or the weak flame will fade). In the case of the salt pile, Claire recalls how she could sense this precarious base for her involvement. As a community organiser, she recognised an issue when the company responsible for the storage of the salt at the border of the Chelsea waterfront was in violation of the law. Having a background in public health, she was aware of the fact that the health burdens of the salt pile accumulate over a long period, and as a consequence that the lack of visible and tangible health impact in the short term would impede a rapid and robust mobilisation of the local community affected by it. Moreover, she knew the owners of the company were locals, and this family was seen as a good neighbour, donating to local organisations. So, she felt she had to proceed carefully, and only when she found out that some of the residents living close to the mountain of salt started to report dust in their homes and on their cars, she saw an opportunity to initiate a campaign.

In other words, Claire felt a legitimate base for her professional engagement with the salt pile based on a fragile balance between her own assessment as an organiser, aware of the health hazards and the violation of public health laws, and the emerging awareness of nearby residents that the salt pile was distributing dust. For her, a threshold for further organising efforts was based on an initial, but yet implicit, consent of a small part of the community.

Sign 2: community engagement with the issue

During the initial and often fragile phase of community and community worker engagement, a form of local consciousness grows or ignites. It is important for community workers to present themselves as possible allies with respect to the essential and tangible aspects of people's everyday lives. If we – metaphorically speaking – consider the lifeworld of a certain community, with its challenges, codes, relationships and habits as a 'bubble' shielded by a social membrane, the worker is to touch that membrane but without too much pressure. He or she, after all, may be a relative outsider and cannot start by pushing or prodding that membrane too hard. Claire quite literally knocked at people's doors (the equivalent of touching the membrane) when she reached out to the neighbourhood that would be affected the most by the dust the wind would blow from the salt storage. Her motivation for being present in an inconspicuous but at the same time deliberate manner was at first derived from her own concerns: "That neighbourhood is one of the lowest income neighbourhoods [of Chelsea], has the most ethnic diversity, and already has significant rates of asthma. They shouldn't have to deal with the burdens from these companies."

However, the second phase of creating consensus and consent starts when people acknowledge that the community worker 'has a point' in addressing what he or she considers as possibly relevant, damaging or crucial for the neighbourhood. Here, the balance in the worker–community relationship tends to shift somewhat. The direction it gravitates towards is more explicit, with a mutual commitment to address the issues at hand. Usually, community workers tend to derive their sense of legitimacy exactly from signs of emerging community engagement. At the heart of this second sign is the emergence of what we came to label as a spirit of 'consensus' in the community that collective actions are needed, appropriate and within in their own interest. This spirit of consensus was what was lacking, and Claire admitted this in retrospect. While in need of signs of community engagement, she experienced divisiveness, and explained that, "Not everybody in this community said it's bad. A lot of people said this salt pile is bad, other people said it's not that bad: 'Oil companies are the worst'. Other people said you're giving these guys a hard time, it's a nice family, they own the land."

Furthermore, she discovered that there "wasn't one clear feeling in the community". While some residents acknowledged the company was violating the law, others pointed out that they weren't really affected by the salt pile, for instance in the summertime. Some shared how, "when the salt pile isn't that tall, I can see the east western waterfront or the Chelsea Creek." Others mentioned that, "when you put a building up there, they would even lose their view on the waterfront completely, and would not be able to see the water." In short, she had to admit there was no large-scale community engagement, as a lot of people said: "we don't want this law enforced". Those words became a verdict for Claire's sense of legitimacy as an organiser in the case of the salt pile. There was no consensus in the community whether to fight against the salt store installation, nor was there consent between her and the local residents. In short, she lacked the sign of local engagement as a basis for her future involvement as a community organiser.

Sign 3: future embeddedness in local structure and community visions

So far one could detect a certain continuity in the signs of legitimacy. It starts with a lucid, somewhat intangible and implicit consent in the opportunity for community workers to be inconspicuously but deliberately present. A second sign that informs the community worker about the legitimacy of their involvement is when some consensus for community engagement emerges around specific issues. But usually, community workers aim towards a more sustainable collaboration, so a quest for continuation of the cooperation tends to emerge in the mind of the worker in what we earlier called phase three. For Claire, this became clear as she states: "I'm from here; I'm a Chelsea person, working with Chelsea, making a difference for Chelsea. I'm not one of those people that say let's make a difference for Chelsea and then move out of the city. I'm here."

Following Claire's attempts to instigate a common framework, we witnessed her search to acquire such a sustainable mutual involvement over time. One of the lessons she drew from that experience was that an organiser should not put herself before the community: "Community organisers shouldn't do that. The community should make a decision and the organiser should listen to the community. The organiser should act on behalf of the community. I didn't do that."

Although the embeddedness in the local structure and community visions were in place for Claire, the consensus and consent were still premature. This was different from Case 2, when the chair was able to connect to the consensus against the workshop reprogramming on the Fridays and to receive consent for further steps. Obviously, most stakeholders were present at the meeting and making an 'ad hoc' programming was a good workaround, but what is more important is that all participants have a long-term relationship with the locality and the Memory of East group of participants. In the process, a new 'symbolic universe' emerged going beyond the earlier consensus.

So far in this section, we have explored crucial signs for community workers to derive their sense of legitimacy for their engagement with local communities. This sense of legitimacy roots the workers in the local recognition that their intentions and actions are appropriate within the locally accepted norms, interests and knowledge of the community. That recognition is the ethical aspect of local consent and is ultimately tangible. As long as the local residents in Chelsea were not convinced a campaign against the local chemical company was in their best interest, Claire was not able to mobilise the people, no matter how disastrous she knew the long-term health burdens of the subtle salt dust in the air would be.

But at the same time, the worker's presence is also a challenge to what is locally held as appropriate and worthwhile. After all, as Saul Alinsky remarked in the still-controversial 1972 *Playboy* interview, a community organiser should even go so far as to 'rub raw the sores of discontent and galvanize them [the people] for radical social change' (Alinsky, 1972). By their presence alone, community workers challenge the local status quo. Earlier, we argued that the 'challenging' presence of community workers requires the creation of a symbolic universe that (1) *legitimises* the involvement of the community workers with local affairs; and (2) integrates the intentions of the community workers with those of the community so that their involvement becomes *sub speci universi*. According to Berger and Luckmann (1991: 113), new 'realities have to be established, other than those of everyday experience, that cannot be experienced in everyday life at all'. In the next section, we address how community workers support the emergence of such new symbolic universes. Community workers do not always have to go to such great lengths as Alinsky proposed. Sometimes a more subtle alignment strategy will build consent in the relationship between community workers and members of local communities.

Everyday *phronesis* as a strategy for building consent

In the previous section, we identified the signs community workers look for in order to deserve consent *from* the community for their involvement *with* the community. This emergence of consent can be construed as ethical, as it forces the workers to acknowledge and value the local ways of being, doing and thinking. However, at the same time, this consent also entails a recognition of the possible added value of the community workers' involvement with people's daily lives. In other words, by accepting community workers in their midst, consent to their intentions is given. Observing *how* community workers create that consent, and at the same time consensus for collective action via 'dialogical encounters' seem to be paramount. In these dialogical encounters community workers tap into the local *phronesis*, 'understood as people's practical wisdom in dealing with both routine decisions and unexpected contingencies (Frank, 2012: 48). Phronesis, being more value-based, distinguishes itself from *techne* ('craftsmanship' or 'know how') and *episteme* (scientific knowledge or 'know why'). To explore this in more depth, we return to the Memory of East case study, focusing on what Sennett (2012) calls 'the subjunctive voice'.

The subjunctive voice

Revisiting Case 2: Memory of East

In the conversation about the 'ad hoc' programme for the Friday afternoons, one of the meeting's participants made a personal comment about the plans. She mentioned how important it was, at least for her, to stay in contact with the sense of why she was involved in this community. This remark led another person, who was more actively involved as a board member, to ask a question about a certain unintended risk of the reprogramming. He introduced his question in a humble and open way, stating he felt that it was somehow connected to the last remark and didn't really know the right words: "Is there any chance that the participants who experience the Friday afternoons as a living room gathering, for some reason might stop attending the new meetings? I am a bit afraid this might happen." In turn, this remark led to a conversation about the ways these participants might continue to feel at home, also with new participants starting to attend. A proposed idea was to look back at this issue after the first sequence of the changed programme to find out whether people stopped visiting the meetings.

This incident illuminates a crucial dimension of how a community worker can ascertain community consent, through the humble, or, what sociologist Richard Sennett (2012: 22) calls, the 'subjunctive' voice of the community worker. 'Subjunctive' is a grammatical term, which refers to the 'mood' of a verb used to describe hypothetical or non-real actions or events, or imaginary, conditional situations. Indeed, in the conversation just described, the board member did not confirm or state a matter-of-fact-situation, but suggested options in a preliminary, open-for-interpretation mode. This involved the use of tentative utterances such as: "Is there any chance the participants ... *might* stop attending...?" or, "I am a bit afraid this *might* happen", to engage the participants in the deliberation and decision-making process about the design of the Friday afternoon programme. One could say that by applying this subjunctive voice and through the content of the question, the board member engaged the practical wisdom of people in dealing with concrete, routine but also unexpected future situations. Both the content of questions like these and the way they are asked are elaborated further in the remainder of this chapter.

Applied phronesis *in action*

Reflecting on the ethical aspects of the content of these conversation(s), we see that it can be framed as *applied phronesis* or a form of value-based exploration. The conversation turns into a new direction because of the content of the question about participants who might stop visiting the Friday afternoons. In the book *Real social science* about applied *phronesis* (Flyvbjerg et al, 2012), one of the editors describes how four questions play a central role in nurturing 'knowledge that can challenge power not in theory but in ways that inform real efforts to produce change' (Schram, 2012: 20). These questions are: (1) Where are we going [with the present practice]?; (2) Who gains, and who loses, by which mechanisms of power?; (3) Is this development desirable?; and, (4) What, if anything, should we do about it? Often, the content of and the build-up across these questions are part of the regular conversations of a community of practice, because one of the participants zooms out of the routine action and introduces a variant of questions (1) or (2). These questions introduce a responsibility for finding a balance between the group interests and the common good in the surroundings of the group. In the case of Memory of East, the question about imagining a future in which certain people might not be participating any more changed the consensus in the present. The 'community worker' introduced a time dimension and a level of interest other than that the one was part of the conversation up to that moment.

Remarkably, it is often the same person who does that in different situations, taking up a reflexive responsibility to always ask difficult questions. If this succeeds on a particular occasion, the group as a whole will investigate the implications of these questions, change their practice wisdom and adjust their actions accordingly. Obviously, one wonders how the intervening questioner not only gets away with these queries but is almost expected to play this role.

In a comparative study on how community workers develop such a rapport with local people, Gradener (2016) discovered they tend to apply a form of *fusing*. This fusing strategy is built up by a skilful merging of the mainly moral, but also pragmatic, interests of community participants with a conditional idea of mutual engagement as a possible fruitful next action. Moral interests are usually the most easy to address and mobilise as they are reactive, automated and direct. They refer to what people value in their immediate lives and reflect the terms on which social interactions are taking place. By accepting someone in their midst who is asking the difficult questions, the local community accepts the worker. But they would not have to do so, if at least the worker had not shown any respect nor willingness to explore the local preoccupations, their practice wisdom and notions of the common good.

Ethical characteristics of intervening

Having discussed the content of the question, we now discuss how the careful way it was introduced by the speaker is crucial for the *phronesis* to shift in the group during the conversation. In the case study, the question had a connection to what was said before in the conversation, and it showed a deep presence of the speaker while being humbly posed. Building on those observations about *how* the question was posed we expand, suggesting that Nieuwenhof and De Weerdt's (2006) four-fold framework is useful. For them what is crucial is first, the conviction that these processes are embedded in the *connection* of the group members and that, in principle, there is a certain harmony hidden in the collisions that are also often there. Second, the practitioner has a mindful *presence* for letting unfold 'what-is' with all beautiful and ugly sides and motives people show for whatever reason is possible. Third, there is a need to remain *humble* about the controllability of the unfolding learning processes, despite a possible urgent feeling of direction based on personal morals and experience. Finally, there is a need for *discipline* to keep the faith in connectedness, presence and humility while searching for a balance between carefulness and perseverance. This latter characteristic relates to what was said earlier about people who tend to take on an everyday role of the 'thorn in the side'. We are convinced that consent arises from a certain kind of admiration of the rest of the group for taking up this difficult, but necessary, role, for 'making things better' in the long term.

Conclusion

This chapter's goal was conceptually and empirically to unpack how community workers in practice obtain consent from members of local communities to become and stay engaged around issues that affect their daily lives. Consent has been shown to be far more 'normative' and far-reaching than consensus: it binds everyone concerned to specific ways of action based on an 'embodied' commitment, even though there is no complete unanimity. Central in this acquisition of consent is the embodiment of an ethic of engagement that also allows for the professional intentions of community workers to be an integral part of the community development endeavours. This acknowledges that community workers in practice are never *tabula rasa*, nor should they be. On the contrary: we have demonstrated how a community worker and community cooperation can be well founded in a successful merging of the interests of both engaging parties building new symbolic universes of cognitive and moral interpretations about what makes life valuable and how they could engage with each other in new ways. Persistently asking questions that stimulate moral and critical evaluation in an open manner evokes people's practical wisdom for decision making with the intention of combining individual, group and community interests in future local developments.

References

Alinsky, S. (1972) 'Empowering people, not elites: Interview with Saul Alinsky', *Playboy Magazine*, March. Available at: www.vintageplayboymags.co.uk/Interviews/Alinsky_Saul.htm

Arendt, H. (2005) *The promise of politics*, New York: Schocken Books.

Baerveldt, C. and Voestermans, P. (2005) 'Culture, emotion and the normative structure of reality', *Theory and Psychology*, 15(4): 449–73.

Beck, E.L. and Eichler, M. (2000) 'Consensus organizing', *Journal of Community Practice*, 8(1): 87–102.

Berger, P.L. and Luckmann, T. (1991) *The social construction of reality: Treatise in the sociology of knowledge*, New York: Penguin Books.

de Kreek, M. (2017) 'Collective empowerment through local memory websites', PhD dissertation, Rotterdam: Erasmus University Rotterdam.

Flyvbjerg, B., Landman, T. and Schram, S. (eds) (2012) *Real social science: Applied phronesis*, New York: Cambridge University Press.

Frank, A.W. (2012) 'The feel for power games: Everyday phronesis and social theory', in B. Flyvbjerg, T. Landman and S. Schram (eds) *The real social science: Applied phronesis*, New York: Cambridge University Press, pp 48–65.

Gradener, J. (2016) 'Keys to the community: A multiple case study into professional legitimation in community development practice', PhD dissertation, Utrecht: Utrecht University.

Harfield, C.G. (1997) 'Consent, consensus or the management of dissent? Challenges to community consultation in a new policing environment', *Policing and Society*, 7(4): 271–89.

Lévi-Strauss, C. (1955) *Tristes Tropiques*, Paris: Librairie Plon.

Nieuwenhof, R. van den and De Weerdt, S. (2006) 'Didactief van de liefde: een pleidooi voor diepgaand leren in coaching, training en opleidingen' [The didactics of love: On deep learning in coaching, training and education], in J. Hovelynck, S. De Weerdt and A. Dewulf (eds) *Relationeel organiseren: Samen leren en werken in en tussen organisaties* [Relational organising: Learning and working together within and between organizations], Leuven: Lannoo Campus, pp 75–105.

Schram, S. (2012) 'Phronetic social science: An idea whose time has come', in B. Flyvbjerg, T. Landman and S. Schram (eds) *The real social science: Applied phronesis*, New York: Cambridge University Press, pp 15–26.

Sennett, R. (2012) *Together: The rituals, pleasures and politics of cooperation*, New Haven, CT: Yale University Press.

Suchman, M.C. (1995) 'Managing legitimacy: Strategic and institutional approaches', *Academy of Management Review*, 20(3): 571–610.

FIVE

Whose ethics counts? Ethical issues in community development and action research with communities facing stigmatisation

Pradeep Narayanan and Sowmyaa Bharadwaj

Introduction

How much do participatory methods in community-based research and development empower communities vis-à-vis not only the facilitators but also other stakeholders, and how much do they disempower and lead to exploitation? Robert Chambers unequivocally presents a talisman: 'At the core are principles and commitments to equity, respect, diversity and human rights. Who finds out, who learns, and who is empowered are core questions. The challenge and opportunity is for participatory methodologies to provide entry points for confronting and changing relationships and power' (Chambers, 2012: 168). Chambers has listed 40 'who?' and 'whose?' questions, the responses to which would define the ethics of participatory research and development. Nevertheless, what is important, which is also what this chapter tries to argue, is that ethics itself is also under contestation and it is even important to ask the question: whose ethics counts?

The question gains far more relevance in the context of communities that face stigmatisation, such as sex workers, people living in areas classed as 'deprived', people of certain classes, castes or religions. Such communities often face a wider social structure that is intrinsically violent towards them. The stigma is externally inflicted on the community and most often also internally experienced and owned by the members of the community, because their behaviours are under the constant gaze of, and compared against, the so-called socially and commonly accepted norms. Despite violence, both physical and emotional, such community members do not resort to open confrontation but, rather, accept themselves as deviants in relation to wider societal norms. Sometimes they 'willingly' conform to the stereotypes with which they are associated, if they feel that this helps them to cope better or survive.

Set against this backdrop are community development practitioners, who also coexist in this very society with its baggage of stereotypes and notions of right and wrong. When they embark on a programme of facilitated mobilisation of such stigmatised communities, hoping to challenge these norms and attempting a reversal of the discrimination, they end up being faced with several contradictions and dilemmas about defying accepted 'progressive' norms of civil society. Not only do they find themselves challenging the dominant societal norms that stigmatise and blame people who are marginalised, but they may also find that the more 'progressive' norms that they are attempting to uphold (working towards empowerment of groups traditionally without voice or supporting community action and protest, for example) may not be shared by the people in the communities they are trying to support. This chapter explores such ethical dilemmas and challenges; and the consequences of efforts to overcome or ignore them. By setting the context of a project with sex workers' collectives in various parts of India, it describes how they face stigma and discrimination and how ethics is located in a complex web of power relationships between facilitators and communities; between communities and society; between perpetrators of stigma and victims; and among community members themselves in programmes and interventions with these collectives. It details the dilemmas that programmes have to take into account and how the decisions made may create conflict between overall or societal ethics and ethics of the communities and how some sex workers themselves are often faced with choosing to confront the dynamics, while others want to cope and accept the stigma to survive.

This chapter is written with a community development practitioner's lens, building up an understanding from the experiences of sex workers themselves, drawn from our research and development work. Sex workers described how condescension and pejorative comments characterised their daily existence because at many levels their lifestyles went against certain accepted and appropriate standards of community living, customs and codes of conduct. Influencing these rules and norms was beyond their control. When this was described in the local language, the authors felt that for the purpose of this article the term 'ethical considerations' was best suited to explain nuances of their collective experience. Drawing on the discussion of the nature of ethics in Chapter One of this book, we regard ethical considerations as relating to matters of harms, benefits, rights and responsibilities. Following everyday English language, we tend not to distinguish between 'ethics' and 'morality', or 'ethical' and 'moral'. However, when discussing the prevailing societal norms regarding sex work, we tend to use the term 'morality'.

In this chapter we first give an overview of sex work in India and community development interventions in this field. We then discuss the ethical issues arising during community development work with sex workers, followed by discussion of some of the ethical dilemmas in measuring or evaluating the effectiveness of interventions designed to mobilise sex workers to form groups and take action for change.

Background: community development with sex workers in India

Praxis Institute for Participatory Practices

Praxis is an Indian organisation that specialises in the use of community-led participatory methods and approaches in an attempt to ensure mainstreaming of the voices of the poor and marginalised sections of society (see www.praxisindia.org). These methods enable communities to research their own realities and hence to own, shape and drive development processes to bring about change. The key aim of these processes is to encourage and ensure participation among people whose lives are affected by an issue in a way that goes beyond merely listening but shapes decision making by building consciousness ('conscientisation'), rather than perpetuating extractive systems of data collection. It challenges a linear approach to development that tends to prioritise the needs of institutions and governments and is led by self-identified and often external experts. Rather it promotes participatory methodologies that are inclusive, community-led, understand issues of power and recognise the complexities, uniqueness and evolving nature of people's realities (see www.participatorymethods.org). Using these principles of engagement, Praxis has over the last two decades been closely involved with sex workers in a variety of community development programmes. Its work has ranged from designing inputs to monitoring of programmes related to anti-trafficking, as well as rehabilitation work and the creation of measurement frameworks for the collectivisation of sex workers in the HIV context.

Sex work in India

While the term 'sex workers' constitutes a meaningful single population for epidemiological purposes, in reality it encompasses female, male and transgender sex workers, who are further categorised based on the location of their work, that is, home based, street based, brothel based and massage parlours (Wariki et al, 2012). In this chapter, the focus is on female sex workers and is limited to the engagement with sex workers in the context of projects where collectivisation attempts of these female sex workers has taken place in HIV projects.

Although sex work is not strictly illegal in India, associated activities such as soliciting in a public place, owning or managing a brothel, prostitution in a hotel, child prostitution, pimping and pandering are illegal under *The Immoral Traffic (Prevention) Act 1956*. While sex work is referred to as the oldest profession in the world (Sarode, 2015) with mention being made in ancient Indian religious and historical texts, sex workers themselves have historically been the targets of scorn because of the perceived immorality of the profession. Though poorly defined, 'morality policy' typically describes any policy field where emotion and ideology rule over rationality and reason, rendering notions of evidence-based policy problematic at best, and impossible at worst (Henricson, 2016). Sex work, alongside issues such as abortion, euthanasia, drugs, pornography, capital punishment and gambling, is classically cited as an example of 'morality policy', one in which different moral standpoints clash, and policy is determined by a sense of what is ultimately felt to be right or wrong in relation to dominant norms. In this sense, any attempt to regulate the consumption of sexual services can be read as an attempt to draw boundaries between 'good' and 'bad' behaviour based solely on the understanding that the commodification of the sexual relationship is sinful or wrong (Hubbard et al, 2016). Set against this understanding, the notions of right, wrong and morality are cemented in India thanks to the *Immoral Traffic (Prevention) Act*, 1956, which ensures that concerns of morality continue to be foregrounded as the core of the discourse around sex work, rooted in a 'nostalgic dream of a long lost golden era of cultural cohesion, family values and a conservative sexual morality' (Kempadoo et al, 2016: 27).

HIV-focused interventions with sex workers

More recently, intervention programmes with sex workers have been influenced by the HIV-prevention agenda. In the early 2000s, India was one among five countries, along with Russia, China, Nigeria and Ethiopia, that were classified by the US National Intelligence Council in 2002 as representing the second wave of nations dealing with the HIV/AIDS epidemic (Amin, 2004). Despite the numbers of people living with HIV in India being more than halved from 5.1 million in 2003 to 2.1 million in 2016 (Sharma, 2018), given the sheer population size, India has the third largest HIV epidemic in the world (UNAIDS, 2017). The HIV epidemic in India is driven mainly by heterosexual sex, which accounted for 87% of new infections in 2015, but there has a been recognition of this epidemic being concentrated among certain high-risk groups since the launch of the first National AIDS Control Programme (NACP) in India, in 1992. Sex workers are one of the so-called high-risk groups targeted by India's National AIDS Control Organisation (NACO) through peer-to-peer HIV interventions (when individuals from key affected populations provide services to their peers or link them to services within healthcare settings; see www.naco.gov.in).

While interventions with sex workers initially focused on largely biomedical inputs (like regular testing) to check for sexual and reproductive health morbidity, over the years it broadened to behavioural aspects (condom usage), eventually to structural interventions (collectivisation, demanding rights and entitlements) and community mobilisation efforts in recognition of the violence and discrimination faced by sex workers (Moore et al, 2014). All of these efforts have been rooted in various notions of morality. The anti-trafficking agenda has traditionally adopted more censorious and repressive attitudes towards sex work (Hubbard et al, 2016) and since 2003 has been strongly influenced by a conservative sexual morality which manifested itself in the nature of messaging for HIV prevention – 'abstinence rather than protection', or building narratives of 'victimhood' among women, thereby justifying protective detention. In the modern approach to sex trafficking the anti-slavery angle is gaining prominence. The emphasis is on understanding whether the trafficked person is being coerced or threatened to work, 'owned' or controlled by an employer through abuse or threat of abuse, dehumanised and/or treated as a commodity or physically constrained or has restrictions placed on their freedom of movement (Anti-Slavery International, 2018). In such an approach, abolitionism or ending sex work altogether claims the moral high ground and mobilises a universalising concept of human rights (Kempadoo et al, 2016).

Since the late 2000s, community mobilisation methods became the way forward because of their ability to improve outcomes and make them more sustainable. They also achieved broader goals of addressing poverty and fostering well-being, as well as providing the scope to develop the capacity of those most at risk of HIV/AIDS to tackle issues of discrimination, stigma, exclusion and powerlessness (Thomas et al, 2012). This was attributable to the significantly low rate of HIV infection and high rate of condom use among sex workers in Kolkata, India through the community-led structural intervention called the Sonagachi Project which mobilises sex workers to engage in HIV education, formation of community-based organisations and advocacy around sex work issues (Ghose et al, 2008).

Given the broad scope of community mobilisation itself, these community mobilisation strategies and models to prevent HIV and sexually transmitted infection (STI) included involving local community groups in designing and implementing programmes for improved STI prevention, community-based condom distribution and peer education, building marginalised communities' HIV-related skills and knowledge, supporting partnerships between marginalised communities and outside agencies, promoting community ownership, reliance on group consensus and the use of gatekeepers to access communities to reduce the risk of HIV transmission (Thomas et al, 2012). Donors across the country (and globally) invested in and adopted one of these many pathways of community mobilisation and created a parallel need to precisely define and systematically measure community mobilisation efforts.

Community-based groups (CBGs) are consequently viewed as the basic unit with which to engage for community development workers and are a collective of community members who are mobilised to take action by one or more representatives, or by peer educators. Peer educators are representative community members, who implement HIV-prevention interventions on the ground through outreach, serving a population with whom they have a similar occupational, behavioural, social or environmental experience and among whom they are regarded as trustworthy and looked on as role models. CBGs may take the form of legally registered community-based organisations (CBOs), with a formalised, democratic process of choosing representatives. The formation of CBGs has emerged as a key factor in ensuring that programmes accurately address the needs of high-risk groups, and in making programmes sustainable by developing the groups' capacity to advocate for the services they require. For example, the Sonagachi Project, which began in 1992 to address the vulnerabilities of female sex workers in the Indian state of West Bengal, was handed over to Durbar Mahila Samanwaya Samiti (DMSC), in 1999. Within two years,

DMSC was able to expand to 15 red–light districts in West Bengal, increasing the coverage of the FSW population in the state to a level of 75%–80%. Parallel to this was a move by the NACP in India, which mandated (in 2007) the transition of intervention programmes to their 'natural owners', which led to a mushrooming of CBGs. Avahan (2008), a programme of the Bill & Melinda Gates Foundation, aimed to accelerate this aim of the NACP whereby CBGs would transform their own roles by taking action to address their vulnerabilities and building strong organisations that would be sustainable beyond the lifetime of the Avahan programme (Wheeler et al, 2012).

Monitoring and evaluation of sex worker programmes

In order to understand the process of this transition, Praxis construed that it was essential to unpack, demystify and measure what community mobilisation meant. Sex worker collectives and networks in India have been seeking legitimacy as well as entitlements, but these have been limited to HIV reduction where community mobilisation efforts are of instrumental value. In the absence of a gold standard to measure community mobilisation, the key challenge for Praxis was to create a framework to measure, monitor and evaluate this process of community mobilisation in the Avahan programme. In an attempt to stay true to the principles of participation and conscientisation, the idea was to evolve a monitoring and evaluation (M&E) framework through a process that included the active participation of sex workers where their agency would be built and they could define their own theory of change in the design of an instrument. This would in turn involve a democratising process where the community members can seek accountability from their leaders. The process is not seen as a monolith and does not create a blueprint for community mobilisation but instead provides space for multiple pathways of achieving an outcome, which is as broad as evolving an empowered community group. This was the most important challenge, especially when a M&E system has to measure both process as well as outcome.

It is pertinent to understand that even these key principles of participation and conscientisation have to operate within a certain framework. While these principles look universal they are not derived in a vacuum, but have evolved as a result of the operation of the same morality framework that underpins what we earlier called the 'morality policies' linked with sex work and HIV prevention. They are just as vulnerable to being 'projectised' and thereby not really challenging the mainstream morality framework.

Moral frontiers: a community ghettoised by wider society

In order to understand the strength and extent of mainstream morality and the consequent stigmatisation that it creates, the first important step is to understand what the Community Mobilisation Monitoring Project (across 83 districts in six Indian states) learned about community perception of 'stigma' and how it related 'stigma' to its problems. The objective was to ensure that the community understanding of stigma informs the measurement system. Through a series of engagements, discussions, workshops and interactions with sex workers belonging to four CBOs across four different states, using a range of participatory methods, it emerged that there is a strong, deeply rooted 'stereotyping' of communities. Community leaders among sex workers listed the following four kinds of stereotypes that society has for them. A section of society denotes them as *law-breakers*, like traffickers, snatchers, thieves and criminals. There are others who just want to say that they are *not like us* by calling them 'lower caste, slum dweller, outsider'. For some, they are just a *high-risk population* in the context of HIV. However, for many, they are *society-destroyers*, who are 'pleasure-seekers', 'family-breakers', and 'breakers of social norms'. The last one is the fundamental one, which is manifested even in the first three forms.

One community member described stigma as "the way in which society has defined *social norms* that refuse to accommodate problems faced by sex workers and sexual minorities". She said, "Wider society continuously reminds us that they exclude us because we are deviants from the socially accepted norms". She added, "We call this kind of exclusion 'stigma'." According to another sex worker, "despite repeated assertion of my rights as an Indian citizen, it took me two years to get a ration card". Knowing she was a sex worker, the local staff deliberately delayed her application. The discrimination did not end there. Another shared how, "When I used to go to the [food] ration shop, they always used to make me wait longer than others. They would always allow others in line to go first." Challenging social norms is difficult, because they are justified based on traditions, customs and faith and take the shape of morality. Some of their narrations reflect the deep-rooted discrimination. For example:

- "The child of a sex worker had to drop out from the school because she was treated badly by teachers."
- "We are not able to get a rented place for DIC (drop in centre) in the neighbourhood."

- "Doctors and nurses don't even touch us to see if we have fever – they leave medicines on the table and ask us to pick it up from there – as if we are untouchable."
- "The police and so many others ask us to have sex with them for free when we go to seek legitimate claims."

An interesting aspect of how the community understood stigma was the fact that the practice of ignoring was sometimes felt more severely than even physical assault. For CBO members, despite the risk and reality of physical violence, it was easier to engage with gatekeepers (*goondas* or *goons*), lodge owners, pimps and other stakeholders with whom they needed to develop only business relationships than with 'mainstream' individuals or organisations, with whom they would need to seek alliances in order to challenge their marginalised positions. Achieving a social standing is often a far more difficult proposition than running a smooth business or even getting social security, as this requires building relationships with some people who are typically most deeply antagonistic, such as faith leaders, people in their own neighbourhood community, and even NGO groups.

Clearly, the fact that their work is stigmatised, gets reflected in everything they do. Community leaders feel that the discrimination caused in them "absolute poverty, absence of family support, insensitivity of government functionaries and the non-existence of safe spaces for them to even meet and discuss". Many of these characteristics together have further 'othered' these communities into isolated groups both in the minds of society at large and the state, which is by law duty bound to realise rights and entitlements for these citizens.

What is often forgotten is, as a sex worker put it, "Once a sex worker – always a sex worker. Even though I quit sex work many years ago, I am not allowed to forget this – right from the neighbourhood grocery store to the teachers in my children's school. Sometimes I feel it is best to go back to sex work." In the case of communities that practise traditional sex work, this notion of societal morality completely dismantles the allowance of the practice. Women who choose sex work as a profession and openly admit to doing sex work are typically ostracised and become 'invisible'. At the end, if these aspects of morality surrounding sex work are not challenged, the stigma faced by the community would continue. Is not the core of the discrimination derived from the so-called *moral* fabric of society? Morality is very hard to change, for the change would challenge the basic concepts of institutions such as marriage and family. Is it not true that in order to eliminate discrimination of sex workers, one has to challenge the way morality gets defined in society? What became clear to us in the course of our work is that morality underlies stigma and discrimination, this despite interventions and possibly to some extent, perpetuated in interventions themselves.

Interventions: benevolent, but do they challenge morality?

Discourses, and accompanying intervention programmes around HIV/AIDS and Indian sex workers, have been shifting – from an invisible and largely insignificant group, to a target of health, welfare and surveillance programmes, to agents of change and as part of an HIV-prevention solution grounded in structural intervention models. Sex worker CBOs have become central to the government's HIV/AIDS response strategy (Magar, 2012). These interventions focused on providing clinical services to the community, and also emphasised behavioural change among sex workers to promote condom use, so that the spreading of HIV to wider society is prevented. The interventions gradually took the form of community mobilisation, wherein collectives of sex workers were encouraged and they even found a place at negotiating tables with regards to policy making and implementation.

This became possible because addressing HIV required the intervention of reaching out to the population of hidden sex workers, which was in turn possible only by actively encouraging the agency of peer sex workers. There was a need for the intervention to work closely with them. And the various collectives of sex workers, peer educators and NGOs were not monoliths. Each of these groups and interventions were faced with a series of subjectivities, conflicts and difficult choices, which were collectively expressed and termed as ethical dilemmas (see Chapter Six in this volume).

Many sex workers who were affiliated with HIV projects shared that initially, "NGO staff often tell us that this work is immoral", asking "Why are you doing things like this – couldn't you find anything better?" This, for the sex workers, demonstrated *a vision-level dilemma* about associating with the HIV projects – since these views were fuelled by a programmatic approach that aimed to make sex workers exit the profession altogether. These statements were often peppered by a reiteration of stereotypes prevalent in wider society. So even with the HIV stigma that NGO staff were working hard to end, sex workers shared "they [NGO staff] initially would not shake our hands as they assumed they would contract an STI from us" or, "even if a non sex worker came for HIV services, they assumed she was a sex worker or judged her as promiscuous". Some NGOs often prescribed uniforms for sex workers who were peer educators, to differentiate between sex workers and staff in NGOs. What became evident is that even after peer sex workers were the backbone of the HIV intervention, there was 'othering' of sex workers in the intervention. Over time, Praxis has recognised that the development interventions need to accept the realities of the existence of sex work and to ensure the dignity of peer sex workers, so that sex workers become the agents of change. It was realised that one cannot reject sex work in a condescending way and still be able to ensure active participation of sex workers.

In subsequent phases of HIV reduction programmes, there was a lot of focus on the mobilisation of sex workers around their rights and entitlements. Interestingly, the entire programme was referred to as 'Targeted Intervention', in which the sex workers were among the targeted communities – with an assumption that, if they were subject to an intervention, then HIV would not spread to the wider society. So even in this more progressive phase of development interventions, which were becoming sex worker–centric, choices related to programme design and funding were governed by a morality of sex workers as agents of change. Yet the change was not centred on the value of their lives as ends in themselves, but borrowing from the utilitarian philosophy, as 'instrumental' in reducing HIV. The importance of sex workers all of a sudden was because of their potential to prevent HIV from spreading. Their empowerment probably had merely an instrumental value. Their acceptance would be tolerated, but with that limit. Despite years of intervening, the programmes are in no way close to legitimising sex work in the legal domain, and way farther from even a trace of acceptance in the socio-religious domain. This raises the question: is it not unethical to envision so-called development programmes in such a way that 'empowerment of sex workers' is seen in a narrow sense – with their threshold being defined by prevention of HIV?

Further, patriarchy continues to play a significant role in defining morality and often sanctions the use of women's bodies as sites of revenge politics. Violence against sex workers was often accepted as 'normal'. It was sometimes assumed that sex workers can never be raped and violence is often normalised as a job peril. The pendulum often swings between the view that they would have been a willing party to the act and the fact that they 'deserve' it. So interventions often located sex workers on the wrong side of morality. Interventions, over the years, were designed to respond to 'addressing the crisis of sex workers' through 'mobilising' and 'attracting' sex workers to programmes and thereby HIV testing centres. There was little effort to create debate around the moralising linked with sex work and the ethical issues facing both those who intervened and the sex workers themselves. In the absence of sociopolitical recognition of the identity of sex workers, at the most, interventions would be sympathetic to their situation, but would rarely accept them for who they are.

HIV interventions, while definitely moving from service-delivery to a rights-based approach, refrained from taking on the societal edifice that made sex work immoral. Reaching out to hidden sex workers was encouraged, the formation of collectives of sex workers was also promoted; and even their fight to seek constitutional entitlements was supported. However, this all happened without making any sociopolitical assertion about their identity in the context of the prevailing negative world view about sex in wider society. Strong environments of 'ethics' defining the boundaries of development interventions become blatantly clear in such a case.

Ethical dilemmas in measuring mobilisation: how to count morality?

Individual and collective systems of ethics define boundaries and parameters of any kind of engagement, determine decision making and guide programmatic interventions (government, non-government and others). Besides, broad research frameworks being conceived by a certain kind of ethical learning, research and especially measurement-based research, such as evaluation and monitoring focused studies, bring in an additional layer of ethics. If the measurement system adheres to the principle of an enhanced role for communities in the programme, it is necessary that the M&E system itself becomes an instrument in the hands of the community to steer the process of community mobilisation. Often, the research has to clearly visualise and define an 'ideal' scenario against which to measure the existing scenario. It is challenging to prevent the prevailing morality from defining what is ideal. Creating a discourse around an ideal scenario would often cause the framework to degenerate into a moral framework that is exclusionary and promotes mainstream power politics.

We can take the example of police harassment and false arrests of sex workers. An 'ideal scenario' that was evolved by the measurement team in consultation with different project stakeholders would be an absence of this police harassment. The stages of the pathway to achieving this ideal scenario were defined as shown in the top layer of Figure 5.1. The research framework viewed this pathway as moving through four more progressively desirable levels from 'basic' to 'vibrant' as shown in the lower layer of Figure 5.1.

For the research measurement framework to acknowledge that the CBOs of sex workers are 'vibrant', the police administration should have a sense of apprehension that the community has the capacity to organise a mass protest demanding that police harassment should stop.

The challenge is to determine the ideal scenarios about the 'hows' and 'whys' of these protests. A CBO shared an example where even the police officers were sometimes clients of sex workers. If anyone from the sex workers' collective was wrongfully detained, the collective sometimes, through their leaders, threatened the staff at the police station that they would 'rat on them' to their families (which would cause them tremendous humiliation). This, in fact, led to the ending of false arrests and harassment and the collective saw this as a tremendous achievement, which they thought deserved to bring the collective up to the level of vibrancy. They felt that it actually saved them the trouble of doing a mass protest at Stage 4.

However, from the perspective of a mainstream moralistic lens, use of such threats is definitely not acceptable. Going by the principle that using constitutional and legitimate means to achieve any purpose is an indication of collective strength, this kind of action would not get rated as 'vibrant', for the constitution is also defined by mainstream morality. The criteria of sustainability and scalability as two key requirements of vibrancy were also missing for the measurement team, as this collective's solution was a one-off and could not be promoted with other collectives as the pathway to adopt. Further, the measurement team was divided, as were the community members, about how to regard the tactic of threatening the police. It was a section of the collective that stated their disagreement with the measurement team by saying that the measurement framework does not take account of

Figure 5.1: A pathway of 'progress' in sex worker communities

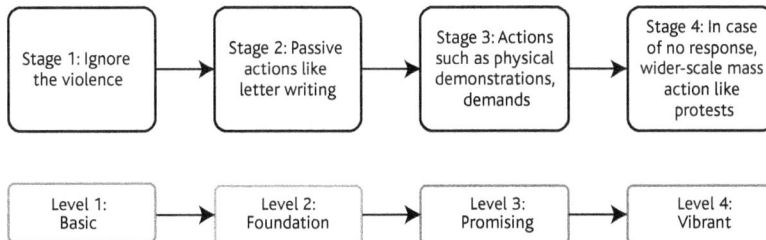

| Stage 1: Ignore the violence | → | Stage 2: Passive actions like letter writing | → | Stage 3: Actions such as physical demonstrations, demands | → | Stage 4: In case of no response, wider-scale mass action like protests |

| Level 1: Basic | → | Level 2: Foundation | → | Level 3: Promising | → | Level 4: Vibrant |

the lived experience of the community, which they felt has to create its own coping pathway to realise members' rights. The path it chooses, even if it is intimidation, is not an easy pathway, but as long as it works for them, they did not want to be concerned with any other issues (especially related to sustainability).

In this case, the measurement framework erred on the side of valuing a 'legitimate' and legally permissible pathway. The principle that the measurement team recognised is that for the process to be effective, it needs to be led by members of the intended-beneficiary community, who should be seen as agents of change, rather than recipients of services. This said, boundaries have to be set within the social rights and justice framework in the context of the community about which the project is concerned. It is necessary to evolve core principles of rights and social justice in discussion with the community, guided by a collective set of ethics – and this process itself is an intervention. The ethics of research, especially of participatory research, is to definitively involve communities even in the development of the research design. However, despite that, when there is a negotiation on what the ideal pathway may be, is it not true that there is not merely engagement of two worlds of people, but also two worlds of ethics? It becomes more challenging when the intervention confronts an issue in which morality is the very basis of stigmatisation for the community that is being involved.

Another instance of an ethical issue linked to participatory research, monitoring and evaluation that became significant for the engagement of Praxis with sex workers was around gaining the consent of community members to participate. Often, it appears, the most significant institution that is created as part of an ethical review process is the requirement that participants are given a 'consent letter'. This outlines the nature of the research to be undertaken and asks potential participants to give verbal or written agreement to take part. While the practice of issuing consent letters is to ensure that the researcher informs the participants about the research in its entirety, before ensuring their participation in the study, what it has now become is primarily a record that the research institution can use in case the researched community challenges the study at a later point of time. In the course of seeking consent per the research norms we followed, one community collective actually reversed the power balance and sought 'consent' from us researchers to their demand that we would not use the data generated without first informing the group, especially where the name of the community-based group was mentioned.

This brought forth for us a series of issues related to the instrument of consent letters in themselves and led us to question the extent to which research ethics is all about seeking community consent. For members of the Praxis team, the feeling of powerlessness, by making ourselves subject to an interpretation of consent at the hands of 'the researched', was itself an issue. We began to wonder whether the way in which consent letters are used in research is actually ethical? Consent letters, we were made to realise, can actually *disempower* a community if they do not allow for people to change their minds or reconsent as the research proceeds. When people know that they have already consented to a research process, they feel they have less space to back out or challenge the study process or findings. This takes away their right to be forgotten. Another challenge is whether the fact that a particular sex workers' collective has given consent can be assumed to be the consent of an entire community, and there is an added layer of complexity if the community itself is not well organised.

This issue was resolved with the community-based group asking the research team to sign a letter that any product that arises out of research with implications for the community group would require a prior approval from the community group (if the community group is to be named in the research). What remains a challenge, though, is to understand whether the institution of consent letters is almost substituting efforts otherwise needed to build trust between the research team and the community.

Conclusion: negotiating *the* ethics

What emerges from the previous section are three kinds of contestations among the different ethical world views. The first contestation stems from the perspective of the community of sex workers who face stigmatisation in their regular day-to-day lives. Their experiences with larger society shape their 'ethics'. They regularly confront people who see sex work as exploitative, and are happy to view sex workers as 'victims'. However, once people know that sex workers are not leaving sex work, they find ways and means of denigrating sex workers. Patriarchal morality is displayed when male clients are not ostracised in the same way as sex workers. Clearly, standing up for their right to be part of society as sex workers is not recognised. They are allowed to exist as victims, without 'agency'. When sex workers demonstrate agency in any form, to take action which they regard as ethical for them, they are dismissed using the lens of mainstream societal morality. So, while they are allowed a platform as victims, their existence as sex workers or people is not legitimised. Above all, society asserts that, morally, female sexuality must be controlled. The primary confrontation is around the prevailing social morality, which decides what kind of work and profession is acceptable, in this case, for women; and the 'ethics' of the community of sex workers, which involves standing up for their rights as survivors, especially when they want to survive within the domain of sex work. This contest is political, for it involves making choices in terms of whose ethics counts.

The second contestation stems from the perspective of interventionists, in this case, community development workers, who conceptualise and implement developmental projects that involve sex workers. The interventionists here often come from the same society that is spoken of previously, but are willing to concede that sex workers have 'agency' of their own; and have citizenship rights. In that sense, the collective and individual agency of sex workers is recognised and valued, but often only as an instrument, to sustain the pre-existing moral framework. They want to influence and shape the agency of sex workers to prevent people from entering sex work, to prevent trafficking, to ensure that they cease to be instrumental in spreading HIV. The overall ethical framework of the targeted intervention programme, which works closely with sex workers on HIV/AIDS, itself could be challenged for 'using' sex workers to benefit wider society, especially when addressing stigmatisation of sex work where the sex workers themselves are the last of the programme's priorities. The intrinsic empowerment needs of sex workers are very different from the instrumental empowerment of sex workers that interventions demand.

The third contestation stems from the research ethics that participatory researchers bring into the layer of measurement that intends to understand and evaluate a programme in a comprehensive way. Researchers cannot be oblivious to the ethical contestations described. Often, especially when there is a need to define a measurement of a change framework, researchers have to take a stand. The principles of ethics in participatory research require the community to be involved in, and to inform, the research framework. Involving the people affected by the issues under study is the bare minimum, providing importance to their views is still possible. However, to provide primacy to their morals, especially when those morals are challenged by mainstream society, of which the research team itself is a part, will be the biggest challenge. Further, it is not difficult to defend the ethics behind the research framework that is developed by the research team, but what matters is whether the research framework that provides primacy to one set of ethics excludes certain voices from finding a place in the study? And if this is the case, is it not also unethical to create a research framework that excludes one kind of voice? In this context, there is an utmost need to institutionalise community-led ethical review processes (Thomas, 2000), where there is a space for the community to define research ethics using their own lens (Narayanan, 2018). It is necessary to prevent 'ethics' becoming an instrument in the hands of mainstream politics to influence research to tread a pathway it wants. Praxis has organised community-led ethical review processes to ensure that community ethics informs the research designs.

Promoting purposive introspection into the ethical frameworks that are central to any intervention is a crying need of the community development sector. Ensuring a community-led ethical review committee process will go a long way towards subverting the institutionalisation of a singular ethical framework. This signals the importance of asking the question: 'whose ethics counts?' as the fundamental starting point in any engagement. Is it the ethics of the communities facing stigmatisation that defines the intervention pathway, or that of the wider and mainstreamed society? We also need to consider whether different institutions that define and police ethics even recognise the ethics of marginalised communities. One of the roles of organisations that promote and undertake community development and participatory research is to raise this question and develop new methodologies for making visible and valuing the indigenous ethics of diverse communities.

Acknowledgements

We are grateful to the sex workers who have worked with Praxis over many years and contributed their views on their livelihoods and challenges. We are also grateful to the Avahan programme of the Bill & Melinda Gates Foundation, and Priya Babu and Nalini Jameela, who advised the monitoring study. We are also very grateful for the conversations with Tom Thomas, Robert Chambers, Sarah Banks, Danny Burns, Jo Howard, Andrew Russell and Jane Macnaughton that helped to nuance and concretise the thinking around this paper, as well as provide it direction.

References

Amin, A. (2004) *Risk, morality, and blame: A critical analysis of government and U.S. donor responses to HIV infections among sex workers in India*, Takoma Park, MD: Center for Health and Gender Equity (CHANGE). Available at: www.hivpolicy.org/Library/HPP000864. pdf

Anti-Slavery International (2018) 'What is modern slavery?' Available at: www.antislavery.org/slavery-today/modern-slavery/

Avahan (2008) *Avahan – the India AIDS initiative: The business of HIV prevention at scale*, New Delhi: Bill & Melinda Gates Foundation. Available at: https://docs.gatesfoundation.org/Documents/avahan_hivprevention.pdf

Chambers, R. (2012) *Revolutions in development inquiry*, Abingdon: Earthscan.

Ghose, T., Swendeman, D., George, S. and Chowdhury, D. (2008) 'Mobilizing collective identity to reduce HIV risk among sex workers in Sonagachi, India: The boundaries, consciousness, negotiation framework', *Social Science & Medicine*, 67(2): 311–20.

Henricson, C. (2016) *Morality and public policy*, Bristol: Policy Press.

Hubbard, P., Sanders, T. and Scoula, J. (2016) 'Prostitution policy and the precautionary principle', *Drugs and Alcohol Today*, 16(3): 194–202.

Kempadoo, K., Jyoti, S. and Pattanaik, B. (eds) (2016) *Trafficking and prostitution reconsidered: New perspectives on migration, sex work, and human rights* (2nd edn), Abingdon: Routledge.

Magar, V. (2012) 'Rescue and rehabilitation: A critical analysis of sex workers' antitrafficking response in India', *Signs*, 37(3): 619–44.

Moore, L., Chersich, M., Steen, R., Reza-Paul, S., Dhana, A., Vuylsteke, B., Lafort, Y. and Scorgie, F. (2014) 'Community empowerment and involvement of female sex workers in targeted sexual and reproductive health interventions in Africa: A systematic review', *Global Health*, 10: art 47. Available at: https://globalizationandhealth.biomedcentral.com/articles/10.1186/1744-8603-10-47

Narayanan, P. (2018) 'Ethics is politics: Whose ethics counts?' *Community Development Journal Plus*, 9 February. Available at: www.oxfordjournals.org/cdjc/ethics-is-ethics-whose-ethics-counts/

Sarode, S. (2015) *Historical study of prostitution trade in India: Past and present*, project submission to University Grants Commission. Available at: http://vcckarad.com/Minor%20Research%20Project%20on%20 HISTORICAL%20STUDY%20OF%20PROSTITUTION%20 TRADE%20IN%20INDIA%20%20%20PAST%20AND%20 PRESENT.pdf

Sharma, S. (2018) 'HIV cases in India drop more than 50% but challenges remain', *Hindustan Times*, 19 January. Available at: www.hindustantimes.com/india-news/hiv-cases-in-india-drop-more-than-50-but-challenges-remain/story-nE8wetmZ8cjDYM0KIZZnwK.html

Thomas, J. (2000) 'The stages and process of developing an ethically sound, community based multi city study among the vulnerable population', paper presented at the satellite conference, International network on community based HIV social research, XIII International AIDS Conference (Track E, 13th July), 9–14 July, Durban, South Africa.

Thomas, T., Narayanan, P., Wheeler, T., Kiran, U., Joseph, M.J. and Ramanathan, T.V. (2012) 'Design of a community ownership and preparedness index: Using data to inform the capacity development of community-based groups', *Journal of Epidemiology and Community Health*, 66(2): 26–33.

UNAIDS (2017) *Ending AIDS: Progress towards the 90-90-90 targets*, Joint United Nations Programme on HIV/AIDS (UNAIDS). Available at: https://reliefweb.int/report/world/ending-aids-progress-towards-90-90-90-targets

Wariki, W.M., Ota, E., Mori, R., Koyanagi, A., Hori, N. and Shibuya, K. (2012) 'Behavioral interventions to reduce the transmission of HIV infection among sex workers and their clients in low- and middle-income countries', *Cochrane Database of Systematic Reviews*, 2: art CD005272.

Wheeler, T., Kiran, U., Dallabetta, G., Jayaram, M., Chandrasekaran, P. and Tangri, A. (2012) 'Learning about scale, measurement and community mobilisation: Reflections on the implementation of the Avahan HIV/AIDS initiative in India', *Journal of Epidemiology & Community Health*, 66(2): ii16–ii25.

SIX

Koorliny birniny, ni, quoppa katatjin[1]: respect and ethics in working with Indigenous Australian communities

Jennie Buchanan, Len Collard and Dave Palmer

Koorliny yeye – introductions

This chapter explores the topic of work with Indigenous Australians, particularly focusing on a range of ethical challenges. Rather than starting with a discussion of conventional English conceptions of ethics the authors introduce *Noongar* frames and discourse concerned with the business of *karnya* (a good disposition and sensibility).

We use the term *Noongar* to refer to people living and those who have passed away, who have long-standing cultural affiliations and connections to the south-west corner of Western Australia. *Noongar boodjar* (country) spreads from roughly north of Jurien Bay (about 250 kilometres north of Perth, the capital of Western Australia); moving inland to north of Moora and down the southern coast between Bremer Bay and east of Esperance (about 750 kilometres south-east of Perth by road). There is evidence that at the point of colonisation there were around 14 different areas with varied geography and spoken dialects. The approximate area of the Single Noongar Native Title Claim is 194,000 square kilometres. In comparison, Scotland is just over 80,000 square kilometres (National Native Title Tribunal, 2003).

Specifically, the chapter examines the place of the following practices: *wangkiny kaya boordier* (talking to the bosses); *gnarl* (sweat); *birniny* (digging and scratching); *quop karnya* (good and sensitive work); *quop koondarn* (respect); *dabakarn dabakarn* (going along steady); *wabaliny quop weirn* (singing out to the good spirits); *boodjar wangkiny* (talking to country); *maar ni* (listening to the wind); and *korunkurl moort* (becoming family and community).

The history of outsiders working with Indigenous Australian groups is long and often horrifying. To say that Indigenous communities have endured pain and trauma at the hand of governments, church organisations, universities, resource companies, and non-government groups is a dreadful understatement. Partly, this reflects a long and lasting history where the vested interests of outsiders (for example, governments, business, universities, even non-government organisations) usurp the goals and aspirations of Indigenous communities.

In a chapter contemplating ethical work with Indigenous Australians some would expect a discussion about the importance of non-Indigenous people understanding the history of colonial Australia and the systematic marginalisation of Indigenous communities (see Haebich, 1992; Kickett-Tucker et al, 2017). Others may want us to talk about the need for community workers to 'decolonise' their minds; or indeed a discussion of principles such as social justice, self-worth, self-determination, inclusion and equity.

However, we will replace this with a discussion of *Noongar* conceptual ideas. We do this for a number of reasons. The first is that many *Noongar* have different concepts in their lexicon for talking about good practice. Additionally, we make the judgement that far too often concepts such as those just mentioned are used to mask a lack of real commitment to good practice with Indigenous communities. For example, in the 'Australian community workers code of ethics' document (ACWA, 2017a), the 'Australian community work practice guidelines' (ACWA, 2017b) and even the International Association for Community Development (IACD, 2017) standards document keywords, such as: 'Aboriginal', 'Indigenous', 'culture', 'language', 'racism', 'colonisation', 'country' and even 'family', are absent. This is particularly disconcerting given that in Australia a significant number of community development practitioners accept resources to 'service' the interests of Indigenous communities.

The conversations that helped shape this chapter have their roots in a long 'yarn' (the Aboriginal English term for the process of the respectful to and fro that goes on between parties as they weave their ideas together). We, as authors, have all known each other for about 30 years and had many long and deep conversations about these matters. However, we also undertook a series of filmed discussions in November of 2017.

Before our dialogue begins we should point out that we will be talking about Noongar and Wedjela (non-Indigenous) experiences, and that these are particular to the history of 'settler' and 'settled' communities in the south-west of Australia. Some of this history has points of similarity to what has happened in other parts of the world. However, we want to make the point that each place and circumstance holds much difference, even within Australia. Indeed, recognising this speaks to a central theme of community development; starting our relationships with a sensitivity to the history, language and cultural context of the particular communities with whom we work.

Wangkiny kaya boordier – starting with respect

DAVE: Let's imagine that this chapter is an exercise in travelling on *boodjar* (country). How about we use the metaphor of 'walking' or 'journeying' to help us think about the ethics of working with Indigenous Australian communities? Len and Jen, what would be our first steps?

LEN: Well, if you are *boodjar koorliny* (travelling on country), one of the first things you should do is 'sing out' to the old people, those who have passed away and are now the spirits of the land and sense of the place. You need to call out to ancestors, to *moort* (family), about who you are and what your intentions are;[2] you'd say something like:

> *Kaya noonarkoort Noongar Wedjela. Gnulla koort karnya barminy noonook nidja koorliny yeye nyinninny. Gnulla koort boola barminy djinanginy noonook ni gnulluk wangkiny yeye. Nidja Noongar boodjar noonook nyinniny. Noongar boordier nidja boojar, koora, yeye boorda. Gnulla koorliny birniny karnya koort.[3]*

> Hello to our friends both *Noongar* and non-*Noongar*. We write this while sitting in *Noongar* country. We believe it is worth remembering that *Noongar* have contributed much to cultural and economic life in the south-west of Australia and that *Noongar* knowledge and systems have long influenced life in this part of the world, particularly in community work. We will go along picking our way through knowledge with a respectful heart.

The other important thing to do if you are going out and away from your home area is to sing out to the living people from the area; to tell them you are coming out their way. You should ring up the local bosses to tell them you're coming out and what you intend to do.[4] This is the old way and the right way.

DAVE: That reminds me of the important part *gnarl*, or sweat, plays in ethical practice with *Noongar*. How would you explain this Len?

LEN: Part of the old *Noongar* practice is to make your *gnarl* (sweat) known to *boodjar* (country) as you sing out to the 'old people', or spirits. This lets them know or, if you have been that way before, reminds them who you are and how you are related to that part of the world. This should be done with your grannies (grandchildren and other family who may be with you) so that they see you go about your business in a respectful way.

This is much the same as how people across the globe behave when they come into other people's houses, districts or countries. It shows respect, good manners and sets up relationships in a healthy way. *Quop koondarn* and *quop karnyan* are two concepts that come from *Noongar* ontological traditions that are important here. In short, this means to have a sensibility of good respect when you come into other people's country. And smelling your *gnarl* helps country know whether you are *quop karnyan* or not.

JEN: Lovely, hey? I can't say I've read too much about the importance of underarms in ethical community development. However, Elizabeth Povinelli (1993: 32) talks about how important it is in Aboriginal philosophy and practice. She puts it this way:

> Aborigines act on the assumption that entities inhabiting the country 'smell' and 'hear' their (visitors) verbal and physical activity and that these beings 'come out' or 'send out' agents in the form of climatic changes, an abundance of foods, spirits of possession, and sicknesses in order to communicate their reactions to human presence. Moreover, speech and sweat are seen to penetrate people and places: speech goes in the human ear and travels through the air, sweat comes out of the body and sinks into water holes.

DAVE: So *boodjar* (country) can tell who you are, what you have been doing, and all about your intentions through your *gnarl* (sweat)? Perhaps instead of saying 'actions speak louder than words', *Noongar* might say, '*gnarl* (sweat) speaks as loud as *wangkiny* (talk)'. Len, could we then conclude that an ethical practice with *Noongar* community would have to be laden with the sweat of community workers?

LEN: Both literally and metaphorically.

Birniny – digging and scratching

JEN: This implies that the way we hold ourselves (stand and carry our bodies) on country and the way we go about moving is very important.

Len, you have taught us much about the practice of *birniny*. As I understand it *birniny* is a deeply philosophical word for *Noongar*. It is also a word about practice. How we do things. It's a word that describes a way of moving through country, and a word that gets used as a powerful and poetic metaphor for life. Could you talk about this a little? How, as a concept and a way of being in the world, *birniny* might shape the approach 'outsiders' take on with Aboriginal communities?

LEN: *Birniny* translates as the act of scratching, scraping and digging. When you scratch, scrape and dig, you produce lots of *gnarl* (sweat). When we *birniny* we are literally trying to uncover both what is on the surface and what is underneath.

The word *birniny* comes from the word *birn* which is a kind of plant that you find in the undergrowth in many parts of *Noongar boodjar* (country).[5] You usually find *birn* off the main track, and as part of the rich ecology of ground cover and botany that sits between the soil and the height of your knees.

A *birn* plant is properly hardy and has prickles and tough foliage that can cut, graze and inflict sores on your legs if you're not careful. From when they were young, *korlangka* (young *Noongar*) were taught to walk through country in a particular way to avoid hurting their legs (see Rose, 2002). This way of walking demands that you are attentive to both the areas ahead of, in proximity to, and below your feet.

Unlike travelling on a well-worn path or road that is clearly mapped out, *korlangka* were taught that our feet needed to be *genininy* (looking), and our *kaat* (head) needed to *koorliny yeye* (go along in the present). Just like the *waitj* (emu) that is constantly picking, scratching and looking for what is available in the undergrowth, when we walk through the *birn* we have to move in and around what is offered up by *boodjar* (country).

JEN: Yes, I love the way the *waitj* (emu) moves. I've often marvelled at their feet, and the relationship they have to the beak and eyes. It's almost as if the emu has eyes in its toes so that when it walks it lifts its claws. Momentarily pausing for the feet to make the decision of where to land.

DAVE: Nice metaphors for community workers Jen. I love the idea that our bodies and our gait take lessons from the old *waitj* (emu). And what you say Len is also very interesting. It reminds me a little of the etymology of the word 'read'. As I understand it, 'read' comes in part from the old Norse word *raten*, in part the Latin *legere*, and in part the old French *lire*, which meant to gather up, collect, pick up and choose. The idea of early readers was to carefully pick through a text much as an emu picks through the undergrowth picking out food and discarding those things that cannot be digested.[6]

LEN: That's right for *Noongar* too. The way I was taught was to dig and scratch and scrape my way through knowledge. In much the same way, we were taught to *birniny* through our relationships with others; struggling and picking our way through the complex systems of community, constantly looking out for the prickly things, and being ready to quickly adjust our movements to deal with those around us.

DAVE: That reminds me of an observation that Western Australian writer Tim Winton makes about the business of seeing things in the Australian bush. He says that though we may stare, try as we might, we often do not first see the objects of our attention when we are looking at them straight on. Rather, he notes that things in the natural world, whether they be sea creatures in saltwater country, or birds and animals in the forests, seem to come to us from the corner of our eye (Winton 2015: 86).

I think this is another good tip for how we might hold ourselves in community development practice; always on the lookout, attentive to what might lie just out of the corner of our eye, and always prepared to adjust to what we see and do. I also like the lesson that this offers about the need to move off the main track in our search for things to sustain ourselves and our community.

LEN: Yes, as *Noongar*, we were always taught that when you walk through *boodjar* (country) you are always *genininy* (looking). Always looking for a feed, for sources of sustenance. Always *aliwa* (looking out) for potential danger. And always looking to *katitjin* (learn). *Birniny* is a philosophical way of being. A way of doing things and holding yourself. And I think an approach to community development too (Collard, 2007).

Quop karnya, quop koondarn – respectful sensibility

DAVE: Len, can I ask you to talk more about manners and everyday ethical behaviour in community development with Indigenous Australians?

LEN: Well, the word *karnya* means good manners, or good moral integrity and sensibilities. *Koondarn* is another word that implies sensibility and good ways of conducting yourself. If someone says that you got no *koondarn* then they are saying you have no manners; you are behaving in a manner that is out of order.

When I was growing up *koondarn* was related to shame. *Karnya* is sensibility or having sense. Nowadays many young *Noongar* use the word *karnya* to mean shame but it was always more about having respect.

DAVE: That's interesting. According to Richard Sennett (2002), the word respect gets poorly used in modern times. Often it gets used as a weapon against communities who are not doing so well; a way of demanding they earn it or gain it by doing things. Sennett reminds us that the social practice of respect is much more reliant on a gift economy. That entering relationships of reciprocity, of giving and receiving, is how respect gets built.

JEN: So, reciprocal systems of obligation are at the heart of respect or *karnya*? This reminds me of the importance in Aboriginal cosmology of the obligations that come with age to nurture those who 'come along after' (Myers, 1991: 211). Brian McCoy (2008: 22), who writes from a strong ethical position of involvement in community development with *Kukatja* (a southern Kimberley Aboriginal group), draws on the Western Desert concept of *Kanyirninpa*.

LEN: *Kanyirninpa* sounds like the *Noongar* word *karnya*. What does that mob mean by *Kanyirninpa?*

DAVE: As I understand it *Kanyirninpa* is expressed in a few interconnected ways. It includes the practice of nurturing the young through law and life; particularly to describe older people taking responsibility and offering protection for those they 'hold'. It involves relationships of teaching and learning, where older people help young people 'grow up the right way' (McCoy, 2008: 22). McCoy also explains that *Kanyirninpa* or 'holding' young people is an act of exercising respect towards others; creating conditions to reinforce social bonds and social obligations (2008: 28; see also Palmer 2012 for a description of how this plays out in a remote area community development project).

Wangkiny – talking and yarning

LEN: As I mentioned earlier, many English words used to talk about ethics are not always accessible to *Noongar*. In my view, this is the first reason why *Noongar* words, intent and meaning are essential if we are to understand how community workers need to conduct themselves with *Noongar* communities (see Trudgen, 2000).[7]

JEN: It strikes me that using *Noongar* language in your practice is an important way of recognising many of the elements that are important to *Noongar* community. Words like *boodjar* (country), *moort* (family and relationships), *katatj* (*Noongar* knowledge), *kura*, *yeye* and *boorda* (the connection between the past, present and future) are all important ideas that better set out how to behave than English concepts.

In our case, the language of the south-west of Australia has come to exist over 40,000 plus years to articulate how to live and 'do' community in this part of the world (Host and Owen, 2007: vii). English is much younger, is relatively unfamiliar to many *Noongar*, and emerged in a different set of communities to explain and achieve things in completely different circumstances. Most importantly, English is an introduced language for *Noongar* and not always the most comfortable language to carry knowledge, practice and insight. So, in a way, a vital ethical obligation for community workers is to recognise where they don't have the language of Indigenous Australia. The act of acknowledging this helps us recognise that we need to do one of two things: either recruit local people as translators or learn the language.

DAVE: Of course. Language is how we hold not just our knowledge but also our ways of being. We hold our ontologies, behaviours and cultural protocols in language. Indeed, words probably shape the way we hold our bodies.

Many of those who have set out conversations about community development have long reminded practitioners of this. One of Freire's first order ethical principles is concerned with the critical part language and local conceptual frames ought to play in setting up work with community (Freire, 1986).

Jen, you and Len are working on a project called *Noongarpedia*. Can you briefly describe this and talk about what you have learned about ethics from this work?

JEN: *Noongarpedia* is a project that has been running for about four years.[8] It's involved using Wikipedia as a platform to support the use and reinvigoration of *Noongar* knowledge and language. It has included academics, language teachers, children, young people and community groups to both create *Noongarpedia* entries as a way to learn, pass on and make public *Noongar* knowledge, and to create relationships across the generations.

LEN: As a *Wedjela* involved in this community development project can you say some things about learning *Noongar*? Some *Noongar* and non-*Noongar* have been critical about *Wedjela* learning language, claiming that it's just another act of cultural appropriation. What are your observations?

JEN: I'm very sensitive to this, so I get nervous and it is complicated. In my case, I'm working in a project where *Noongar* are my bosses.

Two of the three chief investigators are *Noongar* professors. *Noongar* language is an integral part of the work we are doing; and I have been clearly instructed that an integral part of me showing my respect is to build my *Noongar* language skills. If I don't have the will to learn *Noongar* then my ability to learn about the process of doing this with *Noongar* community members is compromised.

On the other hand, I am very aware of the sensitivities and pain that many *Noongar* experience around language. Part of the history of what governments have done over many generations is to make it illegal for *Noongar* to live on their country, marry who they want, raise their children and speak their language. So, for many *Noongar* it is a very painful thing that they now can't speak in the language of their ancestors. As a *Wedjela* woman, for me to show off my language skills can be hurtful and insensitive. I think to do this in an egocentric way is deeply unethical and cruel.

DAVE: So perhaps rather than asking, 'should a *Wedjela* learn *Noongar* language?' we might ask 'how should *Wedjela* learn and practise *Noongar* language?'

JEN: It varies. Sometimes I need to be sensitive to the trauma of *Noongar* who have not had this opportunity, and take a back seat – listening, and resisting the urge to speak. However, in other contexts, when working with *Noongar* who are strong language speakers, I might have an obligation to be less hesitant.

LEN: That's where the concepts *koondarn* and *karnya* are useful. Both are used to imply a way of being in relation to others. It's not possible to practise this unless you are considerate of others, put your ego in your back pocket, watch what is happening, and have some decency and care for how others are feeling.

JEN: Yes, it's a very Western thing to want to show off how much you know. This can be terribly brutal and traumatic for people who have been taken away from their language.

DAVE: This seems particularly relevant to academics. In a university context knowledge is king; we are expected to showcase and promote our knowledge. What you are saying is that in work with *Noongar* it is relationships and respect that trumps knowledge.

LEN: Yes, *Noongar* might say '*moortaliny boordier nidja karnya*' (how we treat family and relationships is the boss and right way to do things).

But it is not always this simple. On the other hand, at home when I was growing up it was expected that you 'show off' to a certain extent. Oldies would say, "*Woolah* (an expression of celebration) *per* (wow), listen to little Lennie talking like a real *Noongar*."

Dabakarn dabakarn – going along steadily

JEN: This is also why it's important for outsiders to come into their work gently and quietly. Here I really like the *Noongar* idea of *dabakarn dabakarn*. This means to go along gently, quietly and steady. To go along *dabakarn dabakarn* involves not only listening to what people say, but also noticing what is happening with people's bodies, what is happening outside and what is happening between people.

LEN: Part of going along *dabakarn dabakarn* involves 'reading the play', watching what's happening and being ready to respond. It doesn't mean that you don't move quickly when you need to. In fact, *dabakarn dabakarn* is a way of preparing you to *kert kert djakoorliny* (jump quickly into action). Dave, you played Australian Rules Football so you recognise how you move like this.

DAVE: Yes, I used to play a position called half-back flank. Many think this is just a defensive position but when I was young I learnt that my job involved being prepared to receive a handball (a ball pass) from a key player by stepping into action from slightly behind the play.

LEN: Jen, how do you know the right speed, whether you sit back or step up?

JEN: I think this is taking us back to our earlier discussion about coming into country. Part of what I do is read my own body. My stomach feels good. I feel good. My breath feels good when I am in the right place and doing things respectfully with people. There might be birds singing, a gentle wind that blows, a warmth. I feel safe. Now some people might find this really strange. I think this is the point. You are a stranger coming into a new community setting. Doing things that feel strange or *wamaluk* is a discipline that reminds you not to take things for granted.

LEN: Obviously I don't think it is strange. I've been raised to look out for responses from the subtle messages that country and the old people give. It is often a little sign, a little bit of wind, a little bird or a leaf dropping a certain way.

JEN: And of course, science has just caught up with some of these old Indigenous insights and practices. The idea that we should sing out to country and sing out to the beings that inhabit country was once thought of as a bit 'out there'. I'm reminded of the beautiful character of Doctor Doolittle, created by writer Hugh Lofting in the 1920s, who used his talents to talk with his animal patients in their own language. Not only does this allow Doolittle to care for animals as humans are cared for by doctors, it also allows him to better understand the natural world and the history of everything (Lofting, 2013).

Now it seems that science is beginning to see the value of humans building relationships with birds like magpies, famous as they are for swooping and sometimes causing serious damage to people during the nesting season. In recently published research, zoologist Gisela Kaplan has established that a magpie only swoops a person if they are unknown to the bird and pose a threat. Communicating with a magpie will earn you their trust and goodwill for the life of the animal (Kaplan cited in Brown, 2017).

DAVE: There are also comparisons being made with the practices of business and the corporate world, and Indigenous community development. For example, at the beginning of an induction onto a production site of an oil and gas company you can't enter the site unless you have gone through a process that often takes considerable time. This process involves changing what you are wearing; putting on colours (bright visible shirts), perhaps what you might describe as 'painting yourself up'. It also involves changing your feet (putting on steel-capped boots), how you are going to step to protect yourself and not put others at risk. You often watch a short video and take instructions on how you should act and behave on site.

Increasingly this comparison is being made by community-controlled Aboriginal ranger groups. For example, the Murujuga Land and Sea Unit, who are responsible for the Burrup Peninsula in the Pilbara region of our state, combines these processes with cultural safety inductions.[9] One of the rangers takes on a role as the occupational health and safety officer and another the cultural safety officer. When you go to their headquarters you need to sign in, much the same as if you are visiting other organisations, government departments or industry sites.

They point out, and industry points out, that it doesn't matter if you believe in this new religion called 'risk management' or think that we have gone overboard with health and safety measures. Similarly, it really doesn't matter if you think it is silly to have someone sing out to the old people. You simply won't be allowed to go on site unless you go through these rituals and processes to keep you as safe as possible.

Boodjar wangkiny – talking to country

LEN: Yes, this is what we were taught as kids. *Boodjar* (country) and *boordier* (local bosses) have voices, ways of communicating and power in influencing things. We were taught that if you're not sure then ask for more signs. Like a *yonga* (kangaroo) making himself known to you might just be a curious *yonga* who accidently stumbles into you, but if it comes towards you instead of racing away and the wind suddenly kicks up at the same time as you see an old *moodjar* (native Christmas tree) then you need to take note that the old people are watching you. Jen, what are some of the experiences of being in the wrong place?

JEN: I can't sleep. If I do go to sleep I might wake up like I am dreaming. There are things that I will see and hear.

And the people from the community will give you signs too. They will stop being involved, they will allow projects to wind down, they will look away from you when you are trying to talk with them. This'll make me sound strange, I bet?

LEN: No, I don't think so. You are talking about things that the old people taught us. While this may sound incomprehensible to many community workers, academics or government officials it is completely understandable to me. And I suspect to Aboriginal people across an array of communities in Australia.

However, it does point to the dangers of sending out young community workers with no knowledge of these things. When we do this, we send them straight into harm's way, both for them and the communities they are working with. We have a moral and ethical obligation to not allow this to happen. Yet, my estimate is that we would be lucky to find more than 10% of community workers employed in this area who know these things.

DAVE: There will be some people who read this, Jen, and think this is way too esoteric; this sounds like community workers are 'oddities', not professionals.

However, one way of thinking about this is to imagine that what we are talking about is a set of literacies. Many of us are raised being 'literate' to signs like a fence telling us that we shouldn't cross over to the other side, or a HAZCHEM sign warning us there are chemical dangers in our proximity. The point of occupational health and safety training is to make us more 'literate' or knowledgeable to the risks. In a similar way in *Noongar boodjar* (country) there are signs that the 'illiterate' will not be able to read. Unless you are familiar or 'literate' in *Noongar* then your work might endanger you and those around you.

And I don't think this is as foreign to Westerners as many might imagine. I think the French poet and philosopher Charles Baudelaire was onto something similar when he wrote about the *flâneur* (Tester,

1994), from the sixteenth and seventeen centuries, who would saunter around early modern European cities, observing society and the ecology of the neighbourhood. Baudelaire's *flâneur* was a talented and attentive spectator of their environment, reading the city as others might read a text. Later, philosopher Michel de Certeau described the act of walking 'was to a network of city streets as speech is to the language spoken' (cited in Morrison, 2017: 145). Len, what are some of the other signs that *Noongar boodjar* offers up?

LEN: There is anxiety. There is conflict. There is mishap. All of a sudden, we will find ourselves in the middle of interpersonal dramas. When good people start to have arguments and things start to go wrong then this is often a sign *boodjar* (country) gives us that what we are doing, where we are or who is involved is not right.

As Jen pointed out, if people can't sleep at night or are anxious, they are jittery and in disputation, and that things don't seem to be working to plan, then the 'old people', the spirits are signalling that due processes have not been followed.

Maar ni – listening to the wind

DAVE: Jen also talked before about wind. It seems extraordinary in a discussion about ethical work in community development to talk about 'wind'. Are we saying that I have to be literate about the wind to work ethically with Aboriginal communities?

LEN: Yes, the wind is very important to *Noongar*. This is where of course the relationship with senior people and cultural leaders who can 'read' these things becomes critical. You need to do more than simply ask or consult with these people; you need to rely on them as your 'bosses', those who literally guide your every step.

JEN: So, to use this example are you saying that a community development project needs to employ someone who knows about wind?

LEN: Well, literate in a whole bunch of stuff including wind.

JEN: Can you explain how this works?

LEN: I can do and will do, but here is another challenge. You are asking me to be the cultural instructor and this is good. As I just said, we need to find ways to draw in *Noongar* as those who help lead the work. However, *Noongar* are not always going to be available to you. Across the nation, Indigenous Australians only represent about 3.3% of the population (Biddle and Markham, 2017) and not all of them have deep cultural literacy. Many are also incredibly busy with dozens of obligations to their family, their jobs, to community-controlled organisations, and negotiating land and management of country.

However, if the cultural and knowledge bosses are not available this is where someone like yourself, with good solid grounding, needs to stand up and show your *boordi*, your leadership and knowledge. This means that you cannot always and continuously get away with not learning about these matters.

So, Jen, I'm going to ask you to speak on this one right now. What has wind got to do with ethics?

JEN: Many of my Aboriginal colleagues have taught me that there is a profound connection between health, one's spirit and wind. There are parallels in old European cultural traditions; though since the Enlightenment the 'high priests' of knowledge, biomedical scientists and health practitioners tell us that our health and well-being is shaped by things like stress, nutrition, disease and poor lifestyle. However, in most of the places I have travelled the wind and breath of people and country is what causes ailments and, conversely, can help heal. Often illness is associated with particular winds. Arrernte knowledge tells us that the north-west wind, *aretharre*, is a bad one (Dobson, 2007: 23–4). According to Clarke (2008: 21–2). Aboriginal knowledge systems in Central Australia interpret the decline of people's health as often caused by malevolent winds and sorcerers who exercise their influence through bad winds.

LEN: Well when the wind starts to blow through the sheoaks[10] then *Noongar* would say that the ancestors are speaking. When I was growing up the old people who had special healing skills would fix people by removing illness through sucking it out and throwing it away in the wind.

It is important to understand that *Noongar* knowledge systems are not as anthropocentric as Western knowledge systems. In *Noongar* community there is a deep and long-standing relationship between people, plants, rocks, animals and the wind. For Aboriginal groups across the country each person in a community is connected with the ecology through a family-based section and subsection system, often called a skin system. The way this works is that each person is born into a skin (group). This sets out how they relate to others in their community. Every person and 'thing' in the same skin, regardless of their biological or genetic connection to others, is treated as a brother or sister. Similarly, all women in one's mother's skin are treated as a mother, all men in the mother's skin group are treated as uncles.

The skin system helps tell us about our rights and responsibilities, our obligations, and our birthright. Different winds are included in this complex set of relationships. These winds help us know where we are in relation to each other and country. In this way wind acts as an ethical barometer (sorry to mix the metaphor), helping guide our movements and behaviour. If we do not 'read' this, then we risk becoming ethically lost. Dave, how would you explain this?

Korunkurl moort – becoming family and community

DAVE: As I understand it, there is a deep connection between three things in the *Noongar* world: *boodjar* (country), *moort* (family) and *katitj* (the law, knowledge and stories of things seen and unseen). This ontological connection is pretty consistent in all the places I've ever visited and worked.

It is through *moort*, or the family system of obligation, that *katitj* is passed on. Children get to know about the world through the key people, according to their skin, whose job it is to educate them. When they get older it becomes their responsibility to take care of these older people and in turn pass on knowledge to younger people. Indeed, this link between the generations is not broken by birth or death (Collard, 2007). As people get older, indeed particularly when they pass on, their obligation to hold future generations becomes more pronounced. The way this works is that senior people who pass away go back to *boodjar* with the job of looking after members of their family. Their main role is to protect the safety of their *moort* (family), ensure that integrity of *katitj* (knowledge), and thereby maintain the health of *boodjar* (country).

If *wam* (strangers) travel to this country then part of the responsibility of those who have passed on is to act as guardians of family. If *wam* (strangers) come onto country unannounced or without proper introductions then they are likely up to no good. It is the job of the 'old people' who have passed away to place barriers, and 'make mischief' on the outsiders. Such mischief might include damaging people's feet, sending them a little crazy, inducing conflict, getting them confused or making them sick.

In describing the ontology and practice of Belyuen people from northern Australia, Povinelli (1993: 31) explains it this way:

> Places are perceived as sentient-like beings or as filled with those beings. Mythic vistas and ordinary jungle patches absorb and evaluate the physical sounds and smells, the

ceremonial names and social identities of the people who walk through them. If the country does not recognize the language and sweat of persons, it inflicts them with bad luck, or worse, mental and physical disease.

LEN: One of the important consequences for community workers is that this way of being, this ontological tradition, demands that people 'buy into' deeper relationships with community. Dave and Jen, my children and grannies (grandchildren) count you as family, and your kids count me as family; I know that you have family connections in the Kimberley as well, and that this brings with it obligations that are not just work related.

JEN: It's interesting isn't it that, as neo-liberal language and mentality has increasingly shaped the way community organisations do business we become more nervous about intimacy and family-based connections. In most discussions of ethics, we are expected to distance ourselves from or 'declare' any conflicts of interests. One of the big things in this regard is declaring if we have family interests in our work. This is kind of counter to the ethical importance in *Noongar* ontology of looking after family. The older I get as a community worker the more I think my obligations to 'become' family with my close *Noongar* brothers and sisters grows.

Boordawan: conclusion

LEN: As I said earlier, I have always found it difficult understanding the concepts and ideas that many use in the community development area. I believe there are at least two reasons for this: (1) *Noongar* is my first language and knowledge system; and (2) community development workers have been too closely implicated in the long, and I think continuing, history of using language as a tool against rather than for *Noongar* families.

JEN: I think the observations of women like Audre Lorde and Chandra Talpade Mohanty about the limitations of Western language and ontology are helpful here. Talking about the circumstances confronting women of colour, Lorde (1983: 100) claims that 'the masters tools will never dismantle the master's house'. She clearly posits that the language of the West has limited value in helping change the circumstances of Indigenous communities. Similarly, Mohanty (1984) points out, that Western conceptual and policy tools function as the norm against which the lives and communities of the Indigenous and developing world is managed and evaluated.

Both point to the profound importance of drawing on the language and ontology of local people if we are to support these communities.

DAVE: What we have tried to do in this chapter is seek out *Noongar* ways of thinking about ethics and the behaviour of those working in the field of community development. While not trying to codify this, we are setting out a number of key themes that might prove helpful. These, we believe, start from the ontologies and conceptual traditions that go back many thousands of years for *Noongar*. As well as arguing that community development practice ground itself in *Noongar wangkiny* and *katitj* (language and knowledge) we invite workers to take on distinct practices such as *wabaliny quop weirn* (singing out to the good spirits) and adopting a way of moving that reflects the way of moving *Noongar* describe as *birniny* (digging and scratching) and *dabakarn dabakarn* (steady steady). We offer a slightly different way of thinking about ethical practice, taking inspiration from the *Noongar* idea of *quop karnya, quop koondarn* (a respectful sensibility). At times this is likely to appear strange and demand new 'literacies' such as *maar ni* (listening to and reading the wind). Finally, often against the conventions of Western professionalism we claim that outsiders adopting community development have an obligation to *korunkurl moort* (become family and community) rather than sitting outside and distancing ourselves from those with whom we work.

LEN: Knowing this and taking account of it allows us to *quop koorliny* (go along) *quop karnya* and *quop koondarn* (in a good and respectful way) creating the *quop weirn* (good spirit). This is what *Noongar* describe as an ethical practice. This is both a metaphor and a literal practice for how we can do things as community workers.

DAVE AND JEN: *Kaya boordawan* (yep, that's right, talk later).

LEN: *Kaya boordawan.*

Notes

[1] *Koorliny* (going); *birniny* (scratching and digging); *ni* (listening); *quoppa* (good); *katatjin* (knowledge).

[2] 'Travel' to Noongar boodjar (country) and enjoy a 'Welcome to country' via YouTube: www.youtube.com/watch?v=FUSuGWH-HrU posted by South West Aboriginal Land and Sea Council (2012).

[3] Visit the YouTube 'Noongar language lessons' to hear the beautiful sounds of Noongar language: www.youtube.com/watch?v=LOYKZox_Szk&t=17s posted by ACE (2016).

[4] The Aboriginal-English term 'local bosses' denotes those who are senior elders with cultural custodial rights to the area.

[5] Visit the Wirlomin Noongar Language and Stories Project to listen to more language: http://wirlomin.com.au
[6] See English Language & Usage: https://english.stackexchange.com/questions/239630/how-did-pick-out-evolve-to-mean-read
[7] See the bibliography for a range of sources for use in work with *Noongar* language.
[8] Visit the *Noongarpedia* site at: https://incubator.wikimedia.org/wiki/Wp/nys/Main_Page
[9] See Murujuga Aboriginal Corporation: www.murujuga.org.au
[10] The sheoak or casuarina is the genus of a tree species that is native to Australia, Indian and South-East Asia. This evergreen tree of slender branches and many small twigs often creates a powerful sound of the wind as it rushes through the air (Huxley, 1992).

References

ACWA (Australian Community Workers Association) (2017a) 'Australian community workers code of ethics', January. Available at: www.acwa.org.au/resources/ACWA_Code_of_ethics_Jan_2017.pdf

ACWA (Australian Community Workers Association) (2017b) 'Australian community work practice guidelines', February. Available at: www.acwa.org.au/resources/ACWA-Practice-guidelines-Feb-2017.pdf

Bessarab, D. and Ng'andu, B. (2010) 'Yarning about yarning as a legitimate method in Indigenous research', *International Journal of Critical Indigenous Studies*, 3(1): 37–50.

Biddle, N. and Markham, F. (2017) 'Census 2016: What's changed for indigenous Australians?' *The Conversation*, 28 June. Available at: https://theconversation.com/census-2016-whats-changed-for-indigenous-australians-79836

Boodjar Nyungar Placenames of the South-West of Western Australia (nd) Available at: www.boodjar.sis.uwa.edu.au

Brown, S.L. (2017) 'Magpies swooping? You should try making friends with them, expert says', ABC Radio, Melbourne, 31 August. Available at: www.abc.net.au/news/2017-08-31/make-friends-with-magpies-to-avoid-swooping-expert-says/8856438

Buchanan, J., Collard, L., Cumming, I., Palmer, D., Scott, K. and Hartley, J. (2016) '*Noongar boordier gnulla katitjin* – The influence of Noongar knowledge', *Cultural Science*, 9(1): 37–53.

Clarke, P. (2008) 'Aboriginal healing practices and Australian bush medicine', *Journal of the Anthropological Society of South Australia*, 33: 3–38.

Collard, L. (2007) '*Wangkiny ngulluck Nyungar nyittiny, boodjar, moort and katitjin*: Talking about creation, country, family and knowledge of the *Nyungar* of south Western Australia', in S. Morgan, T. Mia and B. Kwaymullina (eds) *Speaking from the heart: Stories of life, family and country*, Fremantle: Fremantle Arts Centre Press, pp 261–78.

Collard, L. and Palmer, D. (2006) '*Kura, yeye, boorda, Nyungar wangkiny ngulla koorlangka*: A conversation about working with Indigenous young people in the past, present and future', *Youth Studies Australia*, 25(4): 25–32.

Dobson, V.P. (2007) *Arelhe-Kenhe Merrethene: Arrernte traditional healing*, Alice Springs: Institute of Aboriginal Development Press.

Fesl, E.M.D. (1993) *Conned!* St. Lucia: University of Queensland Press.

Freire, P. (1986) *Pedagogy of the oppressed*, New York: Continuum.

Haebich, A. (1992) *For their own good: Aborigines and government in the south west of Western Australia 1900–1940*, Perth: UWA Publishing.

Horton, M. and Freire, P. (1990) *We make the road by walking: Conversations on education and social change*, ed B. Bell, J. Gaventa and J. Peters, Philadelphia, PA: Temple University Press.

Host, J. and Owen, C. (2007) *It's still in my heart, this is my country: The single Noongar claim*, Crawley: University of Western Australia Press.

Huxley, A. (ed) (1992) *New RHS dictionary of gardening*, Melbourne: Macmillan.

IACD (International Association for Community Development) (2017) 'Towards common international standards for community development practice', Glasgow: IACD. Available at: www.iacdglobal. org/wp-content/uploads/2017/11/IACD-2017-Draft-Standards-Guidance.pdf

Kickett-Tucker, C., Bessarab, D., Coffin, J. and Wright, M. (eds) (2017) *Mia mia Aboriginal community development: Fostering cultural security*, Port Melbourne: Cambridge University Press.

Lofting, H. (2013) *The story of Doctor Doolittle*, London: Vintage.

Lorde, A. (1983) 'The master's tools will never dismantle the master's house', in C. Moraga and G. Anzaldúa (eds) *This bridge called my back: Writings by radical women of color*, New York: Kitchen Table Press, pp 94–101.

McCoy, B.F. (2008) *Holding men: Kanyirninpa and the health of Aboriginal men*, Canberra: Aboriginal Studies Press.

Mohanty, C.T. (1984) 'Under Western eyes: Feminist scholarship and colonial discourses', *boundary 2*, 12(3): 333–58.

Morrison, G. (2017) *Songlines and fault lines: Epic walks of the red centre*, Melbourne: Melbourne University Press.

Muecke, S. (2004) *Ancient and modern: Time, culture and Indigenous philosophy*, Sydney: University of New South Wales Press.

Myers, F.D. (1991) *Pintupi country, Pintupi self: Sentiment, place, and politics among Western Desert Aborigines*, Berkeley: University of California Press.

National Native Title Tribunal (2003) 'Map of proposed native title determination application: Single Noongar #1', 6 October. Available at: www.nntt.gov.au/searchRegApps/NativeTitleClaims/NTDA%20 Extracts/WC2003_006/WC2003_006%205.%20Map%20of%20 claim%20area.pdf

Noongar Boodjar Language Centre (2015) '*Noongar waangkiny*: A learner's guide to *Noongar*' (2nd edn). Available at: http://noongarboodjar. com.au/wp-content/uploads/2017/10/Noongar-Learners-Guide-2edn-web.pdf

Noongar Boodjar Language Cultural Aboriginal Corporation (2017) 'Noongar language centre: Welcome to Noongar culture'. Available at: www://Noongarboodjar.com.au

Palmer, D. (2012) '"We got to look at our old people, use a different school": The Yiriman Project, going back to country and bringing out stories across generations in the Kimberley', in P. Westoby and L. Shevellar (eds) *Community-based education and training: Learning and mobilising within community development work*, Farnham: Ashgate, pp 41–54.

Povinelli, E.A. (1993) *Labor's lot: The power, history and culture of Aboriginal action*, Chicago: University of Chicago.

Rose, D.B., with D'Amico, S., Daiyi, N., Deveraux, K., Daiyi, M., Ford, L. and Bright, A. (2002) *Country of the heart: An Indigenous Australian homeland*, Canberra: Aboriginal Studies.

Sennett, R. (2002) *Respect: The formation of character in an age of inequality*, London: Allen Lane.

Tester, K. (1994) *The flâneur*, London: Routledge.

Trudgen, R. (2000) *Why warriors lie down and die: Towards an understanding of why the Aboriginal people of Arnhem Land face the greatest crisis in health and education since European contact*, Darwin: Aboriginal Resource and Development Services Inc.

Westoby, P. (2016) *Soul, community and social change: Theorising a soul perspective on community practice*, Farnham: Ashgate.

Westoby, P. and Dowling, G. (2013) *Theory and practice of dialogical community development: International perspectives*, Abingdon: Routledge.

Winton, T. (2015) *Island home: A landscape memoir*, Melbourne: Penguin.

SEVEN

Corporate social responsibility and community development in a mining region in India: issues of power, control and co-option

Satu Ranta-Tyrkkö and Bipin Jojo

Introduction

"Earlier, not much care was taken about the local society. Now that awareness is there." This claim was made in an interview with the managing director of a large-scale iron mine in eastern India in January 2015, when he reflected back on his long experience in the Indian mining industry. While the claim encapsulates a long-term corporate trend, in India corporate involvement in community-level matters remains an issue of constant debate, even suspicion. Can corporate and community interests be complementary, and if so, to what extent, especially in cases where the corporate activity has negatively affected the health and well-being of local people? Whose interests are actually at stake – who, locally, is 'the' company, who passes as 'the' local people, and whose interests do not count? How do the mining companies implement their community development programmes under corporate social responsibility (CSR), and how participatory are these programmes? Should social and community workers engage with corporations to get resources, such as funding and other assets for the actual work with people, and what kind of risks or compromises might that entail?

In this chapter, we discuss these dilemmas in the context of the mining area of the eastern Sundergarh District in the state of Odisha in eastern India. In spite of its context specificity, our case connects with universal themes regarding extractive industries, CSR, and community work and development. These include the deterioration of the local ecosystems and ecosystems-based livelihoods in regions of resource extraction, growing disparities and uneven power positions between those who benefit from extractive industries and those who do not, complexities of CSR in a multi-ethnic and hierarchical society, and the subordination of 'extractive peripheries' to broader political and economic structures and tendencies. Related to these issues, the particular, yet also globally commonplace feature of our case is that the resource extraction transforms an area that is home to Indigenous people.

This chapter is grounded in Odisha on the two most easterly of the 17 blocks comprising the Sundergarh District, Koida and Lahunipada, which alone have around 60 mines excavating mainly iron ore. The data for the chapter were gathered collaboratively for the purposes of Ranta-Tyrkkö's postdoctoral research, on the consequences of the mining industry for disadvantaged groups in Northern Finland and Northern Odisha (Academy of Finland, 2014–17) during two relatively short sets of fieldwork in 2015. Ranta-Tyrkkö first visited the area for ten days in January–February 2015, continuing with a joint two-week fieldwork period with Jojo in October–November 2015. The fieldwork took place in the residential and industrial centres of Barsuan, Tensa, Koida (alternatively Koira) and their nearby junctions, all within a 20–30 kilometre radius of each other. The data consist of observations, interviews and casual conversations with a wide range of people. We talked with villagers (men and women), including casual labourers, truck drivers, teachers, priests, *sadhus* (holy men), past and present *sarpanches* (elected heads of village self-governments called *gram panchayats*), mine workers and managers, shopkeepers, medical practitioners and government officers. We also visited six mines and/or mining companies, some of them several times. As part of the discussions, we always introduced ourselves and explained our affiliations and the nature and purpose of the research, including matters of confidentiality. Depending on the situation and wishes of the interlocutors, we recorded some but not all the interviews, relying mainly on handwritten notes made during and immediately after them. For the purposes of this chapter, extracts describing the corporate histories and CSR activities, the life of local people and their welfare needs, the situation of existing welfare services, the perceived environmental and other changes in the region and assumptions and wishes regarding future development have been thematically organised and analysed.

In what follows, we preface our case study with a brief review of community development and CSR in India and the underlying political and economic continuums that feature mineral extraction in Odisha. Thereafter, we focus on how the mineral extraction structures the mining region in question. We conclude the chapter by highlighting the role of CSR and the challenges of community development in the absence of other investment into the region.

Community development in India

Development, as a notion defining the work with communities, emerged in the aftermath of the Second World War, when newly independent India 'was pulled into the train of development', being from the outset identified as 'underdeveloped' and a 'third world' country (Kuruvilla, 2005: 44). Development was assumed to occur through a similar trajectory of economic growth in all societies, including in countries like India, impoverished by colonial rule. Later on, understanding of development as a complex set of processes has grown more nuanced (see, for example, Healy, 2008: 52–63). While it has maintained its position among the central concepts to think about societies and change, criticism has mounted, for example, against the violence made in the name of development and the idea of progress at its core. This is particularly pertinent in cases of development-induced displacement by industrial or infrastructure projects (in the Indian context, see, for example, Mathur, 2008; Meher, 2009; Padel and Das, 2010, 2014; Nathan and Xaxa, 2012).

While social and community development programmes have often succeeded in improving the welfare of people, critics doubt whether development in general can be adjusted to get it 'right'. For example, Padel et al (2013) criticise 'development' as too often distorted and overly materialist, calling for non-predetermined dialogue on what good and desirable life is about and how to achieve it in sustainable and just ways. Pratap and Priya (2009) further emphasise that such dialogue entails listening the views of the 'marginalised majorities', namely those labelled as 'uncivilised', 'underdeveloped' or 'wrong thinking'.

In India, community-based projects had already been experimented with before independence as a way to improve people's well-being. Later on, the five-year plans introduced new ideas to community development reflecting prevailing political and ideological currents. Nevertheless, Jha's (2016) retrospective analysis is that throughout the decades, the community development programmes failed to address the deep-rooted inequalities prevalent in Indian society. Instead, they entertained a 'homogenised and totalising concept of community', discarding the central dividing lines of Indian society, such as caste, class and educational differences. Moreover, they constructed communities and their members as passive objects, not as thinking and acting subjects remarkably differently situated in terms of power and powerlessness (Jha, 2016: 70–1).

More political and identity-based approaches to community mobilisation strengthened from the 1970s onwards, especially within leftist and Dalit ('untouchable') movements, with increasing awareness of the historical and structural foundations of the present inequality. While not always successful, disadvantaged groups have from time to time succeeded in reconceptualising and positively asserting their identities and mobilising around issues of displacement, rights and entitlements. Meanwhile, it has become clear that dominant castes and classes will not renounce their taken-for-granted privileges of their own accord. Moreover, the shift to neo-liberal economic policies and the consequent privatisation of public companies and resources, together with weakening state intervention in social welfare, have had negative effects for India's disadvantaged communities (Jha, 2016).

Corporate social responsibility in India

When corporations are involved in 'community development' or community-based service delivery, their activities usually fall under the conceptual umbrella of CSR, 'responsibility of enterprises for their impacts on society' (CII, 2013: 7). More critical views (such as in Padel and Das, 2010: 54) define CSR as 'covering up the damage corporations cause to society and environment and maintaining public cooperation with the corporate dominated system'. In India, CSR builds on the earlier traditions of corporate philanthropy and industrial and occupational social work. Overall, the shift to CSR as a distinct approach has been gradual and slow and the concept remains vague (Sarkar, 2008: 36; CII, 2013: 7). Common thematic areas covered by the companies include health, education, environment and community development (Bansal et al, 2018: 45–6).

CSR in India is currently in rapid transition. A recent major change, brought by the *Companies Act 2013*, in force from April 2014, is that all major companies have to spend a minimum of 2% of their average profit, based on the previous three years, on CSR. The 'major companies' include those with an annual turnover of INR10,000 million (roughly US$145,000) or more, net worth of INR5 billion (around US$72.7 million) or more, or a net profit of INR50 million (around US$727,000) or more. While the Act thus binds the largest companies only, according to Sarkar (2008: 31) at stake is a broader shift regarding the goals, objectives and priorities of CSR. The business community is now geared to think of CSR as 'a company's commitment to its stakeholders to conduct business in an economically, socially and environmentally sustainable manner that is transparent and ethical' (DPE, 2013). Further, CSR is increasingly conceived as a business management concept integral to the corporation's core business strategy and potentially a great business proposition (Sarkar, 2008: 39). In 2015, Indian mining companies were still developing their ways to respond to the demands of the new Act. The all-India sample-based assessment of Bansal et al (2018) shows that 52% of the eligible companies did not yet report their CSR expenditure in 2014–15, and that the actual CSR expenditure was about 38% of the total expected.

Specific to the mining industry, the *Mines and Minerals (Development and Regulation) Amendment Act 2015* (renewing the 1957 Act) further requires that state governments have to establish District Mineral Foundations (DMFs), which the mining companies have to fund. The task of the DMFs is to work in the interest of the persons and areas affected by mining-related operations. State governments give guidelines for the work, for example, by funding schemes that implement developmental and welfare projects and programmes in mining affected areas, or minimise and mitigate the adverse impacts of the mining industry. Separately from the DMFs, there are also unused funds accumulated from the compensation paid when forestland has been cleared for non-forestry purposes (such as mining) under the Compensatory Afforestation Fund Management and Planning Authority (CAMPA). During our fieldwork in 2015, the idea of the DMFs was so fresh that their organisation and governance was unresolved.

Politics of mineral extraction in Odisha

Odisha is rich with forests, hydropower and mineral resources, but ranks as one of the poorest states in India. Notwithstanding significant minerals-based economic growth during recent decades, Odisha has India's largest proportion of people living below the official poverty line, around 28% versus the all-India average of 15% (Behera, 2016: 31–2). Odisha's poverty is explained by the state's underdeveloped subsistence-oriented agrarian sector, weak industrial base, mass unemployment and repeated natural catastrophes. What is more, Odisha's development has been socially and regionally extremely uneven, benefiting cities and wealthier coastal areas, but leaving rural areas, where more than 80% of the population resides, marginalised and with poor infrastructure (Adduci, 2013: 181; Dayal et al, 2014: 1–3).

The government of Odisha has prioritised mining and industrialisation with policies conducive to investment from India and abroad to infrastructure and industrial projects that are based on harnessing the state's natural resources (Mohanty, 2014: 39). For example, the government of Odisha has promoted the state as the metals, mining and infrastructure hub of India (IBEF, 2015), and publicised big mining and industrial projects as a necessity if Odisha is to rise from its current underdeveloped state to prosperity and welfare (Mohanty, 2014: 44). On the one hand, Odisha's minerals-based growth strategy has succeeded in that the extraction of iron and bauxite, especially, has multiplied, as also has the minerals-based revenue of the state. In early 2018, there were 624 mining leases in Odisha (GOO, 2018), 142 of them in Sundergarh District (for the full list of companies and other details, see DMF Sundergarh, 2018). On the other hand, the strategy has failed to bring welfare to socially and economically marginalised groups. Instead of wealth trickling down, Odisha has become known as a place of growth with no inclusion (see Padel and Das, 2014).

Odisha's commercially most attractive mineral resources are largely located in the homelands of Adivasis, 'original inhabitants', who in India are also known as 'tribal people' or 'Scheduled Tribes', and who are commonly considered as Indigenous peoples. In India, the terms 'Adivasi' and 'tribal' are interchangeably used. The former asserts a positive identity, the latter carries legacies of colonial, evolutionist anthropology. In postcolonial India, the evolutionist and orientalist discourse is alive: 'the tribals' are still today often marked as uncivilised and unmodern, and thus lacking and hierarchically lower (Rycroft and Dasgupta, 2011; van Schendel, 2011: 19–20). According to the 2011 census, there are 104 million Adivasis in India, which is 8% of the population and makes India's Indigenous population the largest in the world. While the official stand of the government of India is that there are no Indigenous people in the country (for example, Shah, 2011: 10; Rousseleau, 2013), India acknowledges the special status and distinctiveness of Adivasis with educational and administrative quotas, reserved seats in government bodies and protective legislation. The latter includes the fifth and sixth Schedules of the Constitution, the *PESA (Panchayat Extension to Scheduled Areas) Act 1996*, and the *Forest Rights Act 2006*, which in principle ensure Adivasi participation and a say in decision making, and the right to land especially in the ('Scheduled') areas with an Adivasi majority. In reality, the implementation of the legislation is often poor.

The Adivasis of Odisha (numbering just over 9 million, 22.1% of the state's entire population of 42 million; see Census of India, 2011) have mostly lived in small communities in geographically relatively inaccessible regions, relying on the forests for their subsistence. With the increasing competition over land and forest resources, they have suffered disproportionately from various industrial and infrastructural projects causing displacement and loss of traditional livelihoods, and jeopardising their community structures, cultures and identities. Mainstream society accords Adivasis a low status, and disrespect for Adivasi rights and encroachment on their lands by corporations and local elites is commonplace (see Padel and Das, 2010; Mohanty, 2014; Behera, 2016). Adivasis have been structurally disadvantaged via disinvestment in their education and health, discrimination in the labour market and general disinterest and inability to understand them and their views. More than 90% of the Adivasi families of Odisha live below the poverty line (Behera, 2016: 31–2).

Communities and their relations in eastern Sundergarh

Sundergarh is a 'Scheduled' District with an Adivasi majority, its eastern part being originally home to the Pauri Bhunia and Munda Adivasi communities. However, when large-scale mining in the region started with the construction of the Barsua Iron Mine (in operation since 1961) and the adjunct railway line, these communities were scared of outsiders and largely withdrew further into the forest. As they did not pick up the low-skilled mining jobs available, other Adivasi labourers already accustomed to wage work and contacts with outsiders moved in from other parts of Odisha and the neighbouring Jharkhand (then Bihar). As a result, nowadays the Adivasis of eastern Sundergarh have diverse origins from 'locals' to 'migrants'. The constellation of the people in the region has further diversified with non-Adivasi retail traders, public sector professionals, mining engineers and others working in or with connection with mines from all over India.

The Adivasis worked initially as unskilled manual labour inside and outside the mines. As mining has become heavily mechanised, today the low-skilled jobs available are subcontracted and comprise driving ore trucks between mines and the railway line, or loading the ore manually into train carriages. Illustrative of the salary level and conditions, in 2015 a truck driver working minimum of 12 hours per day, 7 days a week, earned approximately INR6,000 (around US$87) per month. Access to even basic education being a relatively new thing for most Adivasis, they rarely qualify for other jobs. Having until recently relied on the forest for every need, many do not yet reckon the value of education, and even those who are motivated lack resources and support. The few skilled Adivasi workers employed in the mines do not necessarily earn much more than drivers or loaders, but their jobs are more secure and give access to club-like benefits, such as company-sponsored housing, healthcare and schooling for children. A common denominator for the tiny better-off section of second or third generation migrant Adivasis with good jobs or small enterprises is usually a father or grandfather, whose regular job in a mine enabled compiling social, economic and educational capital for the next generation.

The highly educated professionals in the mines or in the university degree–demanding public sector jobs are usually non-Adivasis from outside, as are the majority of transportation and logistics entrepreneurs, retail traders and the few private mine owners. While some of these people form the elite of the region, they rarely have their families with them, the explanation being that the widespread pollution and the poor educational and healthcare facilities make the place unsuitable for families. Professionals who could improve the situation are not interested to work in the region for the same reasons. In 2015, none of our interlocutors could recall a single NGO working in the region. Besides existing CSR practices, most people had no clue what social work or community development stand for.

While the relations between different groups seemed easy-going on the face of it, there were undercurrents of discontent. We heard, for example, recurrent accounts of Adivasis being stripped of the benefits to which they were entitled, or paid only fractions of the promised or official salaries. A common view was that non-Adivasis cleverly cash in on whatever structural advantage they have and the subsequent inability of the Adivasis to compete. Unaccustomed to fight for their rights, the Adivasis remain silent when misconduct or injustice occurs. In eastern Sundergarh, access to justice is further complicated by the subdued, yet still extant Naxalite (a so-called Maoist, anti-state guerrilla movement), whose presence labels the region, like other potential Naxalite areas, as a dangerous and even a no-go place. Although the movement is more active elsewhere in Odisha, its existence has validated the operation of central security forces and the state armed police in the region. In these circumstances, the survival strategy of ordinary people is to avoid attracting unwanted attention by fighting their own corners. Moreover, Adivasis, and poor people in general, lack knowledge and financial resources to progress their cases through the courts. What is more, money talks, with unwanted criticism silenced by simply paying the criticism off, or through violence. All this results in the poor having only each other to rely on. Thus, they sort out their problems by sitting together and collectively figuring out if there is something they can do, a practice also in line with traditional Adivasi self-governance.

Environmental impacts and welfare needs

As a hotspot of mineral extraction, life in eastern Sundergarh is subservient to the mining industry. The region is brown and shabby because of the iron dust everywhere, which spreads not only from the mines, but also from the uncovered trucks that transport the ore. Rainwater carries the dust to the remaining fields, where it spoils the fertility of the soil and impairs animal health. Bigger quantities of iron, brought by monsoon run-off waters from the mines, make the soil sticky and unsuitable for cultivation. Mining wipes out the forest and disturbs the animals, making hungry wild elephants come to villages in search of food. Overall, as one interlocutor said, "There is an imbalance of the earth; its equilibrium is lost."

After more than half a century of large-scale mining in the region, the necessary infrastructures for people remain poorly developed. The incessant heavy traffic destroys the main roads, which are under constant repair, whereas villages a few kilometres apart from them commonly lack proper connectivity. While there are a few under-resourced government schools, some elders receiving old age pensions, and some government schemes patchily in place (such as the integrated child development scheme and distribution of food grains at a subsidised price for people under the poverty line), overall the level of public services is meagre.

The locals have no alternative but to adjust, for their lives depend on the precarious mining-related employment. In so doing, they suffer from lung diseases, other health hazards due to pollution, the locally endemic severe malaria (which according to locals goes together with mining), diabetes, and traffic and other accidents. What is more, alcoholism is widespread and generates a number of other problems. Locals say that while alcohol has always been part of the Adivasi culture, it has turned into a major problem only with the advent of the mining industry. Many feel that alcohol gives a moment of solace from the taxing work and believe it buffers the body against the dust, and so spend their salaries on alcohol, neglecting the needs of their family members. This hits women and children particularly hard who, unlike earlier when it was possible to earn money with non-timber forest products, depend nowadays solely on their male breadwinners. Ironically, with mining jobs being for men, the only feasible source of income for women may be making and selling rice beer. At the same time, the inflow of lone men to the mining jobs has changed the gender composition of the region. Taken together, the shifts in the modes of production, the environment and gender relations have brought new kinds of vulnerabilities for both men and women.

When asked in 2015 what the welfare needs of the region are, everyone from the poorest labourers to the managing directors of mines listed similar things: properly running primary schools, opportunities for further education, better coverage and quality of healthcare services, better roads. Nearly as unanimously wished for were pollution (especially dust) control, ways to curb alcoholism, and peripheral development, including the need to develop livelihoods other than mining. Poorer people further addressed the need for better housing (with electricity, toilets and access to safe water) and generally services that the poor can afford. Many (rich and poor alike) also acknowledged the importance of just salaries and proper compensation for those who lose their lands to mining, and the importance of political empowerment.

Corporate responses

In the absence of serious government as well as NGO interest to develop the region, community-level welfare investment in eastern Sundergarh rests largely on the resource allocation by the mining companies. All the mining companies that we visited would be regarded locally as middle-sized or large, and financed numerous CSR activities. In these companies, CSR issues were assigned to one or more white-collar workers in the company administration, but could also be negotiated directly with the CEOs. The company representatives described the CSR activities with a wide array of terminology, including community or peripheral development, but without referring to any particular theoretical foundations regarding CSR. In practice, however, CSR was another name for community investment, that is, financing infrastructure and its maintenance, and educational (teacher salaries, vocational training) and healthcare services (such as health camps) to the local villagers. In other words, CSR meant financial support, or, as one company representative said, "sponsoring basic needs in the periphery".

Illustrative of the common CSR activities, according to its own reporting one of the largest mining companies in the region had spent annually (2012–15) between INR5.8 million (around US$84,000) and INR8.4 million (around US$122,000) on CSR. These figures covered annually the salaries of 17–26 temporary/para teachers in the local schools, sponsoring 25–70 youths to vocational training, and financing medical camps in several villages. Moreover, the company had funded numerous construction works from boundary walls and tube wells to a community centre and a cement road to a village, as well as electrification projects (of a community centre, electrical connections to those below the poverty line in one village, a transformer in another village). Costs that were more miscellaneous included, among other things, renovations of water tanks, teaching aids to schools, chairs and a steel almirah (a large cupboard) to a women's association, provisions to sports and culture, and income-generation schemes (mushroom cultivation, goat rearing, a fruit orchard, each in one village). These figures come from the CSR expenditure reports of the company given to the authors in 2015.

As the previous example shows, while many of the sponsored activities involved hiring personnel, such as construction workers, electricians or medical professionals, they were not really about community organising or community development in the broader, more participatory and political sense of the term. While some targets of sponsorship, like teacher salaries, were fairly established, others were negotiated based on what people with some connection to the company's leadership proposed or what those in charge of CSR saw as sensible. There was not necessarily any community-based process behind the CSR decisions, although some community representatives, like *sarpanches*, were sometimes involved in selecting the beneficiaries. Although the companies claim to 'support what people like', much thus depends on who asks for the support and how.

Moreover, companies concentrate their funding on localities where they would like to expand or have interests to secure, but neglect areas where there is not much to achieve. In 2015, two mining companies competed with each other in the favours done to local residents close to mineral deposits that both companies desired. One small hamlet was provided with numerous water posts with company logos, a fruit orchard and even streetlights – a rare sight in a poor Adivasi locality. The neighbouring bigger village had several recently constructed community halls. Overall, there was both significant overlap as well as blind spots in the corporate service distribution and community investment, and a lack of coordination between companies.

There is no shortage of targets for sponsorship, but the companies "cannot manage everything". Their CSR budgets are limited, and the bigger the company the more likely its CSR policy is set at the head office and not locally, which limits the generosity of sub-branches.

Moreover, while it may seem only fair that companies finance infrastructure and services for local people, the effects of CSR are not solely positive. A common downside of CSR is that it in effect boosts a charity-based approach to welfare instead of building broad-based inclusive welfare structures (see Padel and Das, 2010: 539). In eastern Sundergarh, even the corporate representatives constantly pointed out that the government should also take responsibility over the area and its people, and that government investment in the region was not commensurate with the revenue from its mines. On the whole, if welfare investment rests chiefly on the mining companies, it is patchy and directed by corporate interests. This means that it has continuity only as long as it makes sense from the perspective of the core business, the exhaustion of the subsoil resources. Corporate interest in a mining region does not last forever and thus the CSR activities rarely aim to be particularly far-reaching and comprehensive, and therefore are not sustainable.

Whose development?

From a community development perspective, crucial questions regarding CSR policies are who formulates them, on what premises, and whom do they ultimately serve. Besides the usual scope for the use and abuse of power in a hierarchical and unequal society, welfare programmes in Adivasi regions, especially when designed and implemented by non-Adivasis, risk being out of their depth in understanding the Adivasi cultures and world views. Overall, official and mainstream constructions of reality fail to grasp the standpoints of Adivasis, and the reasons behind their continuous marginalisation (Padel and Das, 2014.) Sometimes the clashes between the modern developmentalist and the Adivasi world views are so insurmountable that subtle forms of Adivasi resistance are interpreted as idleness or backwardness. If, for example, Adivasis do not appreciate programmes that have been planned *for* but not *with* them, it is usually the Adivasis and not the planning processes that are seen as faulty (Kraemer, 2014: 321–33). However, solutions that do not understand or mind the complexity and sophistication of the Adivasi relationships to each other and the land reflect first and foremost 'the developers' self-image and worldviews' (Fauset, 2006, cited in Padel and Das, 2014: 51).

According to Padel and Das (2014: 49), the key problem in the implementation of projects of Adivasi development is that what actually happens differs fundamentally from what is supposed to happen. In reality, there is usually very little correlation between the avowed benefits of the mining industry and the lives of the majority of the people in the mining regions. Much of the 'development' in industrialised Adivasi regions has been simply destructive (p 66), the Adivasis in them being 'among the most impoverished in India' (p 54). Moreover, their personal freedom and quality of life, along with the quality of their living environment, have significantly decreased (p 51). In eastern Sundergarh, the common assumption is that in the end, mining will totally spoil the natural environment and the people will have to move elsewhere.

In Sundergarh and beyond, rampant nepotism and corruption further undermine pro-poor change taking place. If, on the one hand, nearly everyone with an opportunity to do so is primarily concerned with personal gain, the interests of subaltern groups remain forever secondary. Corporations, on the other hand, compete in the neo-liberal global economy, which drives them towards ever-greater cost effectiveness, such as increased mechanisation and trimming the efficiency of their labour. While resource extraction may thus generally increase the socio-economic well-being of the nation (Behera and Basar, 2014), in extractive peripheries this is rarely the case. On the contrary, 'development process that alienates the tribes [Adivasis] from their resources marks the continuity of a historical injustice' and mocks the terminology associated with development, such as sustainability, participation and people-centeredness (Behera and Basar, 2014: 21–2). As one of our interlocutors succinctly said: "the Adivasis are simply used" and "getting lost". In such circumstances, there is a limit to corporate and community interests being complementary. While the patchy community investment serves the companies, manufacturing the necessary consent for their activities, it also maintains the structurally disadvantaged position of poor Adivasis.

The situation is likely to continue as long as development is defined primarily in material terms, while its costs to the environment, to less privileged people and to future generations are ignored, and attempts to challenge the status quo are subtly or more overtly suppressed. The mainstream attitude in India, even if not necessarily hostile to Adivasi rights to land as such, is that the rights of the few – such as the relatively small Adivasi communities in resource-rich locations – should not hinder the economic development of the country. The fact that most fruits of development fall to groups already privileged, and that those struggling to survive day in day out have to stick to dangerous and exploitative work, goes largely unchallenged. For the poor, the equation is clear: "if there is no work, there is no food". At the bottom of the precarious labour market, mining-related jobs are what people know, and financially they beat other options available. Nonetheless, people are aware that mining-related work lasts only as long as there are minerals to extract and that low-skilled job like loading or driving may be gone much before that. For the moment, the potential resistance is therefore against further mechanisation of the mineral transportation, not the extraction itself.

Avenues for change

The relations between humans, and between humans and nature, contain always some fluidity and potential for surprise, and can be consciously worked on. Notwithstanding the complexities already discussed, community development in eastern Sundergarh is not rocket science. The basic starting point would be encouraging and allowing the Adivasis themselves define what they want and what development means for them, learning from them and supporting them in their aims. This implies taking seriously the principle of Adivasi communities' participation in all planning and decision-making processes relevant to them. Another important step would be respecting and putting it into practice the existing legislation concerning Scheduled Areas and Adivasi rights. However, as our discussion attests, aspiring towards greater social and environmental equality in the region is a fragile project. The disadvantaged position of the Adivasis and the cheapness (Moore, 2017) of their environment benefit powerful stakeholders, backing up the status quo. Even so, there may be ways to alter the social and environmental realities on the ground.

The position of disadvantaged groups rarely improves without significant political pressure. Improving the position of the Adivasis is thus likely to require broad-based mobilisation of the Adivasis, as well as their allies; the same holds true for other marginalised groups in India. While there are complex structural and personal reasons why some end up choosing violent struggle as part of the Maoist/ Naxalite movement, from a community development and social justice perspective, violence is a highly problematic path. Instead, there is an urgent need for peaceful, constructive Adivasi empowerment. Among other things, this requires identity and meaning-making work in the Adivasi communities and beyond so as not to reproduce further the unequal power relations structurally in society or in the everyday relationships between people. If the ownership of the mobilisation process remains in Adivasi hands, their communities may benefit from various forms of encouragement, support and facilitation. In these ways, community development can play a role. In mining regions, the task is no less than ensuring the fair treatment of the local communities, and the ecosystems affected by mining operations. The work requires the capacity to understand and work on issues of power, without undermining the complexities of the context (Ross, 2013: 193, 200).

Community development is about communities finding strategies to secure and protect what is important for them, while also envisioning how to pursue the kind of changes they seek. Such processes entail, for example, community-level analysis on the challenges at stake, and discussion about what people dream about and what they hold realistic for themselves and their children. In spite of the current centrality of mining-related jobs, taking care of the natural environment is in Adivasi interests. In 2015, notwithstanding the bleak predictions about the environment of the area, many Adivasi interlocutors emphasised that the place is their home, where they want to live and die. In one village, the main concern of the villagers, many of whom worked for the mines, was the restoration of their fields into cultivable land after the damage caused by flash floods from the mines. These villagers emphasised that agriculture is what they have to sustain themselves with once the mining is over. However, besides practices of recycling (one mine) and environmental monitoring, there were hardly any signs of corporate attempts to take care of the region's natural environment and its regeneration.

After all, the marginalised Adivasi communities could benefit from various practical community development efforts, provided these are realised from beginning to end in collaboration with them. Instead of 'mere' community development, there is a need of Adivasi-centred community development and/or social work, which takes Adivasi world views and values, and not mainstream cultural values, as the starting point (see Ranta-Tyrkkö and Jojo, 2017). At a minimum, community workers, whether or not themselves Adivasis, should be alert not to reproduce mainstream hegemonic and discriminating ideologies in their practice. Simple as this may sound, it is something in which the local labour unions have not succeeded. Instead of providing a platform to fight discrimination at work, our interlocutors' unanimous experience was that the unions, which were all ruled by outsiders, enforced class- and ethnicity-based divisions and generated disputes and disunity.

What kind of community workers could then support Adivasi-centred community work, and where does CSR stand in all this? The Adivasi-centred, empowerment-oriented approach could be introduced by any potential community organiser, be s/he activist, ambitious public sector worker, community worker, social worker or NGO worker. At the same time, the Adivasis are also likely to benefit from and need international solidarity for their case, although that may be a mixed blessing in terms of participation and ownership of the cause. However, notwithstanding the apparently genuine community service aspirations of many corporate officers in charge of CSR programmes, the social justice line of community development is hardly in corporate interests. Having until now provided mainly small-scale material help and services in the midst of constantly marginalising processes, politically empowering work carries the risk of leading to demands for better salaries and working conditions, and even questioning the corporate activity overall.

While corporations in eastern Sundergarh certainly continue to have a role in community service and infrastructure delivery, there are thus limits to the community development dimension of their CSR programmes. Should the corporations want to broaden their approach towards community development, they would need to enhance their skill and willingness for genuine dialogue with the local communities, and be open to criticism. If this is not the case, corporate 'community development' risks remaining at the level of sporadic and paternalistic community investment that simultaneously serves as a neo-liberal tool to maintain the local consent for the extractive activity. Although it would be very challenging to do so, overall, there is a need for independent, pro-Adivasi actors to undertake community development and community organising in this area. More important than their mode of organising is that their mandate is based in, and complies with, the interests of the local marginalised communities over those of their donors or employers (for a critical account about NGOs, see Padel and Das, 2010: Ch 18).

Concluding with a critical note

To summarise, eastern Sundergarh is a region where mineral extraction has been going on for a long time, and where the consent of the local communities was never requested. Having served as a source of minerals and resultant profit ever since, much has been lost beyond repair, environmentally and culturally. Meanwhile, the promise that mining-based industrialisation brings welfare to poor Adivasis has largely failed. Rather, the mineral extraction made some people move away and others move in, thus complicating the communities' sense of belonging and rights to the place. While mining has brought jobs – one of the main justifications of mining in an Adivasi region – the best jobs have gone for educated people from outside, leaving the (now second or third generation) poor Adivasis with the bottom rank, insecure, subcontracted jobs. Furthermore, mining has eaten away at the land and deteriorated the ecosystems, superseding other livelihoods and making everyone suffer from mining-related pollution. Yet, mining being the main source of income for the local people, there is no opposition to it beyond occasional dissident voices. If the poor communities become more outspoken and empowered, the currently underlying tensions, especially regarding the prevailing dynamics of power, could unravel in some form.

While the existing CSR programmes are much needed in the absence of anything else, they hardly exemplify community development as comprehensively understood. Remaining at the level of community investment, they cover up some of the damage caused while maintaining public cooperation with the corporate dominated system (for a broader account, see Padel and Das, 2010: 540). More responsible and empowering attempts would require addressing and finding ways to combat the structural oppression and discrimination that poor Adivasis experience on a daily basis, their mining-related jobs included. Further, noting the deterioration of the natural environment because of the mineral extraction, instead of mere utilisation, desperately missed is both corporate and government interest and investment not only responding to the present needs, but also to the future of the region, including its ecosystems. In addition to fostering the general liveability and well-being of the area, this should involve building the base for livelihoods other than mining, and supporting the participation of the disadvantaged local communities. At any rate, community development should be supportive of critical civil society development. In a democratic society, the lives, rights and living environment of people inhabiting the extractive peripheries are equally as valuable as those of others.

All said, much pro-Adivasi community work in mining regions and beyond would need to be about remodelling the attitudes regarding Adivasis, and fostering and putting into practice strategies that support their identity politics and empowerment. This is a challenging task, as it requires time to establish reciprocally good relationships with the Adivasi communities, and also the guts and wit to negotiate the community orientation with other, more powerful stakeholders. However, noting the current absence of critically minded community development workers in eastern Sundergarh, the chances are that pro-Adivasi change will be slow and its results uncertain. If the corporations truly want to embrace community development as a CSR activity, they would need to incorporate the Adivasi perspective as part of their

CSR strategy, come what may. Likewise, the Indian state, even if seeing mining as a necessary evil would need to educate the Adivasis on their rights, and organise and mobilise for their participation in the decision-making processes regarding the mining industry. This work cannot be achieved without networking and advocacy both at regional/national and international level to confirm commitments made in various instruments and policies for the protection and development of the Adivasis.

Overall, the eastern Sundergarh case resembles many other peripheral places of mineral extraction, where the original inhabitants have had to step aside, mining jobs displace other livelihoods and the continuity of ecosystems, and corporations define the modes of action for everybody else. Nevertheless, as Dyann Ross (2013: 200) reflects, based on lessons from a mining struggle in Australia, power and ethics are always context specific and inseparable. As much as 'community development' by corporations is likely to be an ethical minefield for critically minded community developers, little can be achieved without dialogue and constructive relationships with the companies. Whatever the strategy and however difficult the path, 'ethical behaviour involves accountability towards the less powerful stakeholders without antagonising powerful parties' and the ability 'to maintain impartiality, independence and integrity between different stakeholder interests' (Ross, 2013: 206). The crucial and difficult challenge for those involved in community development work is to resist being co-opted by powerful stakeholder interests, including those of their own employers, but find ways to be faithful to the situation on the ground.

Acknowledgements

The authors are greatly indebted for practical help provided by Manju and Basant Kerketta, Thomas Lakra and his colleagues and network, Sugad Surin, translation help from Poonam Kerketta and Nirupama Kujur, and administrative support from the TISS International Relations Office.

References

Adduci, M. (2013) 'Mining governance in India: Questioning the neoliberal agenda', in J.N. Singh and F. Bourgouin (eds) *Resource governance and developmental states in the global South*, Basingstoke: Palgrave Macmillan, pp 172–91.

Bansal, S., Khanna M. and Jain, S. (2018) 'Corporate social responsibility rules in India: An assessment', *Economic & Political Weekly*, 53(14): 44–51.

Behera, P.C. (2016) 'Livelihood crisis in the scheduled areas of Odisha: Relevance of PESA in a weak state', in N. Tiwari (ed) *Tribal self-governance: PESA and its implementation*, Jaipur: Rawat Publications, pp 30–73.

Behera, P.C. and Basar, J. (2014) 'Introduction', in M.C. Behera and J. Basar (eds) *Resources, tribes and development: Competing interests and contours of possibilities*, Jaipur: Rawat Publications, pp 21–46.

Census of India (2011) Office of the Registrar General & Census Commissioner, India. Available at: www.censusindia.gov.in/

CII (Confederation of Indian Industry) (2013) *Handbook on corporate social responsibility in India*, Gurgaon: Confederation of Indian Industry. Available at: www.pwc.in/assets/pdfs/publications/2013/handbook-on-corporate-social-responsibility-in-india.pdf

Dayal, H., Noamani, F., Bagchi, D. and Godsora, J. (2014) *State of the Adivasis in Odisha 2014: A human development analysis*, New Delhi: Skillshare International India/Sage.

DMF Sundergarh (2018) 'Major and minor lessees'. Available at: http://dmf.orissaminerals.gov.in/website/DMFLesseeMMMList.aspx

DPE (Department of Public Enterprises) (2013) 'Guidelines on corporate social responsibility and sustainability for central public enterprises', Delhi: Government of India, DPE. Available at: http://dpemou.nic.in/MOUFiles/Revised_CSR_Guidelines.pdf

Fauset, C. (2006) 'What's wrong with CSR?' Oxford: Corporate Watch Report. Available at: https://corporatewatch.org/wp-content/uploads/2017/09/CSRreport.pdf

GOO (Government of Odisha, Department of Steel and Mines) (2018) 'Mine lease holder'. Available at: www.orissaminerals.gov.in

Healy, L.M. (2008) *International social work: Professional action in an interdependent world* (2nd edn), New York: Oxford University Press.

IBEF (India Brand Equity Foundation) (2015) 'Odisha unveils IPR 2015, to attract Rs1,73,000 crore investment', *IBEF*, 4 September. Available at: www.ibef.org/news/odisha-unveils-ipr-2015-to-attract-rs173000-crore-investment

Jha, M. (2016) 'Community organising and political agency: Changing community development subjects in India', in R.R. Meade, M. Shaw and S. Banks (eds) *Politics, power and community development*, Bristol: Policy Press, pp 65–82.

Kraemer, R. (2014) 'Making sense of resistance: How mining managers construct anti-corporate mobilization', in D. Leadbeater (ed) *Resources, Empire & Labour: Crises, Lessons & Alternatives*, Halifax: Fernwood Publishing, pp 319–33.

Kuruvilla, S. (2005) 'Social work and social development in India', in I. Ferguson, M. Lavalette and E. Whitmore (eds) *Globalisation, global justice and social work*, Abingdon: Routledge, pp 41–53.

Mathur, H.M. (2008) 'A new deal for displaced people: Orissa's involuntary resettlement policy', *Social Change*, 38(4): 553–75.

Meher, R. (2009) 'Globalization, displacement and the livelihood issues of tribal and agriculture dependent poor people: The case of mineral-based industries in India', *Journal of Developing Societies*, 25(4): 457–80.

Mohanty, M. (2014) 'Persisting dominance: Crisis of democracy in a resource-rich region', *Economic & Political Weekly*, 49(14): 39–47.

Moore, J.W. (2017) 'The Capitalocene, part I: On the nature and origins of our ecological crisis', *The Journal of Peasant Studies*, 44(3): 594–630.

Nathan, D. and Xaxa, V. (eds) (2012) *Social exclusion and adverse inclusion: Development and deprivation of Adivasis in India*, New Delhi: Oxford University Press.

Padel, F. and Das, S. (2010) *Out of this earth: East India Adivasis and the aluminium cartel*, Hyderabad: Orient BlackSwan.

Padel, F. and Das, S. (2014) 'Development wisdom and the reality gap', in M.C. Behera and J. Basar (eds) *Resources, tribes and development: Competing interests and contours of possibilities*, Jaipur: Rawat Publications, pp 49–73.

Padel, F., Dandekar, A. and Unni, J. (2013) *Ecology, economy: Quest for a socially informed connection*, Hyderabad: Orient BlackSwan.

Pratap, V. and Priya, R. (2009) 'From democracy to Swaraaj', in M. Ulvila and J. Pasanen (eds) *Sustainable futures: Replacing growth imperative and hierarchies with sustainable ways*, Helsinki: Ministry for Foreign Affairs in Finland, pp 212–23.

Ranta-Tyrkkö, S. and Jojo, B. (2017) 'Scopes for Adivasi-centred ecosocial work in an Indian mining region?', in A.-L. Matthies and K. Närhi (eds) *The ecosocial transition of societies: The contribution of social policy and social work*, Abingdon: Routledge, pp 105–20.

Ross, D. (2013) 'Social work and the struggle for corporate social responsibility', in M. Gray, J. Coates and T. Hetherington (eds) *Environmental social work*, Abingdon: Routledge, pp 193–210.

Rousseleau, R. (2013) 'Claiming indigenousness in India', *Books and Ideas*, 7 February, https://booksandideas.net/Claiming-Indigenousness-in-India.html

Rycroft, D.J. and Dasgupta, S. (2011) 'Indigenous pasts and politics of belonging', in D.J. Rycroft and S. Dasgupta (eds) *The politics of belonging in India: Becoming Adivasi*, Abingdon: Routledge, pp 1–13.

Sarkar, S. (2008) 'Industrial social work to corporate social responsibility: A transformation of priority', *Journal of Human Values*, 14(1): 31–48.

Shah, A. (2011) *In the shadows of the state: Indigenous politics, environmentalism, and insurgency in Jharkhand, India*, New Delhi: Oxford University Press [first published by Duke University Press, 2010].

van Schendel, W. (2011) 'The dangers of belonging: Tribes, indigenous peoples and homelands in South Asia', in D.J. Rycroft and S. Dasgupta (eds) *The politics of belonging in India: Becoming Adivasi*, Abingdon: Routledge, pp 19–43.

PART 3

Envisioning an ethical space for community development

Relational ethics and transformative community organising in the neo-liberal US context

Loretta Pyles

Introduction

Throughout the world, recent decades have been marked, at least in part, by instability and inequality as evidenced by the growing impacts of climate change, economic crisis, terrorism and racism/xenophobia. Tied up in the extractivist and growth-oriented economy of neo-liberal capitalism, the era is distinguished by the grave dangers of climate disasters and threats of mass extinction. In an economy based on infinite growth that extracts from both the environment and workers and that facilitates gross profits for the few, resulting in a shrinking middle class and desperate forms of poverty and suffering for many, some believe that we are at a tipping point (Korten, 2006; Klein, 2014). Other social issues, such as racism and xenophobia, are foregrounded as continued domination of others in the neo-liberal era has been actualised through increased policing of borders, militarisation, incarceration and retrenchment of basic public social welfare supports (Alexander, 2010; Reisch, 2013). Moreover, in a globalised context, the interrelatedness among issues such as racial justice, immigrant rights, worker well-being and environmental justice is coming more sharply into focus. There is good evidence that time-honoured, reform-oriented organising is not enough to gain the kind of traction needed to create change; rather, something far more transformative for both people and planet is required.

Scholar–activists such as David Korten, Joanna Macy, and Grace Lee Boggs have identified the current times as 'a Great Turning', marked by a shift from an extractivist growth-oriented society to one that is life-sustaining. Grace Lee Boggs, who was a Chinese immigrant to America, and an educator and community organiser based in Detroit, Michigan, wrote:

My hope is that as more and different layers of the American people are subjected to economic and political strains and as recurrent disasters force us to recognize our role in begetting these disasters, a growing number of Americans will begin to recognize that we are at one of those great turning points in history. Both for our livelihood and for our humanity, we need to see progress not in terms of 'having more' but in terms of growing our souls by creating community, mutual self-sufficiency, and cooperative relations with one another. (2012: 133–4)

Enter transformative organising. Aligned with transformative justice and transformative social change, transformative organising seeks this kind of sea change through the evolution of self, the economy, institutions, and social policies and practices (Mann; 2011; Dixon, 2014; Pyles, 2014, 2018; Brown, 2017). According to Mann, 'transformative organizing works to structurally transform the system, transform the consciousness of the people being organized, and in the process, transform the consciousness of the organizer' (2011: 201).

In the current moment, organisers and organisations are making unique contributions in the form of what the movement training group Momentum (www.momentumcommunity.org) calls 'story, strategy, and structure', three components that constitute the DNA of a movement. *Story* is how participants understand the meaning and purpose of the movement; *strategy* is how they choose to take action; and *structure* is how they arrange themselves and make decisions. By leveraging the revolutionary visions of social movements, transformative organisers can utilise some of the tried and true *strategies* of the community organising tradition to bring it into action. Transformative organisers strategically utilise tactics to achieve specific goals, such as those developed by organisers in Birmingham, Alabama during the Civil Rights movement where escalation of non-violent confrontation was used to create crisis, pushing the system to a breaking point (Engler and Engler, 2016). It has been noted that many movements, such as the Occupy protests, have not resulted in their intended outcomes because of the failure to incorporate story *and* strategy *and* structure (Engler and Engler, 2016). I would add a fourth component to the conceptualisation of transformative organising – *process*. In this regard, a transformative practice of organising and change attends to personal, interpersonal and organisational relational processes as pathways to heal the wounds inflicted by the dominant paradigm and to rebuild adaptable and resilient communities (Brown, 2017). Attention to process assists organisers in functioning in a way that is sustainable, attends to '-isms', and heals the internalised oppression of themselves and their organisations.

Transformative organising in a globalised, digital context draws from the touchstones of the workers' movements of the Progressive Era, the Civil Rights and Anti-War movements of the 1950s and 1960s, the feminist movements of the 1970s, environmental and AIDS activism of the 1980s, and the World Trade Organization protests of the late 1990s, and carries the message of liberation differently and arguably even further. It strives to employ the utilitarian methods of building organisations (as affirmed by resource mobilisation theory) as well as to leverage mass mobilisations and protest; at the same it strives to create transformative processes that can change the consciousness of organisers and reclaim our interdependence (McCarthy and Zald, 1977; Mann, 2011; Pyles, 2014, 2018; Brown, 2017). Though there are significant differences and divergences based on the issues being addressed and/or the groups doing the work, transformative organising centres on intersectionality, multimodal interventions and healing justice. This is unique in that transformative organising emphasises questions of ethics, especially relational ethics, in ways that previous strands of organising did not.

In this chapter, I will articulate transformative organising and its key elements, using two brief case examples of transformative organising and mobilisation set in the US context as illustrations. Prior to this discussion, I will contrast transformative organising to the dominant tradition of organising, particularly utilitarian, reform-oriented organising in the Alinsky tradition that has favoured issue-centred organising, strategic wins and hierarchical organisations. While there is a dire need to move beyond some of the old forms of organising, it is also the case that there are many elements from these traditions that are indispensable to organisers working to create change and alleviate the impacts of systemic oppression.

Community organising in the twentieth century

The community organising tradition of the twentieth century largely focused on: (1) building a base of people and leaders to address issues that are important to a community, (2) cultivating power, and (3) engaging in strategic actions to achieve goals (Fisher, 1994). It has been associated with the building of strong centralised organisations and leveraging power over targets to create instrumental changes in the environment and to advance incremental reforms, emphasising the issues that were important to a community rather than an ideological framework to which to adhere. It favoured strategic actions over the mass protest and mobilisations of social movements. Community organising has constituted what Rothman (2001) called 'social action' in his framework for community practice methods, which is distinct from other methods which he identified, namely locality development, social planning and social mobilisation.

The impact of the organising methods of Saul Alinsky (1909–72) cannot be underestimated as they influenced people such as Ed Chambers, Cesar Chavez, Dolores Huerta and Barack Obama over many decades and formed the basis of organisations such as the Industrial Areas Foundation (IAF), the Midwest Academy, the Gamaliel Network, ACORN (Association of Community Organizations for Reform Now), and many labour unions. Alinsky, one of the so-called 'fathers' of modern community organising, held a legendary *utilitarian* ethical stance, embracing a belief that tactics should enfranchise the greatest number of disenfranchised people (Pyles, 2014). His pragmatic methods meant that organised groups of 'have nots' pressured a target (an elected official or a chief executive officer, for example) by creating specific demands in order to leverage tensions and force the target to concede to the power of large numbers of organised people (Alinsky, 1971). His approach utilised boycotts, sit-ins, pickets and strikes, as well as creative tactics such as buying shares in the Kodak company in Rochester, New York so that community leaders could sabotage the vote of shareholders to achieve the goal of more jobs in the community. Such confrontational, polarising tactics have been used successfully by organisers who have been trained in the Alinsky tradition for almost a century, resulting in key reforms on a range of issues including labour, economic justice, the environment, education reform and racial justice.

One of Alinsky's significant contributions was the one-on-one organising conversation, or 'relational meeting', the goal of which is to build a relationship so that a person becomes activated to participate in community organising activities. In these strategic conversations, the organiser seeks to identify the self-interest of the person, agitate them, discuss power, offer them hope in organising, and ask them to commit to take a specific action. Building a strong base as well as developing indigenous leaders paved the way for organisers to embrace and engage in some of the classic and clever strategies espoused by Alinsky in *Rules for radicals* and captured in his famous aphoristic rhetoric, such as 'power is not only what you have but what the enemy thinks you have' (1971: 127).

These strategies, and the tactics that materialise from them, rest on the rational ethical impulses for *distributive justice* – the idea that resource allocation should result in equitable distribution in society – and on the *utilitarian principle* of the greatest good for the greatest number (Mill, 1861/2002; Rawls, 1999). But, this traditional organising model has been critiqued (Mann, 2011; Pyles, 2014; Brown, 2017) as being transactional and using people (both organisers and targets) in ways that fail to place relationships prior to knowledge and outcomes. Arguably, as suggested in Chapter One of this volume, it is important that we develop a more relational ethics, grounded in postmodernist, feminist and Eastern thought, which affirms the importance of engagement, mutual respect, embodied knowledge, uncertainty/vulnerability and attention to an interdependent environment (Austin, 2006). One way in which traditional organising has failed to prioritise the relational has been within the organisational context, as individual voices, including those of women and people of colour, have been silenced through efficiency-oriented patriarchal organisational models.

Thus, the limits of traditional organising may be seen in terms of: perpetuation of patriarchy, hierarchy and other '-isms' through organisational structures and polarising tactics; missed opportunities for stories to bring people together and foster a vision for revolutionary change of society thereby scaling up local campaigns to national and transnational levels; and perpetuating organiser burn out. Moreover, critics of this tradition of organising have also noted how victories failed to change the existing system and transform people's consciousness (Pyles, 2014, 2018; Engler and Engler, 2016). Traditional organising of the 20th century tended toward structured, strategic and practical actions grounded in a desire to redistribute resources. What it lacked was spontaneity, symbolic visions of liberation and revolutionary sensibilities. It can be argued that rationalist, including distributive and utilitarian, ethical frameworks are in part to blame as it straitjacketed organisers into formulaic and limited approaches.

On the other hand, mobilisations and mass protest have often lacked effective strategies and have failed to create lasting organisations that can build power over time (Engler and Engler, 2016). The question facing community organising in this moment is: how can it draw from the effective strategies and structures of the past and move forward with new visions for transformation and ways of doing the work that are sustainable and prefigure the future? Such a vision requires an ethical underpinning that can prioritise relationships – with colleagues, with targets and even within oneself. The ethics of care (which focuses attention on relationships between people) has been very influential in inspiring ethical frameworks for many of the 'caring professions', but less prominent in the field of community development (see Chapter One of this volume). One example of such a vision is to be found in the nursing profession, where some nursing scholars and practitioners have been arguing for a relational ethics in the context of a healthcare paradigm that privileges scientific objectivity, biotechnical expertise and the McDonaldisation of healthcare (Austin, 2006).

Transformative change and organising

Environmental activist Joanna Macy has identified three types of work required during this time of the 'Great Turning', in response to predatory systems that are eroding people's basic rights to food, water, safety, shelter and justice, and stripping people of their essential humanity as narratives and practices of domination pervade people's consciousness. These three types are: (1) holding actions, (2) creating new structures and (3) changing consciousness (Macy and Johnstone, 2012). The first type of work, *holding actions*, means that organisers work to alleviate the suffering that the current system is creating, which may include policy change to reform the system, community organising, mobilisation and direct action to prevent further destruction, and other forms of advocacy and social services provision for people who are most disaffected. The second type, *creating new structures*, means experimenting with innovative sustainable economic models and practices, as well as creating and practising new kinds of empowering, equitable and cooperative organisational structures in business, government and non-governmental sectors. The third type, *changing consciousness*, includes popular education, social justice education and various forms of mind–body practices including meditation that can change the internalised cognitive frames and structures of the old order. All three types are 'mutually reinforcing and equally necessary' (Macy and Johnstone, 2012: 27).

Momentum (www.momentumcommunity.org) is a training institute and movement incubator that offers progressive organisers tools and frameworks to build social movements. Similar to Macy's model, Momentum has framed what they call 'movement ecology' as consisting of three parts: (1) dominant institutional change, (2) alternative institutions and (3) personal transformation (Engler and Engler, 2016). They note that acknowledging these different pathways needed for transformation, 'frees us from the burden of having to embody every theory of change ourselves' (Momentum, nd: 10). *Dominant institutional change* is the work that organisers of the 20th and 21st century have engaged in, alongside advocates, attorneys and lobbyists, striving to make the existing system work better for people. *Alternative institutions* experiment with different ways of engaging in the world, whether it is cooperative businesses, collectively run non-profits, community land trusts or communal living. *Personal transformation* means that participants work to heal the ways the existing system has hurt them in body, mind and spirit. Table 8.1 delineates these three transformative approaches to change listed alongside Macy's model, with examples of what these imply in practice. This work is at the heart of contemporary transformative change work, which seeks not just to reform but rather to revolutionise existing systems and social structures and the ways that these systems and structures become internalised in the person. It is built on a liberatory vision of connection, cooperation, equity and sustainability.

Transformative organising, aligned with transformative justice or transformative social change, is a paradigm and practice that seeks liberation through revolutionary change in systems, communities, organisations and people. Like the organising of the past, transformative organising brings together people who share concerns about particular issues or problems so that they can craft solutions to address them and carry out actions to achieve change. However, one of the things that is unique about a transformative approach when compared to a traditional approach is that the *means* may carry as much weight as the ends, which suggests that organisers attend to how they show up individually, how they come together as a group and how they act collectively in the world. Not all groups are able to embody all of these aspirations all of the time, of course.

Table 8.1: Transformative approaches to change

Macy *(Three types of work)*	Momentum *(Three parts of movement ecology)*	Examples
Holding actions	Dominant institutional change	Direct action, protest, organising, advocacy
Creating new structures	Alternative institutions	Solidarity economy, cooperatives, time banks, community land trusts
Change in consciousness	Personal transformation	Group processing, healing justice, mind–body work

Training for Change, an organisation that seeks to build capacities of grassroots social justice actors, points out that there are many roles to play in a transformative movement which include the roles of helper, advocate, rebel and organiser (Hunter, 2015). Solely fixating on 'organising versus development' or 'organising versus social services' or 'organising versus mass protest' precludes possibilities for individual practitioners and organisations to be flexible in their abilities to move between these different modalities. While there is a reasonable argument to be made to just choose one modality and do it well, one may also argue that this fluidity is an ethical imperative in order to undo entrenched narratives, practices and policies. Such fluidity necessitates an ethical framework that widens ethical imperatives, so that the opposition, an organisational member, and even our own selves become subjects of our attention, care and intervention to the best of our ability in a given moment. As we work in a community in real time, for example, we see that the person we are trying to mobilise into action is actually in need of some other form of support, whether it is emotional, social or economic.

In a diverse, globalising, digital world, transformative organisers are emboldened to practise from an intersectionality perspective (Collins, 2002), utilise the digital environment for strategic messaging/framing, and solidify and leverage bonds with actors across national and ethnic lines. Connected to liberation-oriented social movements in ways that traditional organising has not been, transformative organising is also concerned with the ways that oppression and systemic arrangements impact people internally and interpersonally, attending to issues of internalised oppression, conscious communication in organisations, and healing justice. Transformative organising, rooted in feminist, postmodern, environmental, indigenous and spiritually based relational ethical systems, affirms that organising should result not only in external changes in the environment but in a change in consciousness in the organiser (Mann, 2011; Rossiter, 2011; Pyles, 2018). As Foucault (1972) and others have argued, dominant institutions become internalised in people as they learn to self-censor and surveil themselves, rendering them as 'docile bodies' (cited in Pyles, 2018: 77). If organisers fail to attend to these elements, organising is perhaps just perpetuating the status quo and organisers have arguably been unsuccessful in actualising their ethical mandates. Thus, transformative organising affirms that the processes utilised – how organisers facilitate meetings, who the leaders are, how communication functions, how organisers heal and take care of themselves – should not replicate the kinds of injustices that it is trying to disentangle. Attention to relational processes is at the heart of the liberatory practice of transformative organising serving to prefigure the kind of people organisers want to become and the kind of world organisers want to live in.

Transformative organising considered

Now I flesh out the main components of transformative organising as it is currently playing out, focusing on transnationalism, intersectionality, framing and the strategic use of the digital environment, intergenerationality and healing justice. While not all organising and movement groups and efforts always embrace all these elements (either consciously or unconsciously), these dimensions of transformative organising are at least partially reflective of the current practice environment and offer fertile ground for further inquiry into the ethical challenges being undertaken by transformative organisers today.

Transnationalism

Globalisation has generated the push and pull factors that have increased migration patterns to levels never before seen on this planet, facilitated by efficient transportation, technology and familial networks in destination countries (Kley, 2017). While some people are forced from their countries and communities of origin due to neo-liberal economic policies and projects, others seek 'a better life' in countries with more resources. Political, religious and war refugees, as well as people who have been trafficked, also constitute this population. Destination countries in North America, Oceania and Europe are now experiencing unprecedented levels of diversity as a result of these migration patterns, resulting in greater cultural complexity, religious pluralism and linguistic richness. In the US, there are 42.4 million immigrants, the highest in US history with 13.3% of the nation comprising immigrants, the highest percentage in almost 100 years (Camarota and Zeigler, 2016).

This context has impacted the terrain of community organising in unprecedented and complex ways. First, it has expanded the notion of 'community' in community organising and social movement activities. No longer is 'community' solely conceptualised and operationalised geographically or place-based. Now, community may be transnational, ethnically based or identity-based.[1] One example includes immigrant communities, members of which organise and protest around a particular issue facing people in their home country such as natural disasters or political events (Collyer, 2008). Second, as neo-liberal globalisation impacts both workers in the developing world and consumers in the developed world, campaigns such as anti-sweatshop efforts initiated by college students, including students who are immigrants, are organised transnationally in solidarity with workers in places like the Philippines or Mexico (Featherstone, 2002). All of this has implications for the realities of multilingual capacity building, identity politics, intersectionality and the utilisation of the digital environment. Moreover, it has expanded the ethical groundwork on which organisers stand, no longer just concerned with issues facing their neighbours that one can see in flesh and blood, but embodying 'global empathic consciousness' (Rifkin, 2010: 588), an expansion of the human ethical imperative to include people across the globe as well as animals and the biosphere itself.

Intersectionality

Global migration patterns and greater integration of diverse communities have generated an increased need to attend to the ways that people's various social identities may intersect to exacerbate oppression. For example, a paid domestic worker such as a nanny or housekeeper may face the multiple vulnerabilities of being a woman, a person of colour and an immigrant. Thus, the willingness of populations, such as immigrant domestic workers in the National Domestic Workers Alliance, who were left out of previous waves of social movements, to speak out and demand to be seen and heard has helped to motivate the need to attend to intersectionality and the micropolitics of social movements more generally (Chandler and Jones, 2003; Rowe, 2016). Indeed, organisers are striving to redress the sexism that was rampant in the Civil Rights and Anti-War movements of the 1950s, 1960s and 1970s. Transgender, queer and non-binary movements lend more complexity and nuance to grappling with identity as well. Alicia Garza (2014), a queer, Black woman who was a leader/creator of #BlackLivesMatter wrote:

> When you design an event/campaign/et cetera based on the work of queer Black women, don't invite them to participate in shaping it, but ask them to provide materials and ideas for next steps for said event, that is racism in practice. It's also hetero-patriarchal. Straight men, unintentionally or intentionally, have taken the work of queer Black women and erased our contributions. Perhaps

if we were the charismatic Black men many are rallying around these days, it would have been a different story, but being Black queer women in this society (and apparently within these movements) tends to equal invisibility and non-relevancy.

Attention to intersectionality is arguably lending itself toward more multi-issue organising strategies, cultivation of more analytic complexity and greater capability to witness how power operates across systems and issues. Overall, intersectionality expands the ethical purview of organisers.

Framing and the strategic use of the digital environment

Scholars have discussed the ways that organisers and social movement actors must 'break the frame' of status quo messaging and strategically create new frames (Lakoff, 2004; Johnston and Noakes, 2005). This act requires critical inquiry and consciousness-raising on the part of actors as they dismantle and disentangle the narratives of mainstream media, the government and corporations that perpetuate oppression. This process facilitates the unravelling of social messages that get internalised in actors and that serve to continue to oppress. It is this 'change of consciousness' which is an essential element of transformative organising and of the Great Turning. Moreover, the practice of consciousness-raising further congeals the shared identity and solidarity of actors as they creatively generate a new way to frame their issue. Ultimately, the creation of a new frame such as #BlackLivesMatter is a creative process that can forge new neural pathways and liberate the consciousness of the actors as well as those who are the recipients of the message.

These new frames and messages, what are now sometimes called 'memes', are being transmitted through various media, but especially through social media. While the dark side of social media has been and is worthy of continued investigation (Rushkoff, 2014), here technology is arguably having an effective and positive impact as it is used not only to change consciousness and strengthen solidarity but to plan events, boost turnout for actions and reflect on post-actions. Researchers analysed 66,159 Tweets after the killing of Michael Brown by a police officer in Ferguson, Missouri in 2014, and noted the ways that social media allowed a broad audience to engage with and influence the messages of the movement through a process called 'distributive framing'. These frames started with the initial grievances and matured into specific tactics and policy change in which the organisers were engaged (Ince et al, 2017). GPS-based technologies have also been utilised extensively in recent campaigns, actions and mass movements, including the Arab Spring (Castells, 2012).

Intergenerationality

Intergenerational equity and intergenerational human rights are concerned with fairness or justice between current generations and future generations (Ife, 2012). These terms may apply to a range of issues including the economic debt that future generations may be forced to take on as well as the environmental degradation that the youth and unborn will be forced to face. In community organising, it is a term concerned with the ways that organising and movement skills and sensibilities are passed on to future generations at the same time that the movements are infused and nourished by new ideas and ways of doing things.

Youth have played generative and explosive roles in social movements throughout the twentieth century and have continued to this day. Whether it is youth working on issues of civil rights, environmental racism, immigrant justice, school shootings or education reform, their passion, energy, innovation and intelligence have been indispensable to social change work. Youth-adult partnerships between middle and high school age students and adults have served multiple goals including mentoring, skill sharing, transmission of organisational cultures and movement sustainability (Share and Stacks, 2006; Roberts et al, 2012).

Healing justice

Healing justice is a new dimension of transformative organising and social change work undertaken in the last decade (Page, 2010; Brown, 2017; Pyles, 2018). Activist Angela Davis said:

> I think our notions of what counts as radical have changed over time. Self-care and healing and attention to the body and the spiritual dimension – all of this is now a part of radical social justice struggles. That wasn't the case before. And I think that now we're thinking deeply about the connection between interior life and what happens in the social world. Even those who are fighting against state violence often incorporate impulses that are based

on state violence in their relations with other people. (Angela Davis interview, van Gelder, 2016)

A new generation of activists and organisers are attending to their whole selves, including their minds, bodies and spirits, which are often neglected in the wake of oppression, trauma, and the fast and furious pace of organising, especially in the digital age. In 2010, the organisers of the United States Social Forum held in Detroit, Michigan issued this statement about healing justice, defining it as:

> A framework that identifies how we can holistically respond to and intervene on generational trauma and violence and bring collective practices that can impact and transform the consequences of oppression on our bodies, hearts and minds. Through this framework we built two political and philosophical convergences of healing inside of liberation. (Page, 2010)

Thus, organisers are called on to do both the inner and outer work of transformation, work that can no longer be ignored and that is necessary not only for collective liberation but for the sustainability of social movement work that is likely to become more intense in the throes of late capitalism and climate change. After an Orlando, Florida nightclub shooting in 2016 whereby 49 mostly LGBTQ individuals were killed, a queer activist posted #queerselflove, as a way to bring attention to the fact that self-love and healing work are necessary and are, in fact, sometimes the work itself.

Another example of healing justice work is that of the National Domestic Workers' Alliance, which represents nannies, housekeepers and caregivers. They are incorporating mind–body practices into their political and grassroots education, including Aikido and generative somatics (Rowe, 2016). They identify this work as essential not just for personal healing but to prevent the kinds of traumatic re-enactments that can transpire in social justice organisations, replicating 'power-over' relationships through organisational structures and cultures, as well as through disempowering interpersonal communication patterns. In order for healing justice to be more than just neo-liberal narcissistic self-care, it is necessary to create healing justice organisations. This organisational model shares some resonance with organisational structures such as feminist organisations, contemplative organisations, sanctuary organisations and learning organisations (Pyles, 2018). The healing justice organisation embraces the idea that in order for organising work to be sustainable and for workers to have an opportunity to heal from the oppressions and trauma that harm them, it is necessary that organisations be places that promote workers' rights and justice, attending to participatory and transparent decision making, worker autonomy in workload, a culture of self-care and boundary setting, and time for reflection on social change within the organisation. The moral imperative for organisers to expand their sphere of relational care for 'the other' back onto themselves is an ethical turn that organisers of the past likely would find puzzling. But, as poet and activist Audre Lorde famously said: "caring for myself is not self-indulgence, it is self-preservation, and that is an act of political warfare".

Transformative organising case studies

Transformative organising and its underpinnings in relational ethics can better be understood through illustration of specific case examples of this work in action. Now, I discuss transformative organising that is focused on racialised mass incarceration and immigrant worker rights.

Ending racialised mass incarceration

In the bestselling book, *The new Jim Crow: Mass incarceration in the age of colorblindness*, Michelle Alexander (2010) argues that mass incarceration of Black people in America is a system that reflects the racist dynamics that created slavery and the post-Civil War era 'Jim Crow' laws which, much like the apartheid of South Africa, legalised racial segregation. The system entails a host of practices and policies including police brutality, heavy-handed disciplining of Black youth in schools, jails, prisons, parole and probation that results in a caste system of segregation, joblessness and loss of voting rights for a significant portion of the population. After the publication of Alexander's book, communities wanted to know how to act and Daniel Hunter (2015), an organiser and trainer with Training for Change, offered an organising guide for how to effectively create change around the issue of mass incarceration. He notes that the movement to end racialised mass incarceration is employing a wide variety of approaches and campaigns including: (1) stopping prison construction and reducing incarceration rates, (2) addressing prison conditions including the practices of for-profit prisons and shackling pregnant women, (3) ending re-entry barriers and increasing direct services such as establishing voting rights and lifting barriers to employment, (4) addressing other structural issues such as ending the school-to-prison pipelines and the militarisation of inner city schools, and (5) creating alternatives to incarceration including restorative justice programmes. Just as the Black Panthers of the past provided meals, day care and other social services, so too is this movement blurring the lines between organising, movement building and human services as they provide material and social supports to families of victims and incarcerated people. One can argue that this more fluid practice orientation emerges from their responses to what philosopher Emmanuel Levinas called the face-to-face encounter (Levinas, 1969). It is a practice approach that sets aside preconceived knowledge and representations of people in favour of relationship (Rossiter, 2011).

Hunter notes that the movement to end mass incarceration is also working to 'eliminate the smog inside us' (2015: 36). Calling for the retributive justice system to punish a cop for killing a Black man is not enough as it does not address the harm being done in society, to each other and within individuals. In addition to addressing internalised racism, this movement is concerned with empowering leadership among the people who are most impacted by mass incarceration. While allies can bring tremendous resources to the movement, this movement is calling for formerly incarcerated people to be key leaders. Such participatory approaches can bring up significant challenges between marginalised people and allies. According to Alicia Garza (2014), who started the online platform #BlackLivesMatter:

> Progressive movements in the United States have made some unfortunate errors when they push for unity at the expense of really understanding the concrete differences in context, experience and oppression. In other words, some want unity without struggle. As people who have our minds stayed on freedom, we can learn to fight anti-Black racism by examining the ways in which we participate in it, even unintentionally, instead of the worn out and sloppy practice of drawing lazy parallels of unity between peoples with vastly different experiences and histories.

In addition to addressing these challenges related to intersectionality and identity politics, the #BlackLivesMatter movement has affirmed the importance of healing justice through the articulation of a ten-point plan, which emphasises attention to the traumas of the past through care, connection and relationship.[2] By grappling with intersectionality, healing justice and multimodal approaches to change, the movement to end racialised mass incarceration sheds light on transformative models and reveals a more expansive and relational ethical ground that they are intending to cover.

Immigrant labour organising

In the context of declining private sector unionism and unprecedented immigration, worker centres are community-based spaces, the chief purpose of which is to organise a base of workers to take action on their own behalf (Fine, 2011). The major focus tends to be on issues of worker justice, which may include negotiating wages for day labourers, preventing wage theft, and union organising, as well as a variety of issues related to immigrant rights and language justice. Many of the worker centres in large cities have focused primarily on a particular population such as Spanish-speaking immigrants, though a new wave of organising may be trying to bring together groups that have been historically split from each other, such as African American workers and Latinx workers (Bobo and Pabellón, 2016).

Women are particularly vulnerable in the global economy and so the work that immigrant women are doing around labour justice issues is noteworthy, such as that being done by Mexican and Central American women in casinos in Nevada with the labour union for hotel and restaurant employees (UNITE HERE) (Chandler and Jones, 2003). Not only are they engaged in union organising, securing higher wages and better working conditions, they are also supporting workers with issues like citizenship, Deferred Action for Childhood Arrivals (DACA) and Temporary Protected Status (TPS). Through an intersectionality lens, they have devoted their organising resources to LGBTQ rights in the US and Canada, for example, organising against Proposition 8 (which sought to eliminate rights to same-sex marriage) in California. Moreover, UNITE HERE offers internships for young people providing opportunities for youth and college students to learn about and contribute to union organising. Transnationality, intersectionality, multi-issue organising and intergenerationality all play roles in the work of immigrant labour organising.

Ethical challenges going forward

When I was working in New Orleans, Louisiana after Hurricane Katrina in 2005, I remember the programme director of the international NGO I was working with said something very peculiar to me. I had suggested that we bring together the people and leaders of the neighbourhoods we were working in as we made plans for recovery projects and programmes in some of the hardest-hit neighbourhoods in New Orleans. She said something along the lines of, "we must get our own selves together as professionals before bringing them into the conversation". I have written elsewhere (Pyles, 2011) about how paternalistic and disempowering this seemed and I think it is representative of how community development, humanitarian aid and other forms of social work tend to operate, namely that there is 'us' who are the workers, helpers, organisers and professionals, and 'them', the people who are the targets/service recipients and are in need of something. Alternatively, development models such as the ABCD (asset-based community development) approach affirm that local community leaders, groups, associations and institutions already have a swell of assets and it is only the organiser's job to listen to them, help them leverage these assets and find the resources to effect change (Kretzmann and McKnight, 1993). Moreover, many organising models affirm the importance that those most impacted by the issues are the experts and should lead organisations (Pyles, 2014; Brown, 2017). The famous quotation from Lilla Watson (an Indigenous Australian artist, activist and academic), "If you have come here to help me, you are wasting your time. But if you have come because your liberation is bound up with mine, then let us work together" (cited in Pyles, 2018: 3), points not only to all of our shared fates but to a disruption of the often-rigid line between helper and helped. The people who are working in communities trying to undo oppression are often people who have also been affected by internalised oppressions and trauma. Thus, issues of alliance and healing justice become a critical piece of community organising under a transformative paradigm.

Professional social practitioners, including community organisers, community development specialists, social workers and others, have traditionally been trained to maintain a sharp line between their personal lives and the work that they are doing. They are taught to be 'objective' and to maintain boundaries between themselves and the people with whom they work. But transformative workers who embrace a more relational ethics wonder who and what such a distance serves. The reality is that workers carry multiple social identities, both privileged identities and subjugated identities. Community organisers are people of colour, queer people, immigrants and people with disabilities. While they certainly have important privileges (perhaps a salary and access to organisational resources), they often share commonalities with the communities in which they are working.

Community organisers continue to be challenged by the dominant thinking that segregates people into distinct groups and thus multiracial organising and identity politics continues to be a challenge. It can seem difficult to get Asian immigrants, for example, to align with Latin American immigrants or African Americans. This points to a need for 'strategic essentialism', that is, for groups that are alike and marginalised to strategically align themselves with one another (Spivak, 1995). Of course, this approach not only fails to acknowledge the differences that exist among members who are in similar social locations, but it fails to bridge the barriers that exist across distance. In other words, while #BlackLivesMatter served to strategically align all Black people regardless of differences in economic class, gender, sexual orientation or ability, it may have failed to create alignment with Asian, Latinx and other people of colour, as well as align with other marginalised people in general such as transgender people, working class people or people with disabilities. But, perhaps Garza is right that society is not there yet, that society cannot feign some kind of false unity when individual groups are still targeted and their unique differences are not seen and heard. And yet, she also points out 'when Black people get free, everybody gets free' (Garza, 2014). And, this is not unrelated to another existing challenge, namely that organising tends to be siloed around particular issues. There are some excellent examples of multi-issue organising and ways that allies have come to support each other across issues, and it is incumbent on organisers to continue to forge relational connections across issues and to carve out space for solidarity work.

As social movements attend to issues of organisational trauma and process, self-care and healing from internalised oppression and trauma, are they neglecting the opportunities for powerful reforms that they could otherwise be engaged in? Is it ethical to spend time practising mindfulness, engaging in process groups and undoing internalised oppression as the whole world is burning? Such work can easily lead to solipsistic pursuits and perhaps even perpetuate the neo-liberal narcissism of the times. However, it seems clear that when one's cup is empty it is difficult to have much to offer. Organisers, many of whom could be referred to as 'wounded healers', not only have an ethical duty to do healing justice work, but they must continue to explore the balance struck between healing and action.

Conclusion

Past traditions of community organising have modelled how to engage people, build power and confront authority to achieve specific ends. Given the exacerbated inequities among people and the dire straits of the planet today, though, it is necessary for organisers to bring a new lens and a new set of tools to the work. Indeed, this is what a new subset of organisers is doing. By combining the work of movements, organising and services, transformative organisers are leveraging the strategies of the past with a revolutionary and liberatory vision for tomorrow, one that seeks to not only transform systems but to change consciousness and heal the collective and individual wounds of trauma and oppression. The ethical imperative for transformative community organisers is to build on the organising traditions of the past while affirming the values of relational ethics – engagement, mutual respect, embodied knowledge, uncertainty/vulnerability and attention to an interdependent environment.

Notes

[1] This kind of alignment of people or issues across borders is not without precedent. Previous examples would be the International Workers of the World (IWW), an international labour union founded in 1905, and the Pan-African movement which started as early as the 18th century.

[2] See: https://blacklivesmatter.com/healing-justice/

References

Alexander, M. (2010) *The new Jim Crow: Mass incarceration in the age of colorblindness*, New York: The New Press.

Alinsky, S. (1971) *Rules for radicals: A practical primer for realistic radicals*, New York: Random House.

Austin, W. (2006) 'Engagement in contemporary practice: A relational ethics perspective', *Texto e Contexto – Enfermagem*, 15(spe), 135–41.

Bobo, K. and Pabellón, M.C. (2016) *The worker center handbook: A practical guide to starting and building the new labor movement*, Ithaca, NY: Cornell University Press.

Boggs, G.L. (2012) *The next American revolution: Sustainable activism for the twenty-first century*, Berkeley: University of California Press.

Brown, A.M. (2017) *Emergent strategy: Shaping change, changing worlds*, Chico, CA: AK Press.

Camarota, S.A. and Zeigler, K. (2016) 'Immigrants in the United States: A profile of the foreign-born using 2014 and 2015 Census Bureau data', *Center for Immigration Studies*, 3 October. Available at: https://cis.org/Report/Immigrants-United-States?gclid=Cj0KCQiA_5_QBRC9ARIsADVww17kuEz5Yj5vv503vxc0h6HN5im8vH1L3Su99Puv9Cx7yZkEHVH7-uwaAnrNEALw_wcB

Castells, M. (2012) *Networks of outrage and hope: Social movements in the internet age*, Cambridge: Polity Press.

Chandler, S.K. and Jones, J. (2003) '"You have to do it for the people coming": Union organizing and the transformation of immigrant women workers', *Affilia*, 18(3): 254–71.

Collins, P.H. (2002) *Black feminist thought: Knowledge, consciousness, and the politics of empowerment*, New York: Routledge.

Collyer, M. (2008) 'The reinvention of political community in a transnational setting: Framing the Kabyle citizens' movement', *Ethnic and Racial Studies*, 31(4): 687–707.

Dixon, C. (2014) *Another politics: Talking across today's transformative movements*, Berkeley, CA: University of California Press.

Engler, M. and Engler, P. (2016) *This is an uprising: How non-violent revolt is shaping the twenty-first century*, New York: Nation Books.

Featherstone, L. (2002) *Students against sweatshops*, London: Verso.

Fine, J.R. (2011) 'New forms to settle old scores: Updating the worker centre story in the United States', *Relations Industrielles/Industrial Relations*, 66(4): 604–30.

Fisher, R. (1994) *Let the people decide: Neighborhood organizing in America*, New York: Twayne Publishers.

Foucault, M. (1972) *The archaeology of knowledge and the discourse on language*, New York: Pantheon Books.

Garza, A. (2014) 'A herstory of the #BlackLivesMatter Movement', *the feminist wire*, 7 October. Available at: www.thefeministwire. com/2014/10/blacklivesmatter

Hunter, D. (2015) *Building a movement to end the new Jim Crow: An organizing guide*, Denver, CO: Veterans of Hope Project.

Ife, J. (2012) *Human rights and social work*, Melbourne: Cambridge University Press.

Ince, J., Rojas, F. and Davis, C. (2017) 'The social media response to Black Lives Matter: How Twitter users interact with Black Lives Matter through hashtag use', *Ethnic and Racial Studies*, 40(11): 1814–30.

Johnston, H. and Noakes, J.A. (eds) (2005) *Frames of protest: Social movements and the framing perspective*, Oxford: Rowman and Littlefield.

Klein, N. (2014) *This changes everything: Capitalism vs. the climate*, New York: Simon and Schuster.

Kley, S. (2017) 'Facilitators and constraints at each stage of the migration decision process', *Population Studies*, 71(sup1): 35–49.

Korten, D.C. (2006) *The great turning: From empire to earth community*, Bloomfield, CT: Berrett-Koehler Publishers.

Kretzmann, J. and McKnight, J. (1993) *Building communities from the inside out: A path toward finding and mobilizing a community's assets*, Evanston, IL: The Asset-Based Community Development Institute, Institute for Policy Research, Northwestern University.

Lakoff, G. (2004) *Don't think of an elephant*, White River Junction, VT: Chelsea Green Publishing.

Levinas, E. (1969) *Totality and infinity: An essay on exteriority*, Pittsburgh, PA: Duquesne University Press.

Macy, J. and Johnstone, C. (2012) *Active hope: How to face the mess we're in without going crazy*, Novato, CA: New World Library.

Mann, E. (2011) *Playbook for progressives: 16 qualities of the successful organizer*, Boston, MA: Beacon Press.

McCarthy, J.D. and Zald, M.N. (1977) 'Resource mobilization and social movements: A partial theory', *The American Journal of Sociology*, 82(6): 1212–41.

Mill, J.S. (1861/2002) *Utilitarianism*, Indianapolis, IN: Hackett.

Momentum (nd) 'Momentum training packet'. Available at: www.momentumcommunity.org

Page, C. (2010) 'Reflections from Detroit: Transforming wellness & wholeness', INCITE! Blog, 5 August. Available at: https://inciteblog.wordpress.com/2010/08/05/reflections-from-detroit-transforming-wellness-wholeness/

Pyles, L. (2011) 'Neoliberalism, INGO practices and sustainable disaster recovery: A post-Katrina case study', *Community Development Journal*, 46(2): 168–80.

Pyles, L. (2014) *Progressive community organising: Reflective practice in a globalizing world* (2nd edn), New York: Routledge.

Pyles, L. (2018) *Healing justice: Holistic self-care for change makers*, New York: Oxford University Press.

Rawls, J. (1971/1999) *A theory of justice*, Cambridge, MA: Belknap.

Reisch, M. (2013) 'Social work education and the neo-liberal challenge: The US response to increasing global inequality', *Social Work Education*, 32(6): 715–33.

Rifkin, J. (2010) *The empathic civilization*, New York: Penguin.

Roberts, D., Johnson, G.S. and Richardson, N.L. (2012) 'Environmental justice and youth of color at the Westcare Foundation in Atlanta, Georgia', *Race, Gender and Class*, 19(1/2): 192–217.

Rossiter, A. (2011) 'Unsettled social work: The challenge of Levinas's ethics', *British Journal of Social Work*, 41(5): 980–95.

Rothman, J. (2001) 'Approaches to community intervention', in J. Rothman, J.L. Erlich and J.E. Tropman (eds) *Strategies of community intervention* (6th edn), Belmont, CA: Wadsworth/Thomson, pp 27–64.

Rowe, J.K. (2016) 'Micropolitics and collective liberation: Mind/ body practice and Left social movements' *New Political Science*, 38(2): 206–25.

Rushkoff, D. (2014) *Present shock: When everything happens now*, New York: Current.

Share, R.A. and Stacks, J.S. (2006) 'Youth–adult partnership in community organising: A case study of the My Voice Counts! Campaign', *Journal of Community Practice*, 14(4): 113–27.

Spivak, G. (1995) *The Spivak reader*, New York: Routledge.

van Gelder, S. (2016) 'The radical work of healing: Angela and Fania Davis on a new kinds of civil rights activism' *YES! Magazine*, 18 February. Available at: www.yesmagazine.org/issues/life-after-oil/ the-radical-work-of-healing-fania-and-angela-davis-on-a-new-kind- of-civil-rights-activism-20160218

NINE

A Community Economies perspective for ethical community development

Ann Hill and Gradon Diprose

Introduction

In our teaching of community development we have noticed that some students want to be able to define and name 'the community'. They talk about 'the community' as an entity or thing that is somehow knowable. Similarly, many students also express a desire to 'do the right thing' when it comes to working with communities. Most want to act ethically, and some even want a kind of ethical rule-book that they can use to help guide their actions in different situations. These kinds of desires are completely understandable. They reflect teaching materials on community development that emphasise the importance of understanding the demographics, histories and aspirations of communities one might work with. The desire to know how to act ethically and manage uncertainty also makes complete sense when navigating the often complex negotiations and uneven power relations within and between communities, non-governmental organisations (NGOs), funders, state agencies and the private sector.

While these desires to know and act are understandable, they are also sometimes at odds with anti-essentialist or post-structural understandings which suggest that any notion of 'the community' is a fiction or myth (see for instance Nancy, 1991; Bond, 2011; Diprose, 2016). Similar to this idea that a notion of 'the community' is a fiction or myth, post-structural thinking has also queried what it means to be a human subject. So rather than human subjects being understood as individual, stable, autonomous and rational, post-structural understandings frame human subjectivity as always in a process of becoming (see, for instance, Cameron and Gibson, 2005a). This process of becoming is constructed and understood through relationship, what Nancy (1991) calls 'being-with', which as Popke (2010: 442) writes, is essentially 'the sharing of being with co-present others in space and time'. A post-structural understanding of both community and human subjectivity therefore opens us to the possibility that every encounter and relationship carries the potential for an 'agonistic negotiation over the meaning and contours of what we hold in-common with others' (Popke, 2010: 442). For Negri (2003), this is essentially the crux of ethics. He writes that 'ethics is the responsibility for the common' (Negri, 2003: 183). In this chapter we draw on Negri's understanding of ethics, and follow Popke (2010: 436) who describes ethics as concerns around the:

> nature of our interactions with, and responsibilities toward, both human and non-human others. To speak of ethic[s] ... then, is to consider the nature and extent of these responsibilities, both empirically and theoretically, as well as the ways in which our actions and dispositions toward others tend to fulfill or abrogate them within particular contexts or institutional arrangements.

Within our respective fields (human geography and community development) more generally, we have observed shifts over the last few years away from universalising and individualist understandings of ethics, to this more relational and collective approach to ethics that foregrounds caring for, and responsibility towards, others (see, for instance, Popke, 2007, 2010; Pratt, 2009; Gibson-Graham and Roelvink, 2010; McEwan and Goodman, 2010; Hill, 2011; Miller, 2013; Chapter One in this volume). Feminist geographers like Lawson (2007: 3) have argued that 'care ethics begins with a social ontology of connection, foregrounding social relationships of mutuality and trust'. For Lawson, care can articulate a particular form of social ethics premised on the collective concern for the well-being of others. Popke (2010) suggests that one way to approach and better understand ethics is to focus on the everyday actions and labour that people undertake to care for each other and the more-than-human. He suggests that within human geography, the work of Gibson-Graham (2006) is exemplary in illustrating the various 'ways in which our collective labors create the economic as a field of ethical interdependence and decision' (Popke, 2010: 445). Through their action research, Popke argues that Gibson-Graham (2006) and others have sought to bring into being what they call the 'Community Economy' (CE) where ethical questions around care and 'economic being-in-common' are central.

In their recent book, Gibson-Graham and colleagues outlined six key ethical questions relevant for community development. These questions include:

- What do we really need to live healthy lives both materially and psychically? How do we take other people and the planet into account when determining what's necessary for a healthy life? *How do we survive well?*
- What do we do with what is left over after we've met our survival needs? How do we make decisions about this excess? *How do we distribute surplus?*
- What types of relationships do we have with the people and environments that enable us to survive well? How much do we know about those who live in distant places and provide the inputs that we use to meet our needs? *How do we encounter others as we seek to survive well?*
- What materials and energy do we use up in the process of surviving well? *What do we consume?*
- How do we maintain, restore, and replenish the gifts of nature and intellect that all humans rely on? *How do we care for our commons?*
- How do we store and use our surplus and savings so that people and the planet are supported and sustained? *How do we invest for the future?*

(Gibson-Graham et al, 2013: xiii–xiv, original emphasis)

In this chapter we focus on the key question: 'How do we encounter others as we seek to survive well?' And by 'others', we mean both the human and more-than-human world. This chapter begins with a brief overview of CE thinking and then illustrates how a relational CE approach to ethics and encountering others can be applied in grassroots action in two community development case studies. We highlight how a relational understanding of ethics can help us to better consider ethical economic relationships and practices that underpin community development interventions.

Community Economy approaches

CE theory and the Community Economies Collective (CEC, a group of scholars using these approaches) emerged out of the work of J.-K. Gibson-Graham's (1996, 2006) diverse economic theory. Gibson-Graham (1996, 2006) argued that there are two main issues with conventional understandings of the 'economy'. First, the economy tends to be understood as inevitably capitalist, and second, as separate from ecology or the more-than-human world. To challenge what Gibson-Graham called 'capitalocentrism' (viewing everything either in relation to, subject to, or resistant to, capitalism), CEC scholars understand the economy as a wide range of diverse practices (see Table 9.1), bound up with planetary ecosystem processes and negotiated through various sorts of encounters.

This focus on diverse encounters – involving a range of transactions, labour and enterprise forms, and different finance and property arrangements, rather than just capitalist ones – encourages people to see the multiple ways of enacting transformation in our societies (Gibson-Graham, 2008). To mobilise this transformation, CEC scholars have worked to: increase the visibility of the diverse economy; encourage communities to experiment with diverse economic practices; and build connections between ethical economic actors to bring about collective change (see, for instance, Pavlovskaya, 2004; Cameron and Gibson, 2005b; St. Martin, 2005; Gabriel, 2013; Gibson-Graham et al, 2013, 2017). Drawing on insights from psychoanalytic practice, CEC scholars have used the diverse economy reframing to give new meaning and value to people's lives and construct the economy as a space for other choices (see, for instance, Healy, 2010, 2014). A diverse economy framing can also expand the number of people who see themselves as agents of economic change – reshaping the world in ways that matter for people and planet and that might also prompt a willingness to explore collective actions (Gibson-Graham et al, 2016; Roelvink, 2016). When people can see how their actions are connected through the diverse economy, ethical economic actors can recognise one another in more and more places and relationships, enlarging the field of *collective action* (Roelvink, 2010).

In recent work on collective action, CEC scholars have also used the concept of hybrid networks and assemblages to recognise how human and non-human others can work together as acting subjects (see, for instance, Dombroski, 2013, 2016; Cameron et al, 2014; Roelvink, 2016; Gibson-Graham et al, 2017). CEC scholars suggest that hybrid

Table 9.1: The diverse economy

Labour	Enterprise	Transactions	Property	Finance
Wage	Capitalist	Market	Private	Mainstream market
Alternative paid	Alternative capitalist	Alterative market	Alternative private	Alternative market
Unpaid	Noncapitalist	Nonmarket	Open access	Nonmarket

Source: Gibson-Graham et al (2013: 13)

networks and assemblages are based on three critical interactions: *gathering*, which brings together those who share concerns about an issue; *reassembling*, in which material gathered is rebundled to amplify particular insights; and *translating*, by which reassembled ideas are taken up by other collectives so they may continue to 'do work' in the world (Cameron et al, 2014; Hill, 2015).

The interconnected foci of making visible the diverse economy and enlarging the field of ethical collective action allow us to imagine the post-capitalist world as something we can enact in the here and now. So, rather than giving over to pessimism, or waiting for some future revolution, CEC scholars look to the everyday, diverse practices of people and the more-than-human, and seek to amplify these. This emphasis on the everyday (or in other words, 'starting where we are') resonates with work in community development to help practitioners think beyond fixed notions of both subjects and communities. CEC scholars have used action research and research activist methodologies (see Gibson and Cameron, 2001; Cameron et al, 2011; Werner, 2015; Diprose, 2016; Dombroski, 2016; McKinnon et al, 2016;), participatory action research (PAR) approaches (see Cameron and Gibson, 2005; Cameron and Grant-Smith, 2005; Cameron, 2007; Hwang, 2013), and asset based community development (ABCD) approaches in a range of contexts – from minority world post-industrial regions with high unemployment and corresponding socio-economic issues (see Cameron and Gibson, 2005b; Gibson-Graham, 2006; Newbury and Gibson, 2016), to majority world urban and rural contexts (see Hill, 2011; McKinnon, 2011; Mathie et al, 2017).

As CEC scholars we understand community as 'a never-ending process of being together, of struggling over the boundaries and substance of togetherness, and of coproducing this togetherness in complex relations of power' (Gibson-Graham et al, 2017: 5). Some have argued that CEC scholars are 'Pollyannas' who naively gloss over, or neglect to explore the uneven power relations in communities (see Fickey and Hanrahan, 2014, for further discussion). However, increasingly, CEC scholars are focusing on the ongoing democratic struggle involved as people seek to collectively negotiate and renegotiate their material and cultural survival in different contexts (see for instance; Diprose, 2016; Diprose et al, 2017; Mathie et al, 2017; Borowiak et al, 2018). We find CE approaches to community development useful for understanding the never-ending process of being in community, where subjects and communities are unfixed and constantly in a state of becoming. The focus on mapping diverse and everyday practices, and starting 'where we are', helps to shift attention to ethics and relationality during this ongoing process (and struggle) of becoming.

In the two case studies that follow, we highlight how CE approaches can be useful when thinking about ethics and relationships in specific contexts. In case study 1 we illustrate how mapping a diverse economy can open up ethical questions and identify existing and emerging relationships and opportunities for alternative community development trajectories. In case study 2 we show how subjects come together around *shared* ethical concerns (that include the more-than-human world), to pursue collective action, and in the process move from an 'I' to a 'we'. We use these case studies to illustrate how CE thinking can open up ethical questions around how we encounter others (including the more-than-human) when negotiating challenging questions of community development. We suggest that rather than thinking of ethics as individual and universal (in that there is necessarily a 'right' way to act), ethics is best negotiated through relationships – with humans and the more-than-human world on which our collective survival depends.

Case study 1: City of Powell River, British Columbia, Canada

Like many regions in the post-industrial minority world, the City of Powell River has been struggling with how to respond when a major industrial employer goes into decline. For Powell River, this was an industrial mill and pulp and paper factory run by the Powell River Company. From the end of the Second World War until the mid-1970s, the mill was the largest employer in the region, employing 2,527 people at its peak in 1974. However, due to international competition and financial difficulties that began in the 1990s, production and employment has decreased to approximately 400 people, posing significant 'material and symbolic challenges' for the region (Newbury and Gibson, 2016: 185). In what follows we draw on a book chapter by Newbury and Gibson (2016) to show how a CE approach to mapping the economic diversity in the region can open space for ethical reflections on the possibilities for uncertain futures.

Similar to feminist-inspired scholarship (see for instance England, 2006), Newbury and Gibson are explicit about their role and relationships with the Powell River region. Newbury describes how she has been a resident and 'insider' of Powell River for seven years and a founding member of Powell River Voices: 'a civic organisation aimed at widening the debate about Powell River's social and economic future' (Newbury and Gibson, 2016: 185). Gibson describes how she has participated in public conversations around post-capitalist CE approaches as a visiting scholar. Newbury and Gibson describe their approach as 'participant activist research', noting that it differs from more classic participatory action research (PAR). They write: 'PAR typically works with vulnerable and marginalised groups and has an emancipatory focus', whereas participant activist research involves 'working on matters of shared concern with already mobilized collectives of researchers' to explore emergent possibilities (p 194). CEC scholars often use Eve Sedgewick's concept of 'weak theory' to explore ethical questions around community development trajectories that welcome uncertainty and surprise, 'rather than structural dynamics of transformation' or blueprints for change that rest on strong critiques or preconceived outcomes (p 194).

The CE approach of focusing on the 'here and now' reflects ABCD approaches to exploring a community's existing assets, strengths and more-than-human attributes. One of the risks in focusing solely on the 'here and now', though, is that people (including community development workers) may neglect to consider the history of certain places and communities. Working in Aotearoa New Zealand, Bargh and Otter (2009) point out that in post-colonial communities, a key ethical concern relates to understanding what came before and what was dispossessed if intergenerational ethical issues of redress for indigenous people are to be truly considered. They argue that there is no blank space in terms of engaging with communities, and nurturing indigenous people's politics of place may actually involve the exclusion of colonising discourses and certain people from accessing land, resources or community development projects. This exclusion may be needed to allow indigenous people the chance to reclaim what has been lost through colonisation. What this highlights is that beginning with the 'here and now' also requires some knowledge and recognition of the historical processes that contributed to creating the 'here and now'.

So, what did this mean for Newbury and Gibson in Powell River? First, it meant developing understanding of the indigenous groups (Tla'Amin people) who had lived in the region prior to colonisation. Newbury and Gibson outline how colonisation, and the logging industry in particular, prompted the forcible removal of indigenous people from their land onto a small reserve. They describe how the introduction of diseases by European settlers led to further Tla'Amin people's deaths, and how dammed rivers and logged forests altered the life-sustaining ecosystems Tla'Amin people depended on. Finally, they describe how more recently the negotiation of a treaty in 2012 between the Tla'Amin people and the Province of British Columbia and the federal Canadian government, has shifted the nation from being under the jurisdiction of the 'Indian Act' to self-government. This enables significant changes with increased land ownership and expanded hunting and fishing rights for Tla'Amin people.

Second, it meant gaining an understanding of how the Powell River Company had contributed to shaping the lives of people in the region. Newbury and Gibson describe how the mill provided a certain prosperity and material job security for many during its boom, albeit structured around capitalist and gendered hierarchies that shaped the very design and structure of the city. Similar to many single-industry towns, the Power River Company exerted a certain paternalism, contributing wealth that flowed into education and infrastructure services in the region through local taxation. For these reasons, many of the mainstream responses to the decline of the mill have focused nostalgically on replacing the mill with another large industry.

Finally, it meant gaining an understanding of more recent demographic changes in the region. Newbury and Gibson describe how during the 1960s, US Vietnam draft avoiders moved to Powell River, contributing to a certain counterculture in the otherwise relatively conservative working-class community. They also note that more recently, retirees and wealthy urbanites from Vancouver have bought property in the region, further changing the demographics.

Through this description of the Powell River region, Newbury and Gibson hold the history of the place and community (including the uneven power relations and dispossession of colonisation) in tension with the understanding that subjects and communities are in a constant process of becoming and can never be fully 'known'. What their work usefully highlights is the importance of background research and building relationships to better understand some of the politics and processes that have contributed to shaping a community in the 'here and now'.

A key practical CE method Newbury and Gibson have used to prompt ethical questions about potential development trajectories is reading the landscape for economic difference to identify 'existing ethical economic practices that are oriented directly to the growth of wellbeing' (2016: 198). For example, Newbury has been working with other local people and groups to map the diverse modes of work (including unpaid), different forms of enterprise, and various transactions that occur in the region. This has included creating 'cultural capital' maps that highlight the many and various festivals and events, accounting for the volunteer labour that supports these, and documenting the forms of property and resources that support cultural activities (including privately and publicly owned spaces such as galleries, studios and halls). All of these activities and forms of exchange intersect with the money economy in different ways – through ticket sales, art and handicraft sales, wage payments and the hiring of venues. However, they also generate a whole range of non-money exchanges through gifts, cooperative exchange, bartering and borrowing. Newbury and Gibson note that at the time of writing, a project was under way to begin mapping the diverse food economy in the region. They describe the annual Seedy Saturday where participants swap and sell seeds, and engage in food-related workshops to map how food security can be strengthened. They then describe some of the community groups and services (such as church groups, sports clubs, thrift shops, public libraries, the Youth Resource Centre and other extracurricular activities provided for youth), to highlight the often overlooked work, particularly by women, in these kinds of community organisations. The usefulness of mapping economic diversity is that it is creatively descriptive – highlighting and making connections between what is already occurring in a community to provide a more holistic picture of their economic landscape.

These diverse economic maps can then be used as a starting point for communities to consider what matters of concern and existing practices already connect people, and what they might want to build on and amplify. Such maps also help to illustrate the wide range of existing relationships and forms of encounter that already exist within communities. Newbury and Gibson note that this method is about nurturing multiple entry points within a diverse economy rather than a community relying on one employer/industry/practice/relationship to sustain themselves. Creating diverse economic maps is not about covering over or ignoring disagreement and uneven power relations within relationships and communities. The maps for instance, may actually help people in certain communities to identify relationships, encounters and practices that are unhealthy for them, or limit their sense of autonomy. Ultimately, diverse economic maps can help people to identify shared ethical concerns to build relationships, and make visible the diverse ways communities sustain themselves through interconnections with each other and the more-than-human world. To put it another way, mapping economic diversity provides a helpful representation of the diverse ways people are already encountering each other in any community. To connect this back to Negri's (2003) understanding of ethics, diverse economic maps can help to show how people are already taking responsibility for, and caring about, what they hold in common.

Case study 2: The neighbourhood of Banaba, Manila, the Philippines

Like many neighbourhoods decimated by sudden severe storms and extreme flooding, *barangay* (neighbourhood) Banaba, Manila struggled to cope when Typhoon *Ondoy* (or *Ketsana* as it is internationally known) devastated the area in 2009. The nearby Marikina River broke its banks in rapid time. Some 450mm of rain fell in just 12 hours. Metro Manila recorded its highest rainfall since the 1960s. An estimated five million households were affected citywide with infrastructure damage of US$69 million. Barangay Banaba was one of the hardest-hit areas. Banaba is particularly susceptible to severe flooding because it lies between two rivers, the Marikina and the Nangka, and it is the end destination of two creeks and most settlements are located on floodplains. Many of neighbourhood's 20,000 plus population live in congested informal settlements and have been relocated through government schemes from other crowded parts of Manila. In what follows we draw on empirical research by one of the authors (Ann) who visited Banaba nine months after Ondoy with one of her research partners, a community development worker who was part of the post-typhoon livelihoods rebuilding efforts. Drawing on Ann's participant observation and write up the project as part of her doctorate, we show how people in Barangay Banaba came together around shared ethical concerns, including concerns for surviving well within a more-than-human world of extreme weather, and waste and waterways management considerations. We show how collective action was pursued and in the process how Banaba residents moved from an 'I' to a 'we' in their community development efforts.

International donor organisations responded immediately to the 2009 disaster situation. HEKS (Hilfswerk der Evangelischen Kirchen Schweiz/Swiss Interchurch Aid), Swiss Solidarity and Christian Aid worked with Manila-based NGO, COPE Foundation and Banaba-based People's Organisation *Buklod Tao* to provide relief and rebuilding funding to the amount of 10,000,000 Philippine peso (PHP; approx. US$200,000; 47PHP = US$1 in 2009). Initially, the thought was the donor funding would be distributed on a household-by-household basis once a livelihood damage assessment had been conducted to determine who was eligible for assistance. What is interesting about this case is that the Banaba community broke with this classic tale of household-based development assistance and intervention. Instead, more than 1,200 households agreed to waive their rights to a PHP5,000 household cash handout and to pool their funding to develop an experimental community-based social enterprise cluster (Hill and Rom, 2011; Hill, 2013).

There are a number of reasons and circumstances that led to this collective decision. First, there was recognition that many local livelihood strategies were not working particularly well before Ondoy struck. For example, there had been a glut of *sari-sari* (convenience stores) and other small businesses along the main road in Banaba, many of which were established via high-interest microlending schemes. Making loan repayments, let alone generating sufficient income, was difficult for many of these small business owners. So, rather than rebuild what was there before, for many people in the community there was openness to experimenting and trying something new. Second, there were catalysts and change agents working with the community who were already practised at nurturing mesolevel change and fostering community economic experimentation. For example, *Buklod Tao*, the local people's organisation, which oversaw the post-Ondoy livelihood assistance programme had been active for a long time in the local area lobbying against mining activities, and campaigning for environmental protection. The NGO worker employed by COPE was a social enterprise innovator already practised at community-based experimentation. Lastly, a 'Cash for Work' programme implemented by the international donor organisations, COPE and *Buklod Tao* to provide some immediate relief and household income, also helped generate a collective identity and collective consciousness around improving local well-being. While initially small work teams of workers in the 'Cash for Work' programme were assigned different tasks in different areas, when they discovered a vast amount of rubbish illegally dumped in the Nangka River, all 166 workers combined forces in a collective clean-up. Through this clean-up people in the neighbourhood were connecting with each other and also with the river, and out of this project many began to develop a new community consciousness and interest in surviving well together.

The 'Cash for Work' programme was therefore important in cultivating a 'together' or collective mindset. Workers in the programme were paid PHP382 (about US$8 a day as at April 2018) – the minimum daily wage in Metro Manila – and were asked to contribute PHP50 each (about US$1 as at April 2018) to cover the cost of tools and gloves. By making this contribution they became financial contributors in their own right and had something to show for it in the form of quality shovels and rakes which they could then re-use and share via a community borrow and lend tool library. This initial exercise in working together and sharing tools helped generate a new sense of civic 'we-ness' (Hill, 2011) that proved very useful in the next project steps.

In the months that followed the typhoon, 1,232 Banaba households that waived their rights to an international donor agency handout, including those households that had been part of the 'Cash for Work' programme, signed over their allocation for use in group enterprises. They formed groups of at least ten members, attended various training workshops on enterprise ideas and submitted loan applications with business plans for livelihood projects they were interested in. Applications were screened against social and environmental criteria and for economic viability. The focus was on drawing on existing community assets such as people's labour and skills, and waste raw materials, including large quantities of tetrapacks and river silt discovered in the river clean-up. The various groups utilised these local assets and the donor funding to develop enterprises that centred on investing directly into human and more-than-human community survival and well-being. The environmental and economic criteria used to determine what projects received funding, focused on the well-being of people and ecological systems such as waterways.

Five community-based social enterprises were established out of this process. These were urban container gardening (350 member households); organic compost production (150 member households); tetra-pot production (432 member households); fibreglass fabrication (100 member households); and green charcoal trading (200 members). The 'scale up' implications of pooling human and financial resources were significant. For example, the start-up capital allocated to tetra-pot production of PHP1,447,000 enabled the group to buy sewing machines and to set up a small factory in Banaba. The start-up capital of PHP847,000 allocated to urban container gardening enabled the group to develop multiple urban container garden sites with purpose-built plant risers and to purchase the tetra-pots and compost soil required for larger-scale production.

Figure 9.1 provides a pictorial representation of three of the enterprises and gives some clues as to how they work together in an enterprise cluster. Featured top left and right is the tetra-pot factory where discarded waste tetrapacks are sewn into 'tetra-pots'. These pots are then sold to the urban container gardening enterprise which in turn creates container vegetable gardens ready for sale, featured

Figure 9.1: Banaba group enterprises established after Typhoon Ondoy

Photographs © Ann Hill

bottom left and right. The growing medium in the pots is made by the compost enterprise from Banaba household biodegradable waste, sand, silt and other soil, and sold onto the urban container gardening enterprise.

The Banaba enterprises are a CE experiment in how to survive well with human and more-than-human others. Specifically, they are an experiment in how to survive well in a typhoon prone economically vulnerable region. A key aspect of this experiment is that it required people to shift their disposition from 'I' and individual household concerns, to 'we' and collective concerns for community economic development and ecological systems health. People in Banaba drew on waste materials and their own willing labour to experiment together with new enterprises in the aftermath of extreme weather.

The criteria used to fund certain ideas was holistic in that socio-economic well-being was integrated with ecosystem/environmental well-being and the enterprises that emerged were all interconnected and supported one another. In this way the very process of community organising in Banaba after Typhoon Ondoy helped to foster the movement from a focus on individual/household survival to a collective or community sense of 'we' and what was needed for common well-being. To connect this back to Negri's idea, through community organising and engaging with the donor funding, people were moved to consider what they held in common and how they wanted to maximise their collective well-being.

Conclusion

CE thinking has evolved out of a critique of the grand narratives of modernist development, and a reframing of the hopeless cul-de-sacs of strong Marxist critiques of neo-liberal capitalism that shut down hope and desire for change, and the belief that change is possible (Gibson-Graham, 1996, 2006). As CEC scholars we are well aware that there are 'powerful forces that attempt to enclose common resources, exploit and dehumanise people for profit, and reduce the beauty of the non-human world to commodities' (Gibson-Graham et al, 2017: 4). However, we also seek to 'cultivate representations of the world that *inspire*, *mobilize*, and *support* change efforts even while recognizing very real challenges' (Gibson-Graham et al, 2017: 4). In this chapter we have drawn on two case studies to illustrate how CE approaches can be used to explore ethical questions around how people encounter others (including the more-than-human) to collectively survive well. We have argued that mapping diverse economic practices within communities can help to make visible the existing relationships and practices that people already engage in and care about, while also creating space to consider different development trajectories. We have shown how people can come together to experiment through collective action by detailing some of the ways individuals move from a sense of 'I' to 'we' to create more sustainable economic practices. Finally, we have shown how concerns for the more-than-human can be used to open up space for debate and imagine new economic practices amid uncertainty in a climate-changing world.

The two case studies illustrate a willingness and openness to experimentation that foregrounds the crucial role grassroots economic actors and collective action can play. A CE approach to ethics does not prescribe a 'one size fits all' course of action. Rather, ethical actions are understood as being context specific and negotiated through relationships between people and the more-than-human world. Popke (2010: 449) writes that around the world:

> communities are being constructed around the social geographies of being-in-common, and in ways that respect local difference and autonomy. The goal for the twenty-first century, perhaps, is to provide the space for the expansion

of such projects, and to support the proliferation of new ones, not in order to decide in advance the contours of the in-common.

So, what does this mean for those of us concerned with ethics and community development? For us it means being open to the multiple ways communities can coalesce around what they hold in-common, while being mindful of the debates and negotiations that follow as they seek to manage what is held in-common. This includes being mindful of the subjects and voices who might be excluded from, or silenced in such debates and negotiations. For as Popke (2010) notes, these debates and negotiations are increasingly going to involve rethinking the agency we as humans ascribe to the more-than-human world, and also the spiritual world. While this understanding of ethics and action can sometimes mean uncertainty for community development practitioners, students and researchers, it also allows for a certain softness and acceptance that 'we don't always know' what to do or how to proceed. This softness and acceptance can be productive, opening space for the unexpected and hopeful. For, as Negri (2003) notes, ethics is the responsibility for the common, and also 'the terrain of possibility, of action, of hope' (Negri, 1996: 170). Our CEC 'mode of being' and our experience in teaching and practice inspire us to continue in an 'always work-in-progress' vein and we encourage our readers to do the same. Just as community itself is 'a never-ending process of being together, of struggling over the boundaries and substance of togetherness', so, too, is community development. So let us continue in this vein, an ever-unfolding journey.

References

Bargh, M. and Otter, J. (2009) 'Progressive spaces of neoliberalism in Aotearoa: A geneology and critique', *Asia Pacific Viewpoint*, 50(2): 154–65.

Bond, S. (2011) 'Being in myth and community: Resistance, lived experience, and democracy in a north England mill town', *Environment and Planning D*, 29(5): 780–802.

Borowiak, C., Safri, M., Healy, S. and Pavlovskaya, M. (2018) 'Navigating the fault lines: Race and class in Philadelphia's solidarity economy', *Antipode*, 50(3): 577–603.

Cameron, J. (2007) 'Linking participatory research to action: Institutional challenges', in S. Kindon, R. Pain and M. Kesby (eds) *Participatory action research approaches and methods: Connecting people, participation and place*, Abingdon: Routledge, pp 206–15.

Cameron, J. and Gibson, K. (2005a) 'Participatory action research in a poststructuralist vein', *Geoforum*, 36(3): 315–31.

Cameron, J. and Gibson, K. (2005b) 'Alternative pathways to community and economic development: The Latrobe Valley community partnering project', *Geographical Research*, 43(3): 274–85.

Cameron, J., Gibson, K. and Hill, A. (2014) 'Cultivating hybrid collectives: Research methods for enacting community food economies in Australia and the Philippines', *Local Environment*, 19(1): 118–32.

Cameron, J. and Grant-Smith, D. (2005) 'Building citizens: Participatory planning practice and a transformative politics of difference', *Urban Policy and Research*, 23(1): 21–36.

Cameron, J., Manhood, C. and Pomfrett, J. (2011) 'Bodily learning for a (climate) changing world: Registering differences through performative and collective research', *Local Environment*, 16(6): 493–508.

Diprose, G. (2016) 'Negotiating interdependence and anxiety in community economies', *Environment and Planning A*, 48(7): 1411–27.

Diprose, G., Dombroski, K., Healy, S. and Waitoa, J. (2017) 'Community economies: Responding to questions of scale, agency, and Indigenous connections in Aotearoa New Zealand', *Counterfutures*, 4: 167–83.

Dombroski, K. (2013) 'Always engaging with others: Assembling an Antipodean, hybrid economic geography collective', *Dialogues in Human Geography*, 3(2): 217–21.

Dombroski, K. (2016) 'Hybrid activist collectives: Reframing mothers' environmental and caring labour', *International Journal of Sociology and Social Policy*, 36(9/10): 629–46.

England, K. (2006) 'Producing feminist geographies: Theory, methodologies and research strategies', in S. Aitken and G. Valentine (eds) *Approaches to human geography*, London: Sage, pp 286–97.

Fickey, A. and Hanrahan, K. (2014) 'Moving beyond Neverland: Reflecting upon the state of the diverse economies research program and the study of alternative economic spaces', *ACME: An International E-Journal for Critical Geographers*, 13(2): 394–403. Available at: www.acme-journal.org/index.php/acme/article/view/1013

Gabriel, N. (2013) 'Mapping urban space: The production, division and reconfiguration of natures and economies', *City*, 17(3): 325–42.

Gibson, K. and Cameron J. (2001) 'Transforming communities: Towards a research agenda', *Urban Policy and Research*, 19(1): 7–24.

Gibson-Graham, J.K. (1996) *The end of capitalism (as we knew it): A feminist critique of political economy*, Minneapolis: University of Minnesota Press.

Gibson-Graham, J.K. (2006) *A postcapitalist politics*, Minneapolis: University of Minnesota Press.

Gibson-Graham, J.K. (2008) 'Diverse economies: Performative practices for "other worlds"', *Progress in Human Geography*, 32(5): 613–32.

Gibson-Graham, J.K. and Roelvink, G. (2010) 'An economic ethics for the Anthropocene', *Antipode*, 41(s1): 320–46.

Gibson-Graham, J.K., Cameron, J. and Healy, S. (2013) *Take back the economy: An ethical guide for transforming our communities*, Minneapolis: University of Minnesota Press.

Gibson-Graham, J.K., Cameron, J., Dombroski, K., Healy, S., Miller, E. and Community Economies Collective (2017) 'Cultivating Community Economies: Tools for building a liveable world', The Next System Project, 27 February. Available at: http://thenextsystem. org/cultivating-community-economies/

Gibson-Graham, J.K., Hill, A. and Law, L. (2016) 'Re-embedding economies in ecologies: Resilience building in more than human communities', *Building Research and Information*, 44(7): 703–16.

Healy, S. (2010) 'Traversing fantasies, activating desires: Economic geography, activist research, and psychoanalytic methodology', *Professional Geographer*, 62(4): 496–506.

Healy, S. (2014) 'Psychoanalysis and the geography of the Anthropocene: Fantasy, oil addiction and the politics of global warming', in P. Kingsbury and S. Pile (eds) *Psychoanalytic Geographies*, New York: Routledge, pp 181–96.

Hill, A. (2011) 'A helping hand and many green thumbs: Local government, citizens and the growth of a community-based food economy', *Local Environment*, 16(6): 539–53.

Hill, A. (2013) 'Growing community food economies in the Philippines', PhD thesis, Canberra: Australian National University.

Hill, A. (2015) 'Moving from "matters of fact" to "matters of concern" in order to grow economic food futures in the Anthropocene', *Agriculture and Human Values*, 32(3): 551–63.

Hill, A. and Rom, J. (2011) 'From calamity to community enterprise', *Asian Currents*, May, 7–9. Available at: https://web.archive.org/web/20111203024846/http://asaa.asn.au:80/publications/ac/2011/asian-currents-11-05.pdf

Hwang, L. (2013) 'Rethinking the creative economy: Utilizing participatory action research to develop the community economy of artists and artisans', *Rethinking Marxism*, 25(4): 501–17.

Lawson, V. (2007) 'Geographies of care and responsibility', *Annals of the Association of American Geographers*, 97(1): 1–11.

Linebaugh, P. (2008) *The Magna Carta manifesto: Liberties and commons for all*, Berkeley: University of California Press.

Mathie, A., Cameron, J. and Gibson, K. (2017) 'Asset-based and citizen-led development: Using a diffracted power lens to analyze the possibilities and challenges', *Progress in Development Studies*, 17(1): 54–66.

McEwan, C. and Goodman, M. (2010) 'Place geography and the ethics of care: Introductory remarks on the geographies of ethics, responsibility and care', *Ethics, Place and Environment*, 13(2): 103–12.

McKinnon, K. (2011) *Development professionals in northern Thailand: Hope, politics and power*, Singapore: Singapore University Press in conjunction with University of Hawaii and NIAS.

McKinnon, K., Carnegie, M., Gibson, K. and Rowland, C. (2016) 'Generating a place-based language of gender equality in Pacific economies: Community conversations in the Solomon Islands and Fiji', *Gender Place and Culture*, 23(10): 1376–91.

Miller, E. (2013) 'Community economy: Ontology, ethics and politics for radically-democratic economic organizing', *Rethinking Marxism*, 25(4): 518–33.

Nancy, J.-L. (1991) *The inoperative community*, trans P. Conner and L. Grabus, Minneapolis: University of Minnesota Press.

Negri, A. (1996) 'Twenty theses on Marx: Interpretation of the class situation today', in S. Makdisi, C. Casarino and R. Karl (eds) *Marxism beyond Marxism*, New York: Routledge, pp 149–80.

Negri, A. (2003) *Time for revolution*, London: Continuum.

Newbury, J. and Gibson, K. (2016) 'Post-industrial pathways for a 'single industry resource town': A community economies approach', in I. Vaccaro, K. Harper and S. Murray (eds) *The anthropology of postindustrialism: Ethnographies of disconnection*, New York: Routledge, pp 183–204.

Pavlovskaya, M. (2004) 'Other transitions: Multiple economies of Moscow households in the 1990s', *The Annals of the Association of American Geographers*, 94(2): 329–51.

Popke, J. (2007) 'Geography and ethics: Spaces of cosmopolitan responsibility', *Progress in Human Geography*, 31(4): 509–18.

Popke, J. (2010) 'Ethical spaces of being in-common', in S.J. Smith, R. Pain, S.A. Marston and J.P. Jones III (eds) *The SAGE handbook of social geographies*, London: Sage Publications, pp 435–55.

Pratt, G. (2009) 'Subject/subjectivity', in D. Gregory, R. Johnston and G. Pratt (eds) *The dictionary of human geography*, Chichester: John Wiley and Sons.

Roelvink, G. (2010), 'Collective action and the politics of affect', *Emotion, Space and Society*, 3(2): 111–18.

Roelvink, G. (2016) *Building dignified worlds: Geographies of collective action*, Minneapolis: University of Minnesota Press.

St. Martin, K. (2005) 'Mapping economic diversity in the First World: The case of fisheries', *Environment and Planning A*, 37(6): 959–79.

Werner, K. (2015) 'Performing economies of care in a New England time bank and Buddhist community', in G. Roelvink, K. St. Martin and J.K. Gibson-Graham (eds) *Making other worlds possible: Performing diverse economies*, Minneapolis: University of Minnesota Press, pp 72–97.

TEN

Concluding reflections: philosophical perspectives on community and community development

Peter Westoby

Introduction

This chapter concludes the book with philosophical reflections on the nature of 'community' as an ethical space and 'community development' as an ethical practice. While it may be more usual to begin a text with an abstract philosophical framework within which subsequent practice-oriented chapters are placed or judged, in this book we develop a vision of community and community development at the end. This chapter builds on the diverse narratives of the many ethical challenges relating to policies, organisations and practices recounted by the authors in this volume. They are rooted in the daily doubts and dilemmas faced by people working for transformative change – often in challenging circumstances in the context of a profoundly inequitable world. By turning an ethical lens on this practice, we have focused attention both underneath the macro political and institutional structures and beyond the merely technical and practical toolkits for work on the ground. We have been given accounts of the complexities, uncertainties and contradictions of community development work and the fine textures, including the knots and broken links, that make up the fabric of the ethical spaces in which it is located. What does this mean for our conceptions and theoretical understandings of community and for how we characterise the work that creates, maintains, develops, unsettles and even destroys the ethical space of community?

A philosophical angle on community

Community economists Katherine Gibson and Julie Graham (2006) (writing as J.K. Gibson-Graham), drawn on by Gradon Diprose and Ann Hill's Chapter Nine in this book, use the work of French philosopher Jean-Luc Nancy (1991) and North American feminist Iris Marian Young (1990) to argue that 'we need to liberate community from its traditional recourse to common being ... a commonality of being, an idea of sameness' (Gibson-Graham, 2006: 85–6). In a similar vein, Italian political philosopher Giorgio Agamben argues for an 'inessential commonality, a solidarity that in no way concerns an essence' (1993: 19).

In this way of thinking Gibson-Graham and Agamben are trying to disrupt the philosophical idea of community as 'common' or 'unity'. Instead they imagine community *as an ethical space* where there is no essence of community, but instead there are people making conscious ethical choices. Much like Hannah Arendt's argument that ... 'public spaces do not exist naturally; they need to be artificially created by human beings. These are the spaces in which we act, speak, form and test opinions, in debating with one another' (Bernstein, 2018: 89) ... so 'community' is an artificially created space in which people relate, cooperate, build a convivial life and make choices for the inclusion, or exclusion, of others. Gibson and Graham therefore understand community as signifying 'ethical coordinates for a political practice, not a model or plan' (2006: 88). From this perspective community can be reimagined as a geographical or symbolic site of dialogue and deliberation and ethical praxis. In this sense community is a social practice of people coming together and dialoguing and deliberating about the process and trajectory of development that they choose. There is no one fantasy of development, no inevitable or common unifying vision of 'the good life'. Reimagining community as a symbolic site for dialogue and deliberation foregrounds the democratic impulse of community development – people need to be in conversation with one another discussing, and creating their vision together, and then respecting differences.

Such an approach also recognises that the 'practice' of a community development worker is to step into the 'fabric' (Dunne, 2011: 21) of this imagined community as symbolic site with people caught in their 'volatile combinations of human passions and motivations' (Dunne, 2011: 21). The community development worker makes their ethical decisions about what to do, but in no way can control what is unfolding in the 'community' symbolic site. They are intervening into the site with a nudge, perhaps using what Gradener and de Kreek in Chapter Four describe as *the subjunctive voice*. People, in this symbolic site of community, will make collective decisions that impact on themselves and others, and the community worker is called to be a part of that process, nudging, inviting, suggesting, at times protesting, or even at times withdrawing (particularly if the decisions of people in the symbolic site contravene the ethical values of the community development worker).

Community as hospitality

With the focus on community as a symbolic site of dialogue and deliberation, we argue for a community development vision of community animated by the idea of hospitality. Hospitality orients towards a relationship that is welcoming of the Other, as found in Derrida's injunction of 'community as hospitality' (Derrida, 1997). This has resonances with Levinas's (1999) account of 'ethics as first philosophy', derived from the experience of the encounter with the Other. In doing this he calls for the 'wisdom of love', something that can only occur in the 'face-to-face' encounter with another human being who is profoundly different. Community then can be animated by the idea of not just a symbolic site of dialogue, deliberation and praxis, but ideally and ethically an embodied site of care, deep listening, being open to the encounter with another. In contrast, when people close themselves, their groups, their spaces from the Other, then they are no longer experiencing an hospitable community, but some other kind of closed collectivity – or group-think.

Hospitality can also refer to the ethical practice of the community development worker, who determinedly welcomes other people, other ideas and other ways of thinking. In this sense the ethical community development worker is not pushing for any imagined unity or essence – the group-think – but is honouring the symbolic site for which Gibson-Graham argue, the welcoming of difference, dissidence and agonistic politics.

Going further, Mexican post-development thinker Gustavo Esteva argues that hospitality orients towards the principle of non-intervention and 'co-motion'. The inhospitable and instrumental practices of intervention and 'pro-motion' tend to mean that many professional community development practitioners have predetermined what they are going to do with and for people or communities (Esteva, 1987: 149) – and are therefore not sensitive to that earlier mentioned 'fabric'. In a similar spirit to Esteva, North American authors Margaret Wheatley and Deborah Frieze (2011: 160–86) articulate a community development approach that advocates for friendship as opposed to intervention. Such an approach calls for an opening up of spaces with people and to be part of the people, not only with them but *among them*, again, offering that nudge, that invitation or insistence, but from within and on the edge of the fabric of community.

Community as collective and cooperative practice

Acknowledging 'community' as a symbolic site for dialogue, deliberation and ethical praxis, and arguing for a vision of community animated by the idea of hospitality, we also recognise that within community development theory and practice, community usually signifies *collective* processes of social change. For us, community, emergent through people's efforts in ethical decision making (accounting for difference) and extending hospitality (to the Other), becomes the platform for collective social change efforts. By collective, we simply mean *groups of people* (very rarely some unified 'whole' community) who have gathered together for action. It is this collective approach of small groups that distinguishes community development from many other approaches to social change (legal efforts, mass campaigning, trade unions, political parties, public health and so on).

In collectively oriented community development efforts – the movement from 'I' to 'We', so easily said – people learn to work cooperatively together and in choosing to trust one another then hold each other accountable (through mutual obligations). Such collective and cooperative efforts foreground the daily ethical work of actually cooperating, of actually trusting other people, of actually forgiving one another when encountering the inevitable disappointments of collective efforts. Richard Sennett's book *Together: The rituals, pleasures and politics of cooperation* (2012) is a poignant meditation on the difficulties of such practice in an age of increasing narcissism and growing inequalities.

Ethics and development

Community development is not only about 'community'. It is also a call for 'development'. But, what might an ethical view on development mean? Within the vast myriad discourses of development (for example, development as modernisation, or dispossession, primitive accumulation, growth) we argue that development is most usefully, and ethically reimagined within the post-development and post-structural tradition (McMichael, 2012). By this, we mean that there is what Arturo Escobar identifies as the:

possibility of visualising an era where development ceased to be the central principle of social life ... The post, succinctly, means a de-centering of capitalism as the definition of the economy, of liberalism in the definition of society and polity, and of state forms of power as the defining matrix of social organisation. This does not mean that capitalism, liberalism and state forms cease to exist; it means that their discursive and social centrality have been displaced somewhat. (Escobar, 2010: 12)

To align ourselves with the post-development tradition then is to be consistent with a vision of development that understands *diverse approaches* to 'the good life'. From this perspective, as editors, we suggest alternative pluralistic visions for development whereby people collectively, associatively, cooperatively and individually can have control over decisions that impact on their lives – so determining their own futures. As there is no imagined unified community, so there is no one vision of development, no right way.

Ethics and social solidarity

The idea of solidarity also informs our ethical framework for community development. Our take on this is informed by nineteenth-century European mutual aid philosophers such as Peter Kropotkin (1902) and Pierre Joseph Proudhon (1902), and by the 20th-century injunction of southern hemisphere liberation theologies towards a 'preferential option for the poor'. Such a preferential option emphasises relating to *everyone* with hospitality, but with a primary orientation towards people who experience marginalisation. Hence, equity is foregrounded within the ecology of ethics.

An ethical approach to community development supported by social solidarity involves entering into particular kinds of committed relationship, exemplified by Paulo Freire, who observed that 'this solidarity is born only when leaders bear witness to it by their humble, loving and courageous encounter with the people' (1972: 100). Such solidarity requires movement of community development workers and others to step out of comfort zones, and engagement not only with the universal 'Other' but with those particular 'others' who are marginalised in societies. Solidarity requires community development workers to enter into dialogue with those people, listening to them and learning about their social, political, economic, ecological, cultural and spiritual realities. In our experience the idea of solidarity often disrupts naive intentions to 'help the poor' and usually requires significant reflexive capacities to challenge previous assumptions (Land, 2011) which help guard against paternalism.

Re-emphasising community development as an ethical social practice

An ethical social practice signifies a movement towards *reclaiming* the world and organisational contexts as a social world, which is to push against the current emphasis on managerialism and technique. From our perspective, solutions to human problems will be primarily social and only secondarily managerial and technical. Yet, increasingly, technique is seen as the solution to social challenges.

Social practice therefore means reconstituting 'development work' in terms of social agency and political contestation. From this perspective community development as an ethical social practice: (1) fosters ethical social relationships; (2) invokes agency not just in private and personal relationships, but also in collectively oriented public relationships; and (3) strives to reclaim and reinhabit places as spaces of social activity rather than speculative economic activity or managerial or technique-oriented community development.

Freire (1972) has most clearly articulated such a social practice in the context of literacy programmes. He argued that literacy programmes cannot be just technical processes of enabling people to understand the word. They also need to embody a social practice in enabling people to transform their world, through dialogue with others and co-investigation. In the same way community development work cannot be simply reduced to a mechanistic process such as 'toolkits' for community consultation and recipes for 'building social capital' but must hold instead the social practice of solidarity and political contestation.

Foregrounding an ecological sensibility

Another way we have found helpful to think about ethics and community development is to think about the world through a lens of ecological sensibility. We use this sensibility to think about community development in two particular ways. First, it entails rethinking community development's ethical relationship to the environment or nature – ultimately inviting a new post-human perspective on community development. Such a perspective insists on new questions, such as how does hospitality towards the Other include the non-human world; or, what is it to think about community as a symbolic site of decision making and ethical praxis that includes the rights of a river, or a mountain?

Second, this ecological sensibility helps practitioners to see the world ecologically and holistically – which is to understand connections and relations between people, groups, networks, organisations, ideas and perspectives. Quantum physicist David Bohm's work around *Wholeness and the implicate order* (1980) and Capra's (1994) seminal *Ecology and community* inform our understanding of this often hidden layer of life that is crucial to 'work with' if we are to work ecologically and holistically.

Examples of practitioners who foreground this element of ethical practice include Margaret Wheatley and Allan Kaplan along with Sue Davidoff from The Proteus Initiative (www.proteusinitiative.org). For these community, social and ecological practitioners one of the challenges of development practice is the current overuse, and often unconscious use, of a paradigm that is reductionist and technical. Within such a paradigm complexities and uncertainties are reduced to measurable component parts and simplifications. However, community development as an ecological and holistic practice is not a practice of 'solving a puzzle' or 'using instructions to make sense of a machine' (Kaplan, 2002: xv). Instead, social systems are a complex dynamic process of interacting parts (individuals, groups and organisations) and multiple contexts (policies, plans, culture and so forth). An alternative ethical lens of practice requires an ecological or organic understanding of social systems (Midgley, 2000) – bringing to the foreground the interacting dynamics that underlie collective efforts. To work with the patterns of organic life is to then work ethically.

It is often useful to ground such an ecological or holistic understanding through the metaphor of a web. When we observe and interact with a group of people who are part of a community development process we experience a web of connections, some strong, others frayed, still others knotted or even broken (Peile, 1994). The community development practitioners' 'readings' of this web inform their analysis of potential ways forward. There is no point forging forward with collective action if the relationships between people are overstrained. This 'reading' takes place through both creativity and sensitivity, as well as rational analysis and strategising.

Wheatley and Frieze's (2011: 220–1) memes of 'look for the patterns that connect' and 'start anywhere, follow it everywhere' are indicative of social practice that flows from such a sensibility. The wisdom of this ecological and holistic approach is *not* to start with the toughest problem, for example, the 'root' cause of social disintegration within a community, but to start with what people are ready and able to do, based on the strong connections that already exist. Viewing through an ecological lens gives practitioners confidence that changes in one small part of a social system will flow on to impact and influence other parts.

This only comes through the hard work of seeing the whole web, seeing the ethical pinch points, of harms and injustices in the systems, and analysing and justifying action and strategies. This calls for 'ethics work', as described in Chapter One, including ethical seeing, reasoning and emotional work.

Ethics and deconstructive movements

Finally, responding to the growing world of ethical infrastructure – codes, councils, laws and so forth, we highlight an ethics of deconstruction drawing on Jacques Derrida. We draw on John Caputo's most recent take on Derrida as the starting point, where he argues that:

> The most fundamental concern of Derrida is with the distinction between the programmable, the foreseeable effect, the predictable result, which confines our beliefs and practices within parameters set in advance, which normalizes and regulates, and the non-programmable, the unforeseeable, the marginal, the outsider, which allows for the eruption of something new, of the surprise, the fortuitous, the coming of what we did not see coming. (Caputo, 2018: 192)

Derrida explains the meaning of this in relation to the law and justice. For Derrida, justice per se does not exist – for everything is deconstructible – yet, because of this, justice is always coming, always promised – yet never arrives. What does exist is 'the law', but he is making the case that we should never see the law as representing justice. The law reaches for justice, but it is not justice as such. As per the title of one of Derrida's later books, *The spectre of Marx*, justice is spectral, always haunting, ghost-like, never quite present, but always inviting presence. From a hermeneutical, or interpretive perspective, Derrida is asking people always to interpret the law while reaching for justice, or 'under the call of justice' (Caputo, 2018: 197). He is trying to disrupt the tendency for people in the legal field to run on autopilot, assuming the law, or their orthodox interpretations of law, equate with justice.

We hope the reader can see the parallels in the space of ethics and community development. In the same way as law does not equate with justice, so ethical codes, or the ethical infrastructure that is being padded around any profession, does not equate with ethical practice. Ethical practice is always reaching beyond the imperatives of ethical infrastructure. The ethics work that lies at the heart of practice is always responding to 'the non-programmable, the unforeseeable, the marginal, the outsider', to repeat Caputo's words. In fact, Derrida's ethical framework is an important one for anyone engaged in institutional life, as community development workers always are, but he insists on keeping institutions 'open'. He does not want institutions to ossify, to become satisfied in codes, rules, orders or programmes, which ultimately lead to them decaying. He is trying to honour both the traditions of the past in any institution, yet keep them open to the new.

Community development then, as an institutional, yet ethical project in and of itself, recognises the spectral haunting calls of its traditions – social justice, equity, collective action – and yet reaches into the new, being open to new ethical calls – for example, towards the non-human world. At the same time, community development practitioners, in their everyday practice, doing ethics work, cannot afford to sit back in the comforts of any code, rules of conduct, or programmes.

Drawing on Derrida's approach, we offer these final *aporias* (points of difficulty or undecidability) for community development workers doing ethics work. First is 'the suspension of the rule'. Derrida argues, 'each case is other, each decision is different and requires an absolute unique interpretation' (Derrida, 2002: 252). In practice this means not abolishing rules, or codes, but acknowledging the rule has to be held lightly, perhaps in 'mid-air', such that the practitioner can see the singularity of the social situation. The point being, every social situation is singular, requiring its own unique response. The second *aporia* is 'the undecidable', which entails recognising that any ethical rules can conflict with one another. True care of the singular social situation requires recognising – as Lynda Shevellar and Neil Barringham so beautifully articulate in Chapter Three – sometimes following the rule of the vocation rather than the code. Third, 'urgency' involves acknowledging that in the rough and tumble of daily life, many situations call for action now. So, ethical reflection is crucial, yet action is needed.

On that note, it is our aspiration as editors that this book speaks to the reader in 'this moment', a particular time in the evolution of community development as a field of practice or discipline. Even to be discussing ethics and community development is to indicate an invitation for practitioners and others to be more conscious of intention, values, dilemmas and so much more.

References

Agamben, G. (1993) *The coming community*, trans M. Hardt, Minneapolis: University of Minneapolis Press.

Bernstein, R. (2018) *Why read Hannah Arendt now?* Cambridge: Polity Press.

Bohm, D. (1980) *Wholeness and the implicate order*, London: Routledge.

Capra, F. (1994) *Ecology and community*, Berkeley, CA: The Center for Ecoliteracy.

Caputo, J. (2018) *Hermeneutics: Facts and interpretation in an age of information*, London: Pelican.

Derrida, J. (1997) *Politics of friendship*, London: Verso.

Derrida, J. (2002) 'The force of law: The mystical foundation of authority' in J. Derrida, *Acts of religion*, New York: Routledge, pp 228–98.

Dunne, J. (2011) '"Professional wisdom" in "Practice"', in L. Bondi, D. Carr, C. Clark and C. Clegg (eds) *Towards professional wisdom: Practical deliberation in the people professions*, Farnham: Ashgate, pp 13–26.

Escobar, A. (2010) 'Latin America at a crossroads', *Cultural Studies*, 24(1): 1–65.

Esteva, G. (1987) 'Regenerating people's space', *Alternatives*, 12(1): 125–52.

Freire, P. (1972) *Pedagogy of the oppressed*, London: Penguin Books.

Gibson-Graham, J.K. (2006) *A post-capitalist politics*, Minneapolis: University of Minnesota Press.

Kaplan, A. (2002) *Development practitioners and social process: Artists of the invisible*, Chicago: Pluto Press.

Kropotkin, P. (1902) *Mutual aid: A factor of evolution*, London: Heinemann.

Land, C. (2011) 'Decolonising activism/deactivating colonialism', *Action Learning and Action Research Journal*, 17(2): 42–62.

Levinas, E. (1999) *Alterity and transcendence*, London: Athlone Press.

McMichael, P. (2012) *Development and social change: A global perspective* (5th edn), Thousand Oaks, CA: Sage.

Midgley, G. (2000) *Systemic intervention: Philosophy, methodology, and practice*, New York: Kluwer Academic/Plenum.

Nancy, J.-L. (1991) *The inoperative community*, Minneapolis: University of Minnesota Press.

Peile, C. (1994) *The creative paradigm: Insight, synthesis and knowledge development*, Sydney: Avebury.

Proudhon, P.J. (1902) *What is property? An inquiry into the principle of right and of government*, London: W. Reeves.

Sennett, R. (2012) *Together: The rituals, pleasures and politics of cooperation*, London: Penguin.

Wheatley, M. and Frieze, D. (2011) *Walk out walk on: A journey into communities daring to live the future now*, San Francisco: Berrett-Koehler.

Young, I.M. (1990) 'The ideal of community and the politics of difference', in L. Nicholson (ed) *Feminism/Postmodernism*, New York: Routledge, pp 300–23.

Young, J. (1999) *The exclusive society: Social exclusion, crime and difference in late modernity*, Newbury Park, CA: Sage.

Index

Note: Page numbers in *italics* indicate to figures and tables. Page numbers in **bold** indicate discussions of key concepts.

www.ingramcontent.com/pod-product-compliance
Lightning Source LLC
Chambersburg PA
CBHW070921030426
42336CB00014BA/2488